Critical Political Economy

M000288478

How the media are organised and funded is central to understanding their role in society. *Critical Political Economy of the Media* provides a clear, comprehensive and insightful introduction to the political economic analysis of contemporary media.

Jonathan Hardy undertakes a critical survey of political economy scholarship encompassing worldwide literature, issues and debates, and relationships with other academic approaches. He assesses different ways of making sense of media convergence and digitalisation, media power and influence, and transformations across communication markets. Many of the problems of the media that prompted critical political economy research remain salient, he argues, but the approach must continue to adapt to new conditions and challenges. Hardy advances the case for a revitalised critical media studies for the twenty-first century.

Topics covered include:

- media ownership and financing
- news and entertainment
- convergence and the Internet
- media globalisation
- advertising and media
- alternative media
- media policy and regulation.

Introducing key concepts and research, this book explains how political economy can assist students, researchers and citizens to investigate and address vital questions about the media today.

Jonathan Hardy is Reader in Media Studies at the University of East London and teaches at Goldsmiths College, University of London. He is the author of *Western Media Systems* (2008) and *Cross-Media Promotion* (2010).

Communication and Society

Series Editor: James Curran

This series encompasses the broad field of media and cultural studies. Its main concerns are the media and the public sphere: on whether the media empower or fail to empower popular forces in society; media organisations and public policy; the political and social consequences of media campaigns; and the role of media entertainment, ranging from potboilers and the human-interest story to rock music and TV sport.

Critical Political Economy of the Media

An Introduction

Jonathan Hardy

Routledge
Taylor & Francis Group

LONDON AND NEW YORK

First published 2014
by Routledge
2 Park Square, Milton Park, Abingdon, Oxon OX14 4RN

and by Routledge
711 Third Avenue, New York, NY 10017

Routledge is an imprint of the Taylor & Francis Group, an informa business

© 2014 Jonathan Hardy; Foreword, James Curran

British Library Cataloguing in Publication Data
A catalogue record for this book is available from the British Library

Library of Congress Cataloging in Publication Data
Hardy, Jonathan, 1963-
Critical political economy of the media : an introduction / Jonathan Hardy.
pages cm. -- (Communication and society)
Includes bibliographical references and index.
1. Mass media--Economic aspects. 2. Mass media--Finance. I. Title.
P96.E25H37 2014
302.23--dc23
2013048470

ISBN: 978-0-415-54483-2 (hbk)
ISBN: 978-0-415-54484-9 (pbk)
ISBN: 978-0-203-13622-5 (ebk)

Typeset in Baskerville
by Taylor & Francis Books

To Gill, Jessica and Sean

Contents

Foreword

James Curran

There is considerable uncertainty about what the study of media political economy entails.[1] Seeking illumination, I picked up a copy of Vincent Mosco's *The Political Economy of Communication* (1996), which is presented by its publisher, Sage, as 'the definitive critical overview of the discipline' (back cover).

To my surprise, I found that this book had nothing to say about the influence of advertising on the media. Advertising is a major source of funding for commercial media, so presumably it is worth investigating whether this influences directly or indirectly what is produced. But all I discovered from Mosco's *vade mecum* is that advertisers encourage media to reach 'audiences and deliver them to advertisers' (Mosco 1996: 148). Whether this has any consequences for the media is left unexplored.[2]

Another perplexing thing I discovered from this authoritative introduction is that media political economy seemingly has nothing to say also about the effects of public ownership. Thus, whether public ownership of television channels leads to state control and sterile content, or the representation of diverse viewpoints and creative innovation, or makes no difference at all, are not questions that this definitive guide even considers.

Still more surprisingly, Mosco offers no clear insight into whether private shareholders – and those they appoint in senior positions – strongly influence private media, or whether controllers merely defer to the 'sovereign' consumer; and whether this varies in different contexts. His discussion laps at the edges of this issue without really engaging with it.

Instead, discussion of media ownership focuses primarily on one thing: media concentration. We are told, in great detail, that there has been a tendency towards media concentration; that it takes different forms; and that it can be measured differently. But in response to the obvious question – why does this matter? – Mosco's 'definitive, critical overview of the discipline' offers no clear answer, or indeed clear set of alternative answers.

At this point, it is difficult to suppress a feeling of impatience. If political economy has little to say, concretely, about the influence of advertising and ownership on the content and role of the media, what has it to say about anything? The answer, to judge from this much admired book, is: a lot about a lot of things. Mosco takes us on a roller-coaster ride through theories of spatialisation and commodification. Along the way we are invited to consider whether 'the universalization of commodification ... replaces its traditional connection to the transformation of use to exchange value and the production of codes and the hegemony of sign value'. Indeed, is there 'a radical mitosis in which objects and the labor process that gives rise to them break off and dissolve before the free-floating power of the sign'? (Mosco 1996: 155) – a question that Mosco ultimately sidesteps. This ascent into the billowing clouds of high theory is then followed by a crash landing, and a slow cruise through a banal listing of big companies and commercial sectors, reviewed in a mostly descriptive way (Mosco 1996: 181–92).

What unifies the diverse topics and concerns that Mosco defines as the terrain of political economy of communications? A useful way of understanding the field, he says, is to 'think about political economy as the study of *the social relations, particularly the power relations, that mutually constitute the production, distribution, and consumption of resources*' (original emphasis) (Mosco 1996: 25). Think about this formulation for a moment, and it becomes instantly apparent that a blank, pro-missory cheque is being issued. It is difficult to think of any work of substance engaging with the totality of society – written from different viewpoints, in diverse disciplines, in relation to a multiplicity of topics – that does not consider social relations in relation to resources.

This elastic definition enables Mosco to define the political economy of commu-nications as, more or less, anything that interests him. It is the key to understanding the book's inchoate nature, surprising lacunae, and superficial treatment of some topics. However, this is not to detract from the quality of some of Mosco's insights, and the intellectual courage with which he seeks to map a heterogeneous field – virtues that have resulted in a second edition of his book, generating plaudits from such luminaries as Lawrence Grossberg (Mosco 2009: back cover). Nor are the reservations expressed here intended to detract from the quality of his other work.[3]

However, Mosco's introduction leaves unresolved what media political economy is mainly about, and whether it is worth making the effort to find out.

What is it?

The true nature of media political economy is a mystery that deepens. For Karl Marx, 'political economy' was a synonym for bourgeois economic theory, which he attacked as tendentiously representing the economy to be benignly self-regulating and immutably bound by laws similar to those of nature. Indeed, the subtitle of his most famous book, *Capital*, is 'A Critique of Political Economy' (Marx 1983 [1867]).

But if 'political economy' was deployed by Marx to designate centre-right economic theory, the label is sometimes associated with left-wing theory. For example, David Hesmondhalgh (2007: 34) writes: 'This emphasis in political economy work on capitalism and its negative effects should make it clear that, although you don't have to be a Marxist to work here, it helps'. This identification with the left is especially pronounced in media studies. 'The political economic perspective', writes Michael Schudson (1996: 145), 'has been adopted and developed primarily by left-wing critics and analysts of the news media'.

However, although there is uncertainty about whether political economy's home base is on the left or the right, there is much greater agreement that this approach is deeply flawed. It is widely alleged that the political economy approach is 'reductionist', by which is meant that it reduces complex phenomena to simplifying economic explanation. This is usually contrasted with the complexly related multidimensionality of the critic's own rounded perspective (e.g. Tomlinson 1999: 16–17). A stronger version of this criticism is that critical political economy can offer almost cartoon-like simplicity. Thus, Schudson (1996: 145) writes that 'a political economy perspective has sometimes tended toward "conspiracy theory" or simple-minded notions that a ruling directorate of the capitalist class dictates to editors and reporters what to run in their newspapers'. This is contrasted with the multi-perspectival, balanced approach that he advocates.

The implication of these denunciations is that much media political economy is really not worth bothering about.[4] This would seem to be the view of the distinguished editors – including John Hartley and John Fiske – who produced a compendious, 367-page textbook introducing *Key Concepts in Communication and Cultural Studies* (O'Sullivan et al. 1994). In their considered judgement, the existence of media political economy was not even worth registering.

Intellectual contribution

A different case is presented by three good media political economy anthologies. They show why a focus on media political economy illuminates the forces shaping media institutions, and what they produce; and shines a light on the media's relationship to power, and the media's wider role in society. But with becoming modesty, some of the essays in these collections also acknowledge the limitations of the traditional political economy approach, and emphasise the complexity of the interactions and influences that are in play (e.g. Garnham 2011).

Each of these anthologies has distinctive strengths. One pulls together good past work in two massive volumes (Golding and Murdock 1997); another is good at situating the media in relation to the wider economic context (Winseck and Jin 2012); and the third gives more attention to drama and cultural production than the other two (Wasko et al. 2011). These volumes are supplemented by at least a thousand publications on different aspects of media political economy.

But multi-authored volumes also have limitations, while the sprawling literature on media political economy is now so extensive that it is difficult to stay on top of it. The great virtue of this book is that it pulls together the critical media economy *oeuvre* in a single compact volume. It orders and evaluates this literature under different topic headings to establish clearly the terrain of the subject. It is learned and well written. And its synthesis demonstrates why critical political economy of the media is important to an understanding of the media.

This leaves very little to add in a foreword. However, there are perhaps two themes that are worth exploring further. One is that much media political economy is right-wing or at least neoliberal, and this book, centred on leftish media political economy, needs to be read in relation to this. The second point is that simplification is not the exclusive monopoly of one tradition – something that has implications for the future development of media and cultural studies.

Historical media political economy

One way to illustrate the argument that media political economy is a large mansion with many rooms is to take a look at British media history.

A neoliberal political economy interpretation has long held sway in the history of the British press. Two things gave rise, in its view, to a free press in Britain. One was the dismantling of state controls: in particular, the end of press licensing in 1694; the liberalisation of seditious libel and defamation laws in 1792 and 1843; and the abolition of press taxes in the 1850s. The other agency of liberation was the capitalist development of the press. Increasing sales and advertising revenue allegedly rendered newspapers independent of government and party subsidy, and funded increased news gathering resources that freed papers from reliance on government public relations. Above all, commercialisation rendered the press more responsive to the public. 'The importance of sales to newspaper profits', explains a standard textbook, 'forced papers to echo the political views of their readers in order to thrive' (Barker 2000: 4).

The traditionalist view holds that the press had become by the 1850s the Fourth Estate, that is to say an institution independent of government and representative of the people (Barker 2000: 225). A revisionist variant holds that this epiphany took place in the later 1940s only when national newspapers finally disentangled themselves from close party ties (Koss 1981/1984). But while these competing interpretations disagree about timing, their story line is the same. They both argue that the press became free of government and switched allegiance to the people. And in both cases, they agree about the causes of this shift: state deregulation and market freedom.

As noted above, this is a *political economy interpretation*, albeit one informed by an anti-statist, neoliberal version of this tradition. However, it is challenged by a radical political economy interpretation that reaches a different conclusion. The neoliberal and radical approaches overlap in that they both celebrate the dismantling of repressive state censorship.[5] But they differ profoundly in their understanding of market processes. One approach views the market as an engine of freedom; the other as a system of control.

The radical political economy argues that the nature of the press market changed. Initially, press costs were low, making it possible for people with very limited means to launch great national newspapers, in a way that facilitated the rise of popular radical journalism. However, the industrialisation of the press in the mid nineteenth century dramatically raised costs so that ownership of the national newspaper press became increasingly vested in the hands of rich, mostly right-wing businessmen – a trend that was further entrenched by the rise of press concentration. A reduction of cover prices also made the whole of the mainstream press dependent on advertising. This inhibited radical journalism because some advertisers discriminated for political or economic reasons against radical publications. Partly as a consequence of these structural economic changes, it is claimed, the press retained close links to the power structure of society. This counterview now has growing adherents (Curran and Seaton 2010: Williams 2012a, 2012b; Conboy 2004; Hampton 2004; Petley 2009).

This is a necessarily condensed account in that both traditions also interpret the wider historical context differently (albeit in often vaguely delineated ways). The point that is being emphasised here is that media political economy has two wings. The book that you are about to read concentrates, for understandable reasons, on one of these.

Contemporary media

This same point can be illustrated briefly in relation to contemporary media analysis. There is a well-established neoliberal political economy tradition which argues that the free market guarantees the independence, diversity and accountability of commercial media (Murdoch 1989). In this view, the free market ensures that the media are independent of government. It produces a diverse media system since all are free to publish. It also renders the media representative since media enterprises must respond to their audiences' concerns in a competitive market. This perspective has received a boost from the advent of the Internet, which is viewed by some as enabling citizen journalists and users to undermine corporate media power (Benkler 2006). More generally, neoliberal political economy is highly critical of public broadcasting, holding that it can never be free since it is dependent on state-sponsored privileges (Adam Smith Institute 1984).

One part of the radical political economy rejoinder is that the free market can actively subvert media independence. Thus, media moguls colluded with governments in much of Latin America during the era of the dictatorships because they had shared agendas, and benefited mutually from co-operation (Waisbord 2000); and the same pattern can be found in some East Asian countries such as Taiwan during its quasi-dictatorship (Lee 2000). Media–government collusion can also occur in democratic countries, as in Britain during the Thatcherite era when right-wing moguls entered an informal coalition with government in order to regenerate, as they saw it, a failed society (Curran and Seaton 2010) and in Italy where a long-serving prime minister was also the country's leading media mogul (Ginsborg 2004).

These extreme outcomes are usually the result of two trends – media concentration and media partisanship – fusing to subvert media independence (Curran 2011). But markets can also generate incentives for media companies, with extensive economic interests, to ingratiate themselves to power. For example, News Corporation pulled the critical BBC World Television channel from the northern signal of its STAR TV satellite service in order to please the Chinese government, in the hope that it would gain enhanced access to the Chinese market (Dover 2008). Similarly, Hong Kong press owners' desire to expand their diversified business interests in mainland China was a key factor in the taming of the Hong Kong press (Lai 2007).

Markets can also become politicised by governments, as in the case of the creation of a market-based TV system in post-communist Eastern Europe where franchises were allocated mostly to government allies (Sparks 1998), or in many states in the Middle East where advertisers have been reluctant to incur official disfavour by supporting media that governments disapprove of (Sakr 2001).

More generally, it is claimed that online concentration has extended major news organisations' hegemony across technologies (Curran et al. 2012). Commercial pressures encourage insular, decontextualised, entertainment-centred journalism that badly serves democracy (Curran 2010a). By contrast, strong and independent public service broadcasting regimes support higher levels of knowledge about public affairs than commercial regimes (Cushion 2012).

In passing, it is perhaps worth noting that an intermediate position argues that the market has encouraged greater independence from government or party, while increased professionalism has limited negative market effects. This is, in essence, how Sally Hughes (2006), Carolina Matos (2008) and Carmen Sammut (2007) interpret the development of the media in, respectively, Mexico, Brazil and Malta.

This is not the place to arbitrate between these contending claims but merely to repeat the point that the political economy tradition does not have a party line. It actually embraces very different, and sometimes implacably opposed, interpretations. But what these different interpretations have in common – indeed what makes their authors, in a sense, members of the same squabbling family – is that they tend to give considerable emphasis to political and economic influences.

Simplification

But is not a narrow focus on political and economic influence enormously limiting? Does it not confirm what critics complain about – namely its tendency to simplify? The charge can sometimes be true. But this is no reason for ignoring the valuable knowledge and insights that media political economy can offer.

The charge of reductionism usually flows one way, to denigrate media political economy. But exactly the same charge applies with equal force to cultural studies. Cultural studies tends to concentrate on cultural power, to the exclusion of political and economic power – and when it writes about the latter it is usually through the prism of the power of ideas that are assumed to be autonomous. But again this is not grounds for ignoring the valuable knowledge and insights that cultural studies can offer.

Quite simply, the charge of simplification extends in both directions. Let me attempt to illustrate this argument by taking a closer look at two books, written respectively by leading figures in the political economy and cultural studies traditions. Their books simplify *in different ways*. But they also illuminate in different ways.

Let us first consider *Breaking Up America*, a book by Joseph Turow (1997), a media political economist at Pennsylvania University's prestigious Annenberg School of Communication. His central argument is that 'advertisers have been breaking up America' (Turow 1997: IX) because they shifted from mass marketing towards target marketing from the 1970s onwards. This was partly in order to exclude poor sales prospects but also to facilitate the relating of advertising messages to the social identity and life style of distinct social groups. The effect of this reorientation was to redistribute advertising away from mass media in favour of specialised TV programmes, magazines and websites that tended to emphasise group differences. In effect, changing advertising strategies encouraged the development of a 'hyper-segmented media environment' contributing to the 'unrelenting slicing and dicing of America' at the expense of *mass* media that supported the integration of society (Turow 1997: 6, 199).

The central thesis of the book is wrong. Advertisers did not 'break up America' because America was already broken. Turow's narrow industrial focus prevented him noticing the powerful forces that had already fractionalised American society. Thus, in the city where Joseph Turow works – Philadelphia – many African Americans lived, and still live, in districts where there are almost no white faces. The contrast between wealth and poverty in the city was, and remains, extreme, leading to an almost total separation between where the rich and poor reside. Yet, Philadelphia is merely a microcosm of wider divisions in metropolitan American society.

Indeed, the polarisation of wealth in the US is larger than in any other OECD country, save for Mexico (OECD 2008). A recent study of 'affective polarisation' – that is, strong feelings of antipathy towards the other political side – found that America was the second most polarised out of ten countries (Iyengar et al. forthcoming). The US was outstripped only by Colombia, which has experienced thirty years of civil war. A wide range of influences have contributed to this fracturing of American society, from the legacy of slavery, and its aftermath of Jim Crow oppression, to successive culture wars between secular and religious forces. Advertisers are, at best, only one additional, small input to powerful fissiparous forces that have long been in play. Indeed, advertisers were probably responding to pre-existing social divisions, not just contributing to them, when they shifted more towards target marketing.

Turow's narrow industrial focus caused him to overstate the divisive power of advertisers. Had he stood outside this narrow frame, and considered wider influences shaping society, he would have offered a more rounded and proportionate argument. So the weaknesses of his book exemplify what many critics of media political economy complain about: its tendency to simplify through its selectivity.

Yet, his narrow focus brings into sharp relief an important – and widely ignored – dynamic shaping media systems. His analysis is sustained by careful examination of trade journals and interviews with eighty-six executives. It shows the way in which market researchers sought to develop a more fine-grained market analysis. This encouraged new ways of conceptualising and measuring audiences: such as the People Meter which examined individual viewing behaviour within the home instead of relying on the 'household' as the unit of measurement. This fostered in turn advertising targeted towards baby power, grey power, teen power and other categories based on life style and values, which fuelled the growth of specialised cable television channels. In other words, Turow's analysis documents changes in the 'hidden' economic forces – the media's advertising support system – that contributed to changes in the structure and content of the media. It is an original and informative book that has been followed by subsequent studies that develop its central argument in relation to more recent developments in the media (Turow 2006, 2011).

Let us now turn to another book, *Performative Revolution in Egypt*, written by Jeffrey Alexander (2011), a distinguished cultural analyst and a Director of the Center of Cultural Sociology at Yale University. His central argument is that the revolution which brought down the Muburak regime in 2011 was the product of cultural power. He describes the way in which binary moral categories and energising narratives were deployed to mobilise people on the streets, and to persuade the army to stay neutral. Ideas, words and images were, in his account, the bullets that prevailed; digital communications were the artillery that the regime was unable to spike effectively. The Internet and social media also enabled the rebels to win wider support in the West, and resulted, he suggests, in the Pentagon exerting discrete pressure on the Egyptian military to stay out of the conflict.

Alexander centres his analysis on the month of the uprising, and has little to say about the wider context of the revolution except in one respect. We learn about 'the Arab intellectual revolution of the preceding decades' (Alexander 2011: 95–97), inspired by Arab engagement with Western ideas, in particular its concept of civil society, and with liberal values more generally. These especially appealed to the younger generation, we are told, and found expression in a plethora of films, TV programmes and novels. This provided the intellectual antecedents sustaining the 'performative revolution' and helps to explain why the central mobilising themes of the insurgence – freedom and democracy, civil society and national renewal – had such resonance. It also explains the power of the rebels' 'political theatre', as when the occupation of Tahrir Square enacted what a more civil and egalitarian society might look like.

This is a clever and engaging book that has something interesting to say about the power of ideas and awakening public consciousness. It is also written with an authoritative grandeur of tone (almost as if Jeffrey Alexander wore an academic gown, when he tapped on his keyboard). But despite this, an element of doubt begins to creep in when it becomes increasingly clear that Alexander does not actually speak and read the language of the country that he is writing about. He makes do by relying on the news reports of Western media, and the English language service of Al Jazeera and an Arab/Anglo website, supplemented by translations from occasional Arab sources. This is really quite scientific, he assures us, because Western journalists are like 'lay ethnographers' who are 'disciplined by professional ethics' and, 'in their exercise of interpretive judgement … were detached and impersonal' (Alexander 2011: xi–xii). So what we are actually being offered is an interpretation filtered primarily though Western observers, whose attributes, according to a good anthropological study of foreign correspondents (Hannerz 2004), are nothing like as awe-inspiring as Alexander imagines. The book's underlying assumption that the Egyptian revolution was ultimately the consequence of Western ideas and communications technology also sounds suspiciously simple.

A brief examination of relevant area studies offers a more complex picture in which political and economic influences, largely ignored by Alexander, also played a part (Dawisha 2013; Hamzawy 2009; Joshi 2011; Ottaway and Hamzawy 2011; Campante and Chor 2011, among others). The 2011 Egyptian revolution was in fact the culmination of protests and opposition that had grown over decades. Rapid educational advance had not been matched by economic growth, creating large numbers of educated young people who were unemployed or underemployed. Their raised expectations had, in some cases, turned to disenchantment, and they were to play a crucial role in the revolution. A well-organised trade union movement also existed in Egypt, and it had become increasingly resentful of the growing gulf between rich and poor generated by crony capitalism organised through a corrupt regime. A religious bloc was also opposed to the secular regime, and its principal agency, the Muslim Brotherhood, remained highly organised and retained a strong base despite being repressed. And there was growing popular resentment against an arbitrary and oppressive government at a time of rising food prices and unemployment, partly exacerbated by the removal of some government subsidies. In short, Egypt was a powder keg waiting to blow for a variety of reasons, only partly to do with the influence of Western ideas.

Alexander's thesis about the importance of the Internet and social media in mobilising opposition also needs to be contextualised. The 'wiring of the nation', he writes, was the 'Achilles heel' of the Muburak regime (Alexander 2011: 37). In fact, in 2011, Twitter user penetration in Egypt was just 0.15 per cent, much lower than in more prosperous neighbouring countries; and Facebook user penetration in Egypt was 8 per cent, compared with, for example, 15 per cent in Saudi Arabia and 21 per cent in Jordan (Dubai School of Government 2011: 5). Internet penetration in Egypt, in 2011, was also relatively low: 24 per cent compared with 41 per cent in Morocco, 44 per cent in Saudi Arabia and 69 per cent in the United Arab Emirates (UAE) (Internet World Stats 2011). New media, with higher penetration rates, had not destabilised authoritarian regimes like Morocco, the UAE, Saudi Arabia and Qatar. It was the underlying discontent in Egypt (with *multiple* causes) that made new media subversive, not the mere existence of new media.

So, the argument about simplification goes both ways. Alexander's narrow focus on cultural power caused him to simplify, just as Turow's narrow focus on advertiser influence had the same consequence. Reductionism is not a problem confined to one tradition. Yet, both books have something interesting and important to tell.

Moving forward

And both media political economy and cultural studies have much to contribute to each other, and jointly to the future development of the field. An informal division of labour has developed, in which some researchers focus on political and economic influences on media institutions, journalism and government, and others focus on media representations, the cultural power of audiences and the social relations of everyday life. This division gives rise to unhelpful intellectual barriers: for example, the absurd notion that the study of media entertainment is separate from the study of political communication (Curran 2010a).

It also gives rise to inflated turf claims, in which precedence is claimed by each side. There probably is an irreducible difference between the materialist emphasis of media political economy and the idealist emphasis of cultural studies. But we have a long way to go before we reach this irreducible point, and there is a lot we can learn from each other on the way.

Yet, obstacles lie in the way of this proposed reciprocity. Media political economy has been marginalised by recurrent attacks on its 'reductionism'. This tradition has not helped itself by failing to provide a narrative of its development, and compact presentations of its work, in the way that cultural studies has done so frequently and effectively.

This is why this book is so important. It is an original synthesis that pulls together in book-length form a disaggregated tradition of research. It not only serves well all those who work and study in media political economy. It also makes a larger contribution to the field for all those outside this tradition, and for all those who think that we should learn more from each other.

Notes

Foreword © James Curran

1 Jonathan Hardy may well disagree with, or disapprove of, this foreword. When I undertook to do this, in order to honour publication of this important book in a series of which I am the editor, I did so on the understanding that I would do it independently.

2 Mosco (1996: 149) says in passing that the media deliver 'audiences en masse and in specific demographically desirable forms, for advertisers' without exploring the implications of this key point. Mosco (2009) also incorporates, in the second edition of *The Political Economy of Communication*, discussion of some pertinent topics missing from the first edition.

3 See, for example, his illuminating study of ideas about technology and information (Mosco 2005).

4 This is not, however, what Schudson suggests in his effective and elegant overview, the most recent version of which is Schudson (2010).
5 However, the radical interpretation generally emphasises the undemocratic nature of the state in this period, with the implication that the character of the state changed. This prepares the ground for its view of public ownership and regulation of broadcasting as a positive development.

Part I

Mapping approaches and themes

Chapter 1

What (is) political economy of the media?

Introduction

If there have been times when the political and economic aspects of communication could be neglected by scholars then it is surely not ours. Media industries and practices are being rapidly transformed worldwide. The promises of digitalisation to distribute communication power widely through society and the manner in which such promises are hampered are vitally important issues. Our dependence on communication resources, vividly realised across the keystrokes and connections of daily life, is accompanied by increasing interest and concern in how these resources are organised and controlled. Recognition of the importance of the political and economic organisation ('political economy') of media has never been greater.[1]

There is no definitive beginning but if we take the late 1960s as the start date, critical political economy of communications represents half a century of scholarship. Many of the questions asked by radical scholars in the twentieth century remain salient – questions about control over the media, the impact of commercialisation, public and private media ownership, inequalities and power relations affecting communications. Yet the contexts in which these are asked and answered are characterised by rapid and far-reaching changes. This book has two main aims: first, to introduce and explore key features of the political economy of media and, second, to contribute to debates about the salience, value and direction of critical media studies in the twenty-first century.

The political economy of communications describes all forms of enquiry into the political and economic dimensions of communication. This book discusses and promotes such enquiry. Yet a more delimited approach, that of critical political economy, is the main focus of this book. Within the study of media and communications, attention to political and economic dimensions has often been relatively marginal, with greater attention devoted to 'texts' and 'audiences' than either 'production' or the wider contexts in which communication takes place. Critical political economy describes a tradition of analysis that is concerned with how communication arrangements relate to goals of social justice and emancipation. 'Critical', then, divides this tradition off from various alternative, often 'mainstream', approaches. I take the critical political economy approach to encompass studies that consider political and economic aspects of communications and which are critical in regard to their concerns with the manner in which power relations are sustained and challenged. The vitality of critical political economy studies of communication is demonstrated across recent collections of international scholarship (Wasko et al. 2011; Winseck and Jin 2012) and work on regions such as Latin America (Bolaño et al. 2012). There are several contributing factors that can help to explain this revitalisation, but an overriding factor is that the organisation of communication services has returned to prominence. The promise of limitlessness (in digital communications, content creation, creative labour, global cultural flows) encounters the constraining influences of money and power (the economic and political) in a manner that is unavoidable for serious analysis. The tensions here are not only with visions of limitlessness generated by those advancing the wonders of digital capitalism but also for counter-hegemonic visions of global solidarity and cultural exchange. This chapter introduces media political economy analysis and situates this in relation to alternative approaches.

Political economy

Political economy originally referred to a tradition of economic thinking that addressed the production, distribution and consumption of resources used to sustain human existence. For Adam Smith, the eighteenth century Scottish enlightenment thinker, political economy was the study of 'wealth', and was concerned with 'how mankind arranges to allocate scarce resources with a view to satisfying certain needs and not others' (Smith 1776: 161). For Smith this was also the study of *political* decision-making, a 'branch of the science of a statesman or legislator' concerned with the activities of government to aid economic growth. The so-called classical political economists, such as Adam Smith, David Ricardo, James Mill and Jeremy Bentham, were primarily interested in capitalism as a system for the production, distribution, exchange and consumption of wealth. In the nineteenth century Marx (1818–83) and Engels added class analysis, underpinning their radical critique of capitalism.

A general definition of political economy is the 'study of the social relations, particularly power relations, that mutually constitute the production, distribution and consumption of resources, including communication resources' (Mosco 2009: 24). Mosco traces four ideas central to political economy: engagement with social change and history, understanding the social whole, moral philosophy and praxis (Mosco 2009: 26–36). One link between what we will examine as critical political economy and what is known as classical political economy is that the economic sphere is not separated off from related social and political phenomena. The allocation of resources is recognised to involve political, not merely economic, decisions whose moral consequences permeate social life. Political economists sought to explain the emergence of capitalism but also to assess its implications for human life across societies. This 'holistic' approach contrasts with subsequent efforts by 'neoclassical' writers to establish economics as a mathematics-based science, by bracketing out history, politics and ethics. Yet the classical political economists in nineteenth century Britain were associated with cold calculus themselves, from Nassau Senior's opposition to welfare relief during the great Irish famine, Thomas Malthus's arguments for population control and John Stuart Mill and Jeremy Bentham's utilitarian moral philosophy. Their limitations and pro-capitalist class bias are repudiated in Marx's *Capital*, presented as a 'critique of political economy'.

Neoclassical economics

Initially broad in scope, classical political economy influenced the scientific study of economics developed in the late nineteenth and early twentieth centuries that focused on the efficient satisfaction of wants in markets, known as neoclassical economics. Its founders included Alfred Marshall, Vilfredo Pareto, Francis Edgeworth and Leon Walras. Thus mainstream economics evolved largely as a discipline professing value neutrality, while taking existing social relations as a given, and in general supporting core principles of market-based systems, namely that consumer and citizen welfare is best achieved through efficient market mechanisms. Classical political economy had expounded the labour theory of value, which located wealth creation in the surplus value extracted from workers (Smith, Ricardo, Marx). Neoclassical economics propounded a new theory of value derived from consumer preferences exercised in markets. This bypassed the attention to social class divisions and injustice in the distribution of wealth and income, which Marx had made central to his account of the exploitative social relations of capitalism. Taking consumer preferences to be preformed and beyond dispute helped to justify the narrowing of economic analysis to a mathematical-deductive system studying supply and demand in markets.

While neoclassical economics became the orthodox approach in capitalist systems, elements of more classical political economy persisted, alongside Marxian and social welfarist approaches. Some neoclassical tenets are repudiated in behavioural economics, whose analysis of irrationality in markets dethrones rational economic 'man'. There are also more socially oriented economists such as the development economist Amartya Sen and Elinor Ostrom, who won the Nobel Prize for economics in 2009 for her distinguished work on economic governance and common ownership, which informs analysis of the digital 'commons'.

Positive political economy

Today 'political economy' can refer to a range of contending approaches. One such approach, antithetical to Marxism, is that of the so-called Chicago School, also known as constitutional or 'positive' political economy, or as public choice theory (Mosco 2009: 28). This neoliberal approach is associated with Ronald Coase, Gary Becker, Richard Posner and George Stigler. Their work applies and extends neoclassical economic tenets to focus on calculating 'welfare' maximising advantage and by applying this to all forms of social behaviour. It does so, critics argue, by pursuing a narrow and conservative model of welfare based on promoting the activities of acquisitive individuals exercising freedom over their supposedly naturally acquired property rights. The purported aim is to provide 'positive' or value-neutral analysis, yet the base assumptions are anything but.

Critical political economy

Critical political economy refers to approaches that place emphasis on the unequal distribution of power and are critical of arrangements whereby such inequalities are sustained and reproduced. This critical tradition is influenced by, although by no means limited to, Marxism, as we will examine. Marxian political economy provides a historical analysis of capitalism including the forces and relations of production, the production of surplus value, commodification, social class divisions and struggles.

The political economy of communications

Any examination of communications that addresses economic or political aspects may be included in a broad category of political economic analysis. More narrowly, much 'political economic' analysis addresses aspects of the way in which communications are organised and provided as services. Emerging in the twentieth century the main focus has been on mass communication, defined as 'the industrialized production and multiple distribution of messages through technological devices' (Turow 2010: 17).

The political economy of communication represents a broad field of work drawing on economics, political science, communication and cultural analysis. A more accurate term for the tradition that developed in media and communication studies is critical political economy (or CPE). This 'critical' approach is at odds, as we will see, with 'mainstream' traditions in communication research as well as in economic, political and social theory.

Critical scholarship

The term 'critical' is usefully broad and encompassing, but it also has distinctive historical roots in communication research. It alludes to the academic practices and values of critique in intellectual enquiry – questioning, interrogating and challenging the adequacy of explanations of phenomena. For Mosco (2009: 128) political economy is critical 'because it sees knowledge as the product of comparisons with other bodies of knowledge and with social values'. As a descriptor for political economy, however, 'critical' has a more precise meaning for scholarship that is critical of the deficiencies of capitalism and of rule by elites. The term critical is associated with the Institute of Social Research established at the University of Frankfurt in 1923. The 'Frankfurt School', as it became known, investigated culture in ways that revised, and revived, Marxist theory and integrated this 'Western Marxism' with other social theories and with Freudian psychoanalysis.

These scholars rejected positivist claims that knowledge could be value-free and argued instead for a critical–normative perspective that was also reflective about how forms of knowledge contributed to sustaining or challenging existing social conditions. This approach was critical in that it assessed knowledge and social practice against normative values such as fairness in the distribution of wealth and resources. Its origins lie in the analysis of capitalist economies and authoritarian political systems, ranging from fascist to parliamentary, in the 1930s and 1940s. Yet the scholarship that evolved is not restricted to Marxist thought or even socialist principles. Its enduring values are rather liberal and democratic ones; '[i]t is committed to political enfranchisement, freedom of speech and intellectual inquiry, and social justice' (McChesney 2004a: 47).

The term 'critical' then helps to connect together traditions of critique as well as values of investigating and questioning arrangements. Yet it also has 'negative' associations: we do not (always) appreciate criticism; naysayers with relentlessly negative attitudes may be viewed as rigidly prejudging events, or just not great company. Whether 'critical' is too constraining and self-limiting an organising term for the approaches discussed here is an important question, but descriptively at least it helps to delineate approaches which I hope to show are anything but rigid or 'negative'.

Critical political economy rests on a central claim: different ways of organising and financing communications have implications for the range and nature of media content, and the ways in which this is consumed and used. Recognising that the goods produced by the media industries are at once economic and cultural, this approach calls for attention to the interplay between the symbolic and economic dimensions of the production of meaning. One direction of enquiry, then, is from media production to meaning-making and consumption, but the other is to consider the relationship of media and communication systems to wider forces and processes in society. It is by combining both that CPE seeks to ask 'big' questions about media.

CPE analysis is not defined or limited in respect of its object of analysis. CPE considers all kinds of communication processes, although it tends to ignore some, such as psycho-cognitive and affective processes. It is not defined or limited in respect of methods of analysis. A great variety of research methods are used, although documentation analysis, historical research, textual and media content analysis, economic, statistical and market analysis are the most prevalent. What characterises CPE above all are the questions asked and the orientation of scholars. Whose voices and concerns get to be heard? How are people, ideas and values represented in media discourses – and what is it that affects how this occurs? What is the quality of information, ideas and imagery available through media, and to whom is it available? This tradition asks questions about power in communications and the conditions for realising democracy. These connect, in turn, to two major influences: Marxism, and the theories and practices of democratic politics.

Karl Marx's work and legacy has had a profound influence on ways of understanding power, domination and inequality within the CPE tradition. Marx contributed to socialist and revolutionary politics but his major legacy is derived from his elaboration of a materialist philosophy (historical materialism) and critical analysis of capitalism. CPE draws on this complex legacy in analysing capitalist production and social relations. Mansell (2004: 98) summarises '[i]f resources are scarce, and if power is unequally distributed in society, then the key issue is how these scarce resources are allocated and controlled, and with what consequences for human action'. Critical political economy insists on connecting the study of media to broader patterns of social existence and in particular to questions of the allocation of resources. As British political economist Nicholas Garnham argues, this means identifying how communication and culture relate to processes of production and reproduction within capitalist society. The political economy of culture needs to be situated within an overall analysis of capitalism with 'a political economy of mass communication taking its subsidiary place within that wider framework as the analysis of an important, but historically specific mode of the wider process of cultural production and reproduction' (Garnham 1979: 123). Mosco (2009: 94–95) describes this approach as 'decentering the media'.

One key influence, then, is Marxism, although political economists have grappled with the limitations and criticism of 'classical Marxism' to a greater extent than many dismissive criticisms allow. In particular, the revising of a Marxist tradition within political economy has occurred through the confluence of two other influential currents – democratic theory/politics and cultural theory/politics. Political economy shares many of the democratic aspirations of liberal pluralist accounts of the media in serving citizens, but it challenges the ability of corporate-owned media to adequately do so, and mounts a critique of the capitalist market relations on which liberalism is contingent. Political economy draws upon classical democratic theory's insistence that democracy is based on an informed, participating citizenry, to assert that such political culture can only be generated by a more diverse, democratised media system. Shaped by Marx's critique of capitalism, the Western Marxist critique of commodification, reification and the 'culture industry' (Adorno and Horkheimer 1997 [1944]), and by theories of 'strong', participatory democracy, political economy criticises the capitalist market system for its failure to deliver economic fairness, social justice or the basis for a democratic polity (McChesney 1998, 2008; Mosco 2009; Murdock and Golding 2005; Hardy 2010b).

The principle of democratic governance, rule by the many, has been a guiding inspiration for critical scholars and a corrective to the ideas and legacy of centralised state control exercised by Communist states under the influence of the Comintern. Western Marxism embraced tenets of participatory democracy in its rejection of Soviet Communism and embarked on a positive reassessment of the institutions and processes of civil society, for instance in Habermas's influential analysis of the public sphere. Democratic theory has thus served to complement, challenge and exceed the limitations of Marxism in theory and practice. This connects to the third key influence, that of cultural theory/politics. CPE scholars have been influenced by and have contributed to a wide range of radical traditions that examine and contest forms of discrimination and oppression based on gender, race, sexuality, disability, age and geocultural relations. How these connect to class conflict and class relations are ongoing debates, but CPE is shaped by the influence and tensions across Marxism, democratic theory and organisation, and cultural theory and politics.

CPE approaches to media

Critical political economy of media examines how the political and economic organisation ('political economy') of media industries affects the production and circulation of meaning, and connects to the distribution of symbolic and material resources that enable people to understand, communicate and act in the world. This has three main implications for studying media. First, it requires careful study of how the communications industries work. Here, political economists focus on ownership, finance and support mechanisms (such as advertising), and on how the policies and actions of governments and other organisations influence and affect media behaviour and content. Another key concern is the organisation of cultural production, addressing questions of labour processes and relations, managerial control and creative autonomy for cultural producers. This opens up to the second main topic, the influences and consequences of different ways of organising the media: commercial, state, public and their complex combinations. Analysts engage in historical and contemporary studies of the changing nature of 'structural' influences, such as dependence on advertising finance, the range of political, social and cultural influences on media institutions, and the interactions of all those seeking to influence the media. This connects with the third main area: the relationships between media content and communication systems, and the broader structure of society. To understand any specific media form requires addressing 'how it is produced and distributed in a given society and how it is situated in relation to the dominant social structure' (Kellner 2009: 96). In particular, CPE asks a question that distinguishes it from various 'mainstream' approaches that either ignore, support or accept prevailing social relations: what contribution do the media make in reinforcing or undermining political and social inequality? (McChesney 2003).

For Murdock and Golding (2005: 61) political economy approaches are distinguished in four main ways. They are *holistic*, seeing the economy as interrelated with political, social and cultural life, rather than as a separate domain. They are *historical*, paying close attention to long-term changes in the role of state, corporations and media in society. They are 'centrally concerned with the balance between private enterprise and public intervention', between the private and public provision of services. Finally, 'and perhaps most importantly of all', they go beyond 'technical issues of efficiency' (in terms of market transactions between producers and consumers) 'to engage with basic moral questions of justice, equity and the public good'.

Culture and industry

CPE takes up the notion of the industrialisation of culture, and culture as industry, from the Frankfurt School theorists, notably Theodor Adorno and Max Horkheimer. Media, argues the Western CPE tradition, are 'first and foremost industrial and commercial organisations which produce and distribute commodities' (Murdock and Golding 1974: 205–6). The study of media production has intrinsic value in understanding how and under what conditions media are 'made'. However, CPE rests on a larger claim, that understanding 'production' is necessary in order to fully understand media 'content' and 'audiences'. To repeat a central proposition: different ways of organising and financing communications have implications for the range and nature of media content. For Golding and Murdock (1977): 'It is only by situating cultural products within the nexus [interlinking] of material interests which circumscribe their creation and distribution that their range and content can be fully explained'. According to a later formulation (Murdock and Golding 2005: 60) CPE 'sets out to show how different ways of financing and organising cultural production have *traceable consequences* for the range of discourses, representations and communicative resources in the public domain and for the organization of audience access and use' (my emphasis). This formulation bears traces of a debate on the relative importance of economic factors for a full understanding of the (ideological) meaning of texts. As a much earlier essay puts it, to understand the production of meaning requires not only analysis of how ideology is inscribed in texts and readings, but 'grasping the general economic dynamics of media production and the determinations they exert' (Golding and Murdock 1979: 210). We will address these issues of 'determination' further below.

Core themes

So what has been the focus of work coming from this CPE tradition? According to Murdock and Golding (2005: 64) 'five historical processes are particularly central to a critical political economy of culture: the growth of the media; the extension of corporate reach; commodification; the universalization of citizenship; and the changing role of state and government intervention'. These important themes also serve to emphasise CPE's efforts to examine how the media connect to broader social arrangements. I want to begin though with a more media-centric overview of themes.

A conventional mapping divides media analysis into three areas: production, content and audience. Numerous problems and limitations with this model have been highlighted. It is more suited to a transmission model of 'mass communication', of one-to-many communication, and locates production and audiences at opposite poles. This framework has been found particularly ill-suited to grapple with more recent shifts in relations between production and consumption, signalled by terms such as 'produser' and 'prosumer', with user-generated content, demassification and convergence between 'vertical' mass media and 'horizontal' mediated communications. Nevertheless the model is useful in mapping what remain core foci in media analysis, as well as helping to identify points of 'divisions' in the field.

Production

CPE is most associated with the study of 'production' and in a caricatured, but prevalent, version is limited to an account of media ownership and finance. A related, and more nuanced, criticism is that CPE has tended to offer a limited account of media texts (content) and has tended to ignore important aspects of audiences and consumption – how audiences and users read and make meaning from texts. These are important criticisms that we will address, but the equation of CPE scholarship with 'production' is inaccurate and must be rejected. What does characterise CPE analysis is an insistence on addressing the organisation of production. Against analyses that narrowly focus on textual construction ('textualist') or on the consumption of media meanings, CPE calls for analysts to engage with the manner in which media communications are produced and, more broadly, with the conditions that influence production practices. Amongst the key topics examined are media ownership, finance, governance and regulation, the organisation of media work, influences on media, including owners, managers, advertisers, sources and users.

Content

If production matters for CPE analysis it can nevertheless be distinguished from approaches that deal solely with the economic aspects of media industries and markets, because CPE calls for attention to the 'interplay between the symbolic and economic dimensions' of the production of meaning (Murdock and Golding 2005: 60). Attention to the production of culture is combined with regard for the complex nature and properties of cultural commodities (symbolic value). The goods manufactured by cultural industries 'play a pivotal role in organizing the images and discourses through which people make sense of the world' (Murdock and Golding 2005: 60).

A key focus for CPE is to examine how media and communications serve to sustain the interests of the wealthy and powerful. Media are connected to the ways in which power is sustained through meanings. There are tensions, however, in regard to analysis of ideology, of ideas that serve to sustain relations of dominance (Thompson 1990; Eagleton 2007). First, such ideology critique has been regarded by some political economists as too textualist, disconnecting the interpretation of texts from an appreciation of the conditions in which they were formed. A second criticism is of over-simplistic readings of dominant ideologies within texts. Third, has been criticism of the supposed effects and influence of ideology on audiences. A fourth area of dispute concerns epistemology. Ideology critique involves challenging the construction of reality in discourse, and truth claims. Poststructuralism, which vies as a leading paradigm in media and cultural studies, regards 'reality' as a product of language. As Lee (2003: 154) writes of one influential grouping, the Yale school deconstructionists such as Paul de Man and Stanley Fish, there are 'no facts, only interpretations; no truths, only expedient fictions'. Can appeals to reality be sustained without falling back into naïve realism? CPE adopts a critical realist epistemology. Critical realism is a philosophy of science that distinguishes between real structures, actual processes or events and empirical evidence (traces of events) (Jessop 2008: 45). It recognises 'the reality of both concepts and social practices' (Mosco 2009: 128) and engages in efforts to use empirical evidence to help assess which concepts and theories are more or less valuable. It rejects epistemologies based on ideas alone (ideographic) or 'facts' alone (positivism) and seeks to engage and balance theoretical and empirical considerations, conceiving reality as 'made up of both what we see and how we explain what we see' (Mosco 1996: 2). For the Marxist scholar Christian Fuchs (2011: 265):

> Empirical ideology critique tests whether certain claims about reality can be questioned by looking for counter-evidence that supports the assumptions that the claims are mythological and contradict evidence about the state of reality. It introduces a different level of reality to claims about reality and thereby tries to increase epistemological complexity. It is based on the assumption that reality is complex and contradictory and that one-dimensional representations of reality lack complexity and should therefore be questioned.

CPE scholars challenge the perceived image of their subfield as confirming, over and over, that ownership of the means of media production by capital manifests itself as, and explains, control over meaning. For Garnham (1979: 136) 'Because capital controls the means of cultural production … it does not follow that these cultural commodities will necessarily support, whether in their explicit content or in their mode of cultural appropriation, the dominant ideology'. Critical scholarship needs to examine both iterations of ideology and yet remain alert to signs of conflict, contestation and contradiction in the production and consumption of meanings (Mosco 2009: 96).

Audience

A common view associating CPE with the study of 'production', to the relative neglect of media consumption and audiences, needs revision. There has been very strong and extended engagement with audiences within CPE scholarship.

What characterises this work, however, is an insistence on connecting audience experience to the economics and power dynamics of media provision. There has been historical and contemporary analysis of how audiences are commodified and sold to marketers (Meehan 2005; Wasko and Hagen 2000; chapter six). Another key focus has been on the implications of audience valuation for media finance, examining how advertising serves as a system of subsidy that privileges media serving audiences valued by advertisers, from Oscar Gandy's work on the consequences for Black and minority media, to Turow's (2011) work on the implications of profiling and targeting across the Internet. The ways in which wealth, time, gender and other factors structure access to communications is another central theme. Yet, CPE scholars have acknowledged the tradition's relative neglect of meaning-making processes in the reception, consumption and use of media products, and made various efforts to remedy this by drawing on the insights of cultural studies and other traditions to examine the production and circulation of meaning. As feminist political economist Ellen Riordan (2002: 8) maintains 'it is not sufficient to look only at how corporations limit and constrain cultural representations; we must also interrogate the consumption of these ideological images by groups of people who are in turn sold to advertisers as a niche market'. One ambitious effort to combine political economic contextualisation and audience reception analysis was the *Global Disney Audiences* project (Wasko et al. 2001; Biltereyst and Meers 2011).

Media scholarship involves choices and decision about which aspects of the circuit of communications, encompassing production and consumption, to focus investigation on. Despite its caricature image as being focused on 'production', CPE analysis can claim to have a greater regard for holism (Deacon 2003) than many other approaches, not least those that ignore conditions of production. It is certainly true that the demands of holism are rarely fully realised, but the effort to trace relationships and consequences of the organisation of communications is a principal feature of CPE analyses. Curran (2006) gives an example of such an approach in examining crime coverage in US local television news. In the context of deregulation and marketisation, increased competition in supply and rising pressure to meet corporate owners' and investors' expectations for profit, coverage of crime sharply increased in US television in the 1990s, being both cheap and popular. By the mid 1990s reporting violent crime accounted for two-thirds of local TV news output in fifty-six US cities (Klite et al. 1997). Incessant coverage contributed to a growing proportion of Americans judging crime to be the most serious problem facing the nation, despite crime levels actually falling. Research by Iyengar and others showed that 'Local TV news tended also to focus on decontextualised acts of violent crime by black perpetrators in ways that strengthened racial hostility, and fuelled demands for punitive retribution' (Curran 2006: 140). Such analysis requires that we address the organisation and culture of journalists, the influence of sources, news agendas, media discourses and media influence. Yet equally, it shows that we must address the political economic context and policy changes to fully grasp why news changed, with consequences for the way in which both public issues and socio-ethnic groups were 'framed'.

How do media relate to power sources in society? Whose interests are represented? Who is represented in media? Who has access to communication resources – and what can they do with them? Political economy argues that to answer such questions we need not only the analysis of texts, or texts and readers, but analysis of the forces and interests shaping media and the conditions of production. How you judge political economy will depend on how you view the focus of investigation – the questions it poses and tries to answer. It will also depend on whether you share perspectives that insist there are 'problems' in our media systems, whether you are persuaded that it is important to examine these problems and consider how to try to put them right. *Critical political economy of communications is a critical realist approach that investigates problems connected with the political and economic organisation of communication resources.*

Critical political economy and its others

The tradition of critical political economy is commonly defined, in part, by way of its distinction from three main alternatives: neoclassical/mainstream media economics, liberal pluralist communication studies and cultural studies (Mosco 2009: 128; Hesmondhalgh 2013). Two are broadly defined as 'mainstream' traditions (media economics and liberal communications) while the third is a rival cluster of radical approaches. Defining CPE from its 'others' has value but also limitations; it risks perpetuating a tired, rigid classification and entrenching crude and out-dated divisions of a field that is ceaselessly changing. It is also important to resist imposing a false coherence upon any of these approaches, all of which have great internal diversity, dynamic interconnections and complex affiliations. We will engage with the value and validity of these divisions more fully, but they do have some explanatory value. They help us to trace, recover and reassess the influences, points of difference, as well as the often coded shorthand, through which analysts have worked, disagreed and debated.

Neoclassical/modern media economics

Critical political economy starkly diverges from principles of neoclassical economics that continue to influence 'mainstream' economics. Neoclassical economics presumes the desirability of a capitalist market economy. This set of values is most pronounced in neoliberal thought, where economics is harnessed to a political programme whereby the creation of efficient and unfettered markets is the principal goal of public policy. Neoliberalism 'refers to the set of national and international policies that call for business domination of all social affairs with minimal countervailing force' (McChesney 2001). Market competition is promoted as the best mechanism not only for economic 'growth' but also for social organisation and the distribution of resources. Yet, modern economic thought is far from unified, and some economists, including ones working on media and communications, critique the neoclassical assumptions of rational actors calculating utility maximisation, or the conditions for perfect and imperfect competition, drawing on economic history, psychology and psychoanalytic theory (Sackrey et al. 2010; Miller 2008).

Media economics is a subfield of economics that analyses the media, communications and cultural industries using economic concepts. This work takes different forms with varying levels of 'integration' into media and cultural analysis. The influence of specialist economic analysis on communications research media has been rather limited historically. It has informed legal policy studies, 'political economic' analysis, and to a lesser extent 'cultural economy' work, but has generally remained a largely separate, specialist domain. This is changing, however. Recognition of the importance of economics in understanding dynamic changes in media markets has informed mainstream communications research and teaching. The significance of financing, business operations and markets to understanding the challenges and transformations of media services, underscores this. There is an expanding body of literature on media economics, examining media markets, convergence, digitalisation, transnationalisation and labour (Doyle 2002b; Hoskins et al. 2004; Alexander et al. 2004; Hesmondhalgh 2013).

Critical political economists draw on this media economics literature but highlight certain limitations arising from either the 'uncritical' application of economic concepts, or claims made for free-market mechanisms. What is at issue is less the tools and techniques of economic analysis, or even its insights, than the conceptual and value framework. The CPE tradition is sceptical concerning claims made for markets; it challenges the neglect of asymmetry in regard to the power of actors in markets, and it challenges the contraction of 'value' to the measure of market-based exchanges.

Liberal pluralist communication studies

In the post-war period Western scholarship was dominated by what Pietilä (2005: 105–26) calls 'classical behavioural mass communication research'. According to the behaviourist paradigm, researchers should examine only those behaviours that can be directly observed and measured, with the goal of deriving propositions that could be tested, thus applying methods from the physical sciences to the social sciences. This privileged empirical research and techniques while leaving unquestioned the social organisation of media provision and tended to neglect ethical and critical perspectives. Most influential in the United States, this positivist tradition prompted critical reaction elsewhere (see Nordenstreng 1968; Christians et al. 2009: 184). Early researchers in the CPE tradition did not reject empirical investigation, in fact they insisted on gathering material evidence, but did reject empiricism, 'the reduction of all intellectual activity to the production of falsifiable statements about observed behaviour' (Mosco 2009: 79). Instead scholars argued for a critical approach that acknowledged the relationship between observed reality, truth claims and power interests, an approach developed in the influential work of the Frankfurt School.

The main division between CPE and liberal pluralism concerns the analysis of power and power relations. Liberal pluralist political thought conceives of interest groups who vie for power in a manner which is open and contingent. Inequality in power and resources between interest groups is acknowledged, but no group dominates. Sustained dominance is rejected because it would undermine the affirmation of the 'democratic' political system that liberalism defends, and distinguishes from authoritarian systems. This means that forms of systematic and structured inequality are 'downplayed in favour of an implicitly optimistic notion of society as a level playing ground where different interest groups fight for their interests' (Hesmondhalgh 2007: 32). A rich strand of liberal media sociology offers much needed empirical and ethnographic studies of media organisations, media work, as well as participation and engagement by users. However, this work has also been challenged for its relative neglect of economic influences (Golding and Murdock 1979: 200). Differences between liberal pluralist and radical approaches to media are examined more fully in the next chapter.

Cultural studies

Cultural studies emerged as another strand of radical scholarship. Its origins lie in the work of British social historians and literary scholars including Richard Hoggart, E.P. Thompson, Raymond Williams and later Stuart Hall. Cultural studies explores the dynamics of power and culture across an unbounded terrain, including cultural globalisation and diaspora, analyses of race, gender, sexuality and disability. It has challenged narrow, often elitist, orderings of what constitutes cultural value, to embrace a very wide range of phenomena and to apply insights and approaches to broader sectors including the economy. It has drawn on a wide range of sociocultural theory from work on psychoanalysis, semiotics, language and affect, to cultural theories of social organisations, behaviour and interaction, and cultural policy and politics.

Very much has been written on the 'long-standing theoretical and methodological affinities and tensions' (Chakravartty and Zhao 2008: 10) between CPE and cultural studies, and the institutionalised debate that has flared with often bitter heat for nearly three decades. The 1980s and 1990s saw sometimes vitriolic exchanges from traditions that both claimed a radical legacy and mission, and defended themselves against the putative existential threat posed by the other. Divisions between cultural studies and political economy structured the field of media studies in some educational environments, notably the UK; relations between these 'camps' became hostile, combative and 'adversarial' (Mosco 2009: 80). There are compelling arguments both for and against revisiting this 'cultural studies vs. political economy' divide. The principal case *against* is that many of the heated divisions are of their time, marking out the intellectual and material environment of the 1980s and 1990s, and are arguably of greatest interest to historians. The principal case *for* revisiting is that the division can help new generations of students to map and decode differences formulated in contemporary as well as historical writings.

The shared intellectual roots of cultural studies and political economy have been described by many scholars (Babe 2009). This excavation has often been allied to an effort at reintegration or a redrawing of the map to realign critical scholars working across cultural studies and CPE traditions (Meehan 1999; Couldry 2000; Fenton 2007; Hesmondhalgh 2007). This is vital work, to which this book seeks to contribute. For Babe (2009: 4):

> *Cultural studies* may be loosely defined as the multidisciplinary study of culture across various social strata, where culture refers to arts, knowledge, beliefs, customs, practices, and norms of social interaction. *Studies in political economy of media*, in contrast, focus on the economic, financial, and political causes and consequences of culture.

Babe argues that there are common roots in cultural materialism, an approach developed in the work of Raymond Williams. Williams (1983: 210) called for a 'cultural materialist' approach that should pursue 'analysis of all forms of signification [...] within the actual means and conditions of their production'.

Williams (1980: 243–44) outlined 'a theory of culture as a (social and material) productive process and of specific practices, of "arts", as social uses of material means of production'. This emphasised that cultural forms and activities needed to be comprehended in more encompassing social processes. The legacy was complex, though. As Schiller (1996: 187) discusses, Williams's cultural materialist theory generated an 'ambiguous oscillation, for it explicitly assigned to language, communication and consciousness as such "a primacy co-equal with other forms of the material social process, including ... 'labour' or 'production' "', yet reproduced the dualism in the terms used in discussion, tending to separate language (or consciousness) and production (or being). The field of communications, argues Schiller (1996) has struggled to overcome such dualistic thinking, dividing mental and material and cultural and economic in Western thought, a dualism that Peck (2006) argues structured the mid 1990s debates on political economy versus cultural studies between Nicholas Garnham and Lawrence Grossberg.[2]

The formative intellectual context in which CPE and cultural studies developed has been mapped, albeit in fragmented ways. Schiller (1996: 186) highlights the turn to culture in the 1960s and 1970s, informing political economic analysis of 'transnational corporate communication' and British cultural studies' 'engagement with the history and present status of the British working class and, soon, with the anti-racist and feminist movements that began once again to burgeon. In both cases "culture" appeared to satisfy, or at least, to raise the prospect of satisfying the need for drastic conceptual revision of entrenched Marxian formulations'. Curran (2004) traces how the influence of Marxism and literary studies led to British cultural studies and along a path through textual analysis, psychoanalytic theory and ideology to postmodernism and towards idealist thought and acquiescence. Likewise, McGuigan (1992) charts the shifts from cultural materialism to cultural populism and a more celebratory account of consumer/user power in cultural markets. Against the much better known Birmingham School of British Cultural Studies (whose first directors were Richard Hoggart, then Stuart Hall), Curran (2004) describes a Westminster tradition where Nicholas Garnham, Curran and others took a more materialist path focused on policy and regulation, media institutions and work, technology and history. Babe (2009: 84) argues that in their formative years political economy and cultural studies approaches 'were fully integrated, consistent, and mutually supportive'. CPE shares common roots and integrates well with critical cultural studies (characterised by Raymond Williams's cultural materialism) but the other scion of postmodernist cultural studies is inimical. Critical of the postmodernist (and populist) turn in cultural studies, Babe advocates the reintegration of a cultural materialist, critical cultural studies with political economy. We will return to examine these issues at various points but to do so it is important to identify key differences informing relations between varieties of cultural studies and CPE, some of which remain salient. However, divisions at the level of ontology, epistemology, methods, political philosophy and outlook belie easy summary, much less synthesis (see Ferguson and Golding 1997; Mosco 2009; Curran 2002; Meehan and Riordan 2002; Cottle 2003a; Babe 2009). Three key areas of division are epistemology, politics and political and social theory, and theories and analysis of culture and communications.

Epistemology

Epistemology is the study of knowledge and is concerned with the nature, sources and extent of the knowable, and the justifications for beliefs. As discussed above, CPE generally operates in an epistemological framework of critical realism. This realist epistemology is based on the 'assumption that there is a material world external to our cognitive processes which possesses specific properties ultimately accessible to our understanding' (Garnham 1990: 3). That reality is only accessible to us through concepts and discourses, but there is a material reality independent of discursive construction. For some culturalist critics such 'realism' is conflated with positivism, a crude belief in the capacity to determine 'objective' facts from external reality. Cultural studies, influenced by postmodernist thought, tends towards post-positivist, constructionist and subjectivist epistemologies (Hesmondhalgh 2007: 46). Yet, plenty of culturalist scholars share the main tenets of critical realism. Instead, a more general critique made of CPE is that it is empiricist, privileging observable 'facts' at the expense of interrogating meaning systems and articulations with rigour, in other words doing precisely what the Frankfurt School decried. The charge itself reflects tensions traceable to the humanities' influences on cultural studies and the social scientific influences on CPE (Philo and Miller 2001). Some observations; first, it is problematic to conflate empirical analysis with naïve realism since this tends to discount the methods and material of empirical analysis which are indispensable tools for investigating media and for any 'cultural materialism'. Second, debates on realism are ongoing within contemporary critical scholarship, with notable efforts to provide theoretical sophistication (Garnham 2000; Fuchs 2011). Third, there are, as Babe examines, deeper and more irreconcilable divisions between critical realism and postmodernism.

Politics and political and social theory

Cultural studies has been particularly associated with pluralising what constitutes the political. This has been influenced by feminist, LGBT, postcolonialist, and new social movement critiques of the exclusivity, selectivity, narrowness and hierarchisations of what constitutes the ground of politics. At a theoretical level Foucault's rejection of a conception of power as repressive in favour of one where power is productive, diffused through discursive interactions, has been particularly influential. Identifying with the marginalised and subaltern, cultural studies has aligned with radical social movements but has tended to remain suspicious and disconnected from 'organised' labour movement politics, in contrast to stronger links within CPE with labour and organised working class movements. There are, of course, vital debates about the scope, orientation and organisation of 'progressive' political change. Writers in the traditions of cultural studies and political economy have sought to clarify, and sometimes exacerbate, these divisions and so this remains fraught territory to navigate, with a legacy of reductive positioning and caricaturing. For some CPE writers, cultural studies approaches privilege social identity at the expense of addressing the political and economic forces that structure entitlements, inequality and oppression under capitalism (Mosco 2009). Cultural studies writers in turn have challenged CPE as privileging class-based politics and organised labour movements that are regarded as complicit with, or less radical in countering, other forms of oppression, notably those based on gender, sexuality and ethnicity.

One key division has been in regard to the politics of recognition and associated power dynamics. Much of this is traceable to an older debate about Marxian class politics and its privileging of social class over gender, race and other divisions of power. The industrial working class as subject of history was challenged by both the evident failure of this unified subject to overthrow capitalism and the ordering of power which displaced other sources of oppression including those generated by the revolutionary (male) subject. However, it has been an unfortunate characteristic of radical 'left' movements to engage in often bitter and arcane sectarian divisions amongst themselves. The struggle has had added heat in academia for various reasons. It is much more a 'war of words', as shared commitment to praxis (theory-in-practice) and public–political engagement is more difficult to realise. Further, the debate strikes at core values and self-images for avowed radicals. As many now argue, in Euro-America at least, the times demand that those seeking to sustain and advance critical work find common cause against neoconservatism (Hesmondhalgh 2007: 47), and the threat to criticality arising from marketisation pressures in higher education.

Cultural theory

A core organising tenet for cultural studies is to challenge the condescension, elitism and cultural hierarchism that justifies denigrating or disregarding ordinary, everyday culture. Here cultural studies identifies elitist perspectives from the political left, as well as right-tending conservatism, with the Frankfurt School's critical pessimism ritually condemned in textbook accounts. Within cultural studies a reading of contemporary culture emerged that challenged at key points the critical perspectives of CPE. Cultural studies 'had a fairly positive perspective, counting on the potential resistance of working-class culture in the face of capitalist domination' (Christians et al. 2009: 185). The critical concerns with mass media power and influence were mitigated and minimised by counter-assertions. Commercial mass media dominance was less consequential because its content was raw material used for refashioning into more autonomous and oppositional cultures and meanings (Jenkins 1992). For Lull (1995: 73) 'Popular culture ... is empowering. The mass media contribute to the process by distributing cultural resources to oppressed individuals and subordinate groups which they use to construct their tactics of resistance against hegemonic strategies of containment'. This perspective became dominant in a more optimistic version of cultural studies variously described as 'cultural populism' (McGuigan 1992) and 'celebratory cultural studies' (Babe 2009). A key dynamic in cultural studies was to reject the assumed passivity of audiences and emphasise instead the interpretative capabilities of 'active audiences', the productive refashioning of cultural texts by subcultures and fans, and more recently interactivity and co-creation online. Cultural studies has foregrounded issues of 'textuality, subjectivity, identity, discourse and pleasure in relation to culture' (Hesmondhalgh 2007: 42). The 'new' audience researchers emphasised the active construction of meaning and the appropriation of media products to fashion independent, even oppositional, cultures.

The CPE critique is that cultural studies progressively abandoned attention to the structural factors that influence the production of media content (McChesney 2004a: 43). CPE scholars have charged that the relative absence of analysis of capitalism and the structuring influence of class relations restricts the explanatory reach of cultural studies and contributes in some versions to an uncritical account of market provision ('cultural populism'). In some areas of enquiry what began as an informed criticism of economism and reductiveness in analysis ended up as an evasion of problems of power in all but the most micro of contexts.

The problems of corporate control over communications, emphasised by critical political economists, could be answered by a more consoling account that granted independent creativity and agency to audiences. Political economists argued that active audience accounts reproduced liberal 'uses and gratifications' research, taking media provision as given (offering an uncritical account of what was made available for audiences) and downplaying the highly unequal power dynamics between producers and consumers (Mattelart 1994: 237).

An influential model developed by scholars at the Open University (UK) conceptualised a 'circuit of production linking processes of representation, identity, production, consumption and regulation' (Du Gay: 1997). They argued that all these foci are required to 'complete' a study, and that any can serve as entry points for analysis. By contrast, CPE scholars argue for an ordering and sequencing of analysis that recognises the antecedence of production; 'production is processually and temporally prior to consumption' (Born 2000: 416). For Murdock (2003: 17) analysing 'the dynamics that are currently reshaping the professional production of public culture' is 'an essential first step to understanding the symbolic textures of everyday life'.

Today the re-examination of production and consumption stimulates fruitful dialogue and integration across CPE and culturalist work, for instance in work on the dynamics of corporate synergy and intertextuality. Corporations seek to exploit their brands and intellectual property across a wide range of media platforms, forms and allied merchandise, which are promoted and cross-promoted through their various media outlets. The strategies of recycling, reversioning and repurposing have been analysed by CPE scholars as strategies to maximise revenues, including using corporate forms of transmedia storytelling, as in the *Matrix* trilogy and spin-off products, to create 'narratively necessary purchases' (Proffitt et al. 2007: 239; Meehan 2005). Within culturalist literature such 'top down' critiques of power tend to be reversed in favour of a more celebratory account that takes themes of active audiences and resistant readings into an analysis of fan-generated production. The best work, however, is alert to the contradictory tensions in fandom (Hills 2002) and draws on the strengths of CPE and cultural studies to examine the nature of the constraints and opportunities of inter-textuality. Jenkins (2006) examines the contradictions for media companies in their desire to police intellectual property while encouraging lucrative forms of immersion by fans. Waetjen and Gibson (2007) argue that Time Warner's *Harry Potter* films and merchandise created a 'corporate reading' that supplanted the contradictory and polysemous discourses on commodification encountered in the J.K. Rowling books. Such studies highlight the value of considering how corporate activity seeks to order '(inter) textual space', encouraging analysis of the contending forces and sites of communicative exchange involving user-generated content alongside corporate promotions and journalistic commentary (Hardy 2010a, 2011). In turn this allows for a critical political economy that is alert to contradictions within cultural production and exchange, and can draw on the insights of cultural theory. Far from diminishing critical accounts this strengthens analysis of power dynamics, including corporate strategies to impose proprietary control over symbolic meanings.

Criticisms of critical political economy

We can understand the relations between CPE and its others better by assessing key critiques. Critics of political economy accuse it of reductionism and economism, reducing the complexity of forces shaping cultural expression and communication to an underlying economic explanation derived from the dominant forces and relations of production. Reductionism means attributing 'complex cultural events and processes' – such as a film, TV show or new output – 'to a single political-economic cause, such as the interests of the social class that controls the means of production' (Hesmondhalgh 2007: 47). This is, in large part, a critique of the conceptual foundations of Marxist thought on which CPE is deemed to lie and so requires some elaboration. Charges of reductiveness and economism are traceable to a criticism of determinism. In its most 'vulgar Marxist' form, this posits that the 'superstructure' (the state and political, societal and cultural institutions including the media), reflects the economic base (the economic forces and social relations arising from the dominant system of organising production), leading to an account of the media as a transmitter of ruling class ideology and a usually impoverished account of media output and performance being *determined by* state power (serving the capitalist class) or by the economic and political interests of capitalist media owners and advertisers. Such 'vulgar Marxism' was strongly rejected by scholars who shaped and defined the CPE approach. Golding and Murdock (1979: 200–201) reject as reductionist the view that mass media are instruments of the capitalist class such that media products are regarded 'as a more or less unproblematic relay system for capitalist interests and ideologies'. They argue that this reductionist formulation had its heyday in Britain between the 1930s and 1950s. In their 1973 essay 'For a Political Economy of Mass Communication', they propose a systematic analysis of the processes of corporate consolidation and the implications of commercial power, but they insist that '[to] describe and explicate these interests is not to suggest a deterministic relationship, but to map the limits within which the production of mediated culture can operate' (Murdock and Golding 1974: 226). CPE approaches do lay claim to determination (see below); however, the major contributions within CPE have been much more acutely aware of the problems of reductive analysis than critics allow. Golding and Murdock define CPE in opposition to two tendencies in Marxist analysis, a crude model of base–superstructure (instrumentalism) on the one hand and the theoreticist form of Marxism inspired by the work of Louis Althusser (structuralism) on the other.

Base and superstructure

Idealist thought regards reality as constructs of ideas and creations of the mind. By contrast Marx argues that the way we think is intimately connected with what we do, with what kind of animal we are, and with the social conditions of our existence. As Eagleton (2011: 135) summarises '[f]or Marx, our thought takes shape in the process of working on the world, and this is a material necessity determined by our bodily needs'. Marx (1980 [1859]: 181) outlines what became known as the infamous base and superstructure doctrine as follows:

> In the social production of their existence, men invariably enter into definite relations which are independent of their will, namely relations of production appropriate to a given stage in the development of the material forces of production. The totality of these relations of production constitutes the economic structure of society, the real foundation on which arises a legal and political superstructure, and to which correspond definite forms of social consciousness.

Superstructures for Marx include institutions like the state, law, politics, religion, education and culture, whose function is to support the 'base', including through generating ideas which legitimate the system. Marx and Engels assert the connections between ruling ideas and the interests of their advocates, and highlight the formation of what Foucault calls discursive regimes. However, while challenging idealist thought, the base–superstructure formulation is overly mechanistic. One of the problems with the model – really a metaphor – is that it places culture and the economic on different levels. This was an impediment to understanding the integration of the cultural and the economic. The cultural industry model of Adorno and Horkheimer addresses this problematic by describing the collapse of the superstructure of twentieth century industrialised cultural production into the economic base (Garnham 1979: 130).

In 'vulgar' Marxism or Marxist functionalism the 'superstructure' reflects the economic base: it is enough to know how the media are organised as economic entities to 'read off' their content and symbolic meaning. To regard cultural expression in this way is an example of economism, the meaning and significance of culture being located in the determining structures of the forces and relations of production. According to this view media content (symbolic meaning) must be explained as expressive of fundamental ways in which the economic structure of society is organised. Media content may be understood by the primary function of media as the transmission of the ruling values and ideologies (functionalism). Such an interpretation informs Miliband's (1977: 50) account of Marx and Engels's theory of ideology: 'But the fact remains that "the class which has the means of material production at its disposal" does "have control at the same time of the means of mental production" … Nor is the point much affected by the fact that the state in almost all capitalist countries "owns" the radio and television – its purpose is identical'. This overly mechanistic and instrumental notion of ideology was challenged in turn by structuralist Marxism. For critical cultural scholars the main attraction of structuralist Marxism was that it rejected crude models of economic determination. Its account of ideology addressed the psychic dimensions of identity formation and regarded ideological processes as complex, contested and incomplete. Culture was rescued from its derivative, epiphenomenal position and granted 'relative autonomy' from the base.

However, amongst its deficiencies, notably in the influential account of Althusser (1984), structuralist Marxism shared two features with earlier accounts. First, it tended to infer from the study of output of media (texts) the assumed intentions and deliberations of the producers. Second, following Althusser's account of the mass media as 'ideological state apparatuses' (ISA), it tended to generalise the ideological function and effects of media without regard for variations in their organisation and composition within different sections of the media and across different media systems. Amongst other things this collapsed together vital differences between state-controlled media, public service and private media – and tended to ignore historical specificity. Althusser's own account needs to be read in terms of the French State's grip on national broadcasting under De Gaulle which informed the construction of a more abstract and totalising general theory of ISAs.

Both these points were made in a seminal essay by Golding and Murdock (1977): 'Capitalism, Communication and Class Relations'. Likewise another influential figure, Nicholas Garnham (1990: 23), in an essay first published in 1979, warned that a political economy of culture must avoid the 'twin traps of economic reductionism and of the idealist autonomization of the ideological level'. Garnham argued that the material, economic and ideological are 'analytically distinct, but coterminous moments both of social practices and of concrete analysis' (23).

Few CPE scholars would wish to defend base–superstructure in its mechanistic Marxist formulation, but CPE *is* defined by the claim that culture is linked to economic structures and that any attempt to understand the products of media needs to include understanding of how they are produced and how that relates to broader structures of society. As Golding and Murdock (2000: 74) put it: 'we can think of economic dynamics as playing a central role in defining the key features of the general environment within which communicative activity takes place, but not as a complete explanation of the nature of that activity'. At the other extreme, however, are those theories – for CPE 'idealist' thought – which delink culture from the economic. In place of base–superstructure, a favoured approach – which retains the central concept of determination – is to focus on the economic as constraint. This was the influential approach taken by Raymond Williams in *Marxism and Literature* (1977: 83–89). Williams interpreted determination as setting limits and exerting pressures. This affirmed human agency while retaining stress on examining the conditions shaping how such agency could be exercised, at both individual and societal levels.[3] For Williams (1961), this reformulation was linked to a broader claim of a 'long revolution' in Britain involving three main processes: an industrial revolution, the extension of democracy and the expansion of education and cultural systems, all of them interacting and with no single sphere of activity exercising a determining influence on the others. Concepts of co-evolution and interaction also aid routes out of mechanistic models of determinism. Harvey (2011: 123) proposes seven distinctive 'activity spheres' within capitalist development: 'technologies and organisational forms; social relations; institutional and administrative arrangements; production and labour processes; relations to nature; the reproduction of daily life and the species; and "mental conceptions of the world". No one of the spheres dominates even as none of them are independent of the others'.

CPE writers have insisted that production remains determinant in Raymond Williams's sense of exerting pressure and setting limits regarding the interpretation and use of the cultural goods produced (Murdock 2003: 16–17). A key constraint in capitalist media systems is the drive to ensure profits. This is a pressure of the system and a 'structural' force; it is beyond the control of individuals' agency and constrains how they behave and make choices. The system of production, and the division of labour, is co-ordinated by money 'in the form of price signals on a market' (Garnham 2000: 42). This is determining in one crucial sense, in that we have little choice but to participate in a system of monetary exchange for labour, what Marx (1983 [1867]: 689) called the 'dull compulsion of economic relations'. As Garnham (2000: 195; 1990) argues, the capitalist mode of production has certain core characteristics (waged labour, commodity exchange) which 'constitute people's necessary and unavoidable conditions of existence'. These conditions shape, in determinate ways, the terrain of cultural practices – 'the physical environment, the available material and symbolic resources, the time rhythms and spatial relations … they set the cultural agenda'. The system is structurally determining in a further sense 'because it produces systemic results which no single economic actor planned or desired'. Yet, as Williams insisted, agency remains, and so how individuals behave – for instance individual creative workers – cannot be 'read off' from the 'structure' alone. Garnham (1990: 6) refers to Williams's reformulation as 'soft' determinism, 'not as fixing a simple causal relationship, but as a setting of limits'. Mosco (1996: 5) quotes Aijiz Ahmed who refers to determination as 'the givenness of the circumstances within which individuals make their choices, their lives, their histories'. Determination does not mean that human action is predetermined but that 'some courses of action are more likely than others, if only because it makes some more difficult than others' (Garnham 1990: 6).

These revised conceptions of determinism draw then on cultural theory and sociological theories of structure and agency (such as Giddens's structuration theory and Bourdieu's efforts to overcome the limitations of structure–agency formulations in his theories of habitus and field) (Benson and Neveu 2004). Cultural studies' dissatisfaction with the supposed remnants of economism, in the formulation of economic determination 'in the (lonely) last instance', led to shifts from Williams's 'soft determinism' towards concepts such as articulation (Hall 1980) emphasising discursive construction. Mosco (2009: 185) proposes a conception of structuration as 'a process by which structures are constituted out of human agency, even as they provide the very "medium" of that constitution'. This seeks to redress the criticisms that CPE adopts an overly rigid structural determinism (Turner 2002). The sociological problem of the structure–agency duality has been subject to extensive critique and efforts to overcome its limitations by more dynamic models (Jessop 2008: 38–47; chapter eight). The revised account of determination as pressures, constraints and linkages, opens up questions for cultural research – how far can certain groups of workers exercise creative autonomy (journalists; news anchors; filmmakers; music producers, etc.)? How is power and autonomy organised within firms? How is control changing as a result of dynamic forces – ownership, regulation, competition and technological changes? Today CPE scholars invariably reject the notion that the economic provides the essential causal impetus and that other influences are derivative or non-essential.

Origins and emergence of critical political economy

What came to be known (variously) as the political economy of communication (or culture, or media) has its foundations in the Frankfurt School work of the 1930s and 1940s. Yet, in so far as it draws on criticisms of culture and media its roots go back much further. One source was the social criticism from the 1890s and early 1900s directed at the unchecked growth of large corporate interests in the United States which included criticism of the business interests shaping US journalism by writers such as Upton Sinclair (2003 [1920]). In the early twentieth century there were emergent, left-wing critiques of commercial advertising, mainstream journalism and the private control of broadcasting, some of which is collected in McChesney and Scott (2004). The origins of an academic political economy approach to modern communications lie in efforts to understand the organisation of mass media in the early twentieth century, the expansion of electronic media, the growth of large-scale entertainment and the shift from small-scale or family-owned enterprises to large corporate media and communications businesses. It was in the 1960s that CPE became a distinctive approach with institutional visibility, notably when it was introduced to the curriculum at the University of Illinois, first by Dallas Smythe and then Herbert Schiller (Maxwell 2003; H. Schiller 2000). Media political economy approaches developed in the context of a broader resurgence of radical politics, and were then explicitly formulated in the 1970s (Wasko 2004: 312–13). As Mosco (2009: 68) identifies, there is 'no simple way to examine the wider influences on a field that encompasses the diverse contributions of several generations of researchers scattered around the world'. It has formed out of disparate intellectual currents concerned with the growth of national and transnational communication businesses, government involvement in communications and debates on the appropriate governance of communications and culture across state, public and private actors.

The Frankfurt School

One of the explicit influences on critical political economy was the work of the Frankfurt School notably Adorno, Horkheimer and others including Walter Benjamin and Ernst Bloch. Adorno's analysis of the emerging entertainment industry complex formed part of a broader investigation of processes of domination. He was amongst the earliest theorists to assert that the entertainment industry was a key site of elite domination and to connect that domination with broader structures of political–economic power in contemporary capitalist societies. Yet Adorno also brought a theory and valuation of aesthetics that resulted in an account subsequently read and condemned as elitist, overly pessimistic and 'conservative' by later writers in Marxist and critical cultural theory. Adorno viewed the commercialised American culture of mass-entertainment and consumption as instituting the same kinds of psychological dependency and conformism realised under fascism. This work then occupies an ambivalent position in critical media studies and its influence was also complex and uneven, with key works such as the Culture Industry essay, from *Dialektik der Aufklärung*, not published in English until 1977 (Babe 2009: 18). Culture has been thoroughly industrialised and commodified in a total system of standardisation, yet, anticipating the emphasis on differentiation and segmentation in late twentieth century media, Adorno and Horkheimer (1997: 123) see the emergence of market stratification:

> Something is provided for all so that none may escape ... The public is catered for with a hierarchical range of mass-produced products of varying quality, thus advancing the rule of complete quantification. Everybody must behave (as if spontaneously) in accordance with his previously determined and indexed level, and choose the category of mass product turned out for his type.

For Adorno artistic expression ('high art') was capable of serving critique through 'negative knowledge'. The culture industry collapses together both high and low art, generating a system that produces commodities for profit, sustains conformist art and hinders individuals from coming to critical consciousness, substituting pseudo-individuality and co-option for freedom. Adorno and Horkheimer's perspective was notoriously bleak and totalistic, despite its affirmation of a resistant criticality. Media culture manipulated and acculturated mass audiences into obedience (Kellner 2009: 9). Yet Adorno's work requires a sophisticated reading which textbook narratives have unjustly caricatured, including its rich, sardonic humour and effort to pursue 'negative dialectics' (see Peters 2002; Jay 1996). For the 'Western Marxist' Adorno the optimistic Marxist teleology of the inevitable triumph of the proletariat over the capitalist class had been replaced by a bleaker account of elite domination and control, yet via Freud, Adorno sees ongoing conflict generated between the repressive demands of the system and the individual's psychological needs and drives.

British scholars Graham Murdock and Peter Golding (1977) drew on the Frankfurt School's work in their efforts to develop a critical theory of mass communications. Yet, while they applauded the Frankfurt School's efforts to trace the roots of cultural domination in the economic dynamics of the 'culture industry' they criticised the tendency 'to assert that the capitalist base of the "culture industry" necessarily results in cultural forms which are consonant with the dominant ideology' (1977: 18). Likewise, Thompson (1990: 105) argues that Adorno and Horkheimer 'try to read off the consequences of cultural products from the products themselves'. For Garnham, the Frankfurt School's weakness lay 'not in their failure to realize the importance of the base or the economic, but insufficiently to take account of the economically contradictory nature of the process they observed and thus to see the industrialization of culture as unproblematic and irresistible' (Garnham 1979: 131). This insistence on the contradictory nature of industrialisation and of cultural processes was influenced by the work of British cultural historians, notably Raymond Williams, with whom Garnham had collaborated as a television producer.

Harold Innis and institutional political economy

Another influence on critical political economy came from historical accounts that emphasised the profound effects on social organisation and consciousness arising from the introduction and adoption of successive forms of communication. This analysis was non-Marxist, forming part of a broader 'institutionalist' approach (Mosco 2009; Babe 2009) and its account of communication is generally referred to as 'medium theory'. The leading figure is Harold Innis (1894–1952) a Canadian economic historian who focused on media late in his career although his earlier work had examined broader forms of communications, notably transportation. Innis integrated the control of communication resources into broader histories of political and economic power, and affirmed a dynamic set of relationships between communication power and consciousness. Changes in media technologies were related to changes in political and economic power and to the manner in which knowledge was organised and distributed through societies. In *Empire and Communications* (1950) and *The Bias of Communication* (1951) Innis argued that the physical properties of media (heaviness, durability, storage capacity) generate a bias towards different systems of control through time and space, with printed paper, for instance, being a more space-binding medium for governance across large geographical areas than stone or parchment. This work informed historical studies that foregrounded the influence of communications systems, as well as versions of medium theory that regard media as having intrinsic properties that bring about social change (a technological determinism that Innis himself rejected but which was developed by others, notably Marshall McLuhan). Babe (2009: 22, 32–46) seeks to recover Innis from relative neglect, as someone whose own integration of political economic and cultural analysis could inform efforts to reintegrate these fields today.

Dallas Smythe and Herbert Schiller

Two 'founding' figures, Dallas Smythe and Herbert Schiller, are regarded as especially influential upon North American research, and indeed internationally

(Maxwell 2003; Schiller 2006; Mosco 2009: 82–91). Smythe was a Canadian who established the first course on the political economy of communication at the recently formed Institute of Communications Research at the University of Illinois in 1948–49. This became one of the few established centres for political economic research and provided continuity for generations of scholars, including Herbert Schiller who followed Smythe in teaching the political economy course (H. Schiller 2000).

Dallas Smythe studied economics for his PhD (1937) at the University of California, Berkeley. Attracted by New Deal policies he worked for various government departments, including the Department of Labor where he monitored labour relations in the media and telecommunication sectors, before becoming chief economic advisor for the US Federal Communication Commission (1943–48). Smythe was radicalised by the anti-fascist struggles of the 1930s, by his observations of labour relations and, at the FCC, by the commercial lobbying to secure control over broadcasting (Mosco 2009: 82–84). Smythe's landmark monograph *The Structure and Policy of Electronic Communication* (1957) was followed by an influential essay 'On the Political Economy of Communications' (1960). His major work *Dependency Road* (1981) examined US dominance over Canada's media system and economy. Yet Smythe left the US in the 1960s having struggled against the conformism accompanying McCarthy era attacks on radicals, in search of a more hospitable environment for critical research. Smythe returned to his home town Regina in 1963, becoming Chairman of the Social Sciences Division, University of Saskatchewan. Here, he developed an interdisciplinary programme which attracted scholars and students from around the world, work he continued when he moved to Simon Fraser University in 1974.[4] Smythe was influential in promoting research and policy work on international communication flows under the auspices of UNESCO in the 1960s and 1970s (chapter seven). Travelling widely, he researched communication policies and practices in China, Japan, Chile (under socialist President Salvador Allende) and across Europe. In a tribute his colleague Bill Melody (1992) wrote:

> Much of Smythe's research and writing created discomfort for mainstream social science researchers, teachers, and policy-makers. He resisted deterministic and administrative theories and analyses of all kinds. To him the whole point of independent research was to critically examine the major institutions in society so as to better understand their contradictions and limitations, as a platform for changing them.
>
> […]
>
> He insisted on linking research and knowledge to policy and practice. The first responsibility of those who develop new knowledge is to apply it to improve the human condition, especially for the disenfranchised and powerless.

Herbert Schiller trained in economics and took over Smythe's political economy course at Illinois in 1963. Like Smythe, Schiller's political experience was shaped by the Great Depression, New Deal politics and corporate expansion in North America in the 1930s and 1940s. Schiller attended City College in New York, whose provision of free education to the city's working class and Jewish students (excluded from Protestant elite private schools) contributed to a radicalised educational environment. Schiller worked for the US government on the reconstruction of Germany after the war, then returned to New York to teach and complete a doctoral thesis on the political economy of post-war relief efforts. Securing a visiting position at Illinois, his interest in resource allocation led to work on the radio spectrum and prompted a deepening analysis and critique of business power. His first major book *Mass Communication and American Empire* (1969) was followed by *The Mind Managers* (1973), *Communication and Cultural Domination* (1976) and a host of books and articles up to his final retrospective *Living in the Number One Country* (2000).

Schiller's work helped to define the political economy of communication approach in the US, examining communication in the wider context of business expansion and corporate influence on government. Yet it was his critique of Western cultural imperialism that helped to make Schiller better known abroad than in America and a huge influence on critical scholarship worldwide (chapter seven). Central concerns for both Smythe and Schiller were to examine the growth and power of transnational communications companies and their linkages with other businesses and capital, notably advertising, with states and state policy, and with governing elites. Their work examined corporate media in North America but was also internationalist and Marxian, placing a critique of capitalism and interests in class, social justice and cultural imperialism at its centre.

Mosco (2009: 88–89) describes a conference he attended at Illinois in 1979 which brought together a new generation of students of Schiller and Smythe under the auspices of Thomas Guback, including Janet Wasko, Eileen Meehan, Oscar Gandy, Manjunath Pendakur and Fred Fejes. The political economy approach now broadened with the work of a new generation including Herbert Schiller's son Dan Schiller, and Robert McChesney, both at Illinois, Gerald Sussman, Stuart Ewen, Emile McAnany, Robin Anderson, Andrew Calabrese, John Downing, Oscar Gandy and Robert Hackett, amongst many others. From the early 1980s political economy of communications began to develop as a 'collective enterprise' across North America and Europe.

European research origins

A political economy approach was explicitly propounded by scholars in the United Kingdom, notably Graham Murdock, Peter Golding, Nicholas Garnham and James Curran. In contrast to the United States a critical Marxian framework was embedded in the institutional efforts to establish degree courses in media studies in the 1970s and advanced and explicated as an alternative to mainstream liberal approaches (chapter two). Golding and Murdock worked at the Centre for Mass Communication Research, at the University of Leicester, established in

1966 as the first academic centre for the study of media in the UK, and led by James Halloran. Murdock and Golding's (1974) 'For a Political Economy of Mass Communications' was the first of a series of papers that set out the rationale and research agenda for political economy.

Nicholas Garnham worked as a BBC television producer and film critic, became involved in the audiovisual trade union and began teaching part-time before helping to establish the first media studies degree at the Polytechnic of Central London (renamed the University of Westminster in 1992) (Curran 2004; Mosco 2009: 77). Garnham's influential essay 'Contribution to a Political Economy of Mass Communication' (1979) outlined the theory and tasks for political economy analysis. An inchoate 'Westminster School' emerged, but most scholars in this emerging subfield were scattered institutionally and also tended to integrate cultural and sociological analysis. The sociological focus was strong throughout, in studies of news and documentary producers in press and television by Phillip Elliot, Jeremy Tunstall, Paul Hartmann, Philip Schlesinger, Murdock and Golding. Other key influences, as mentioned, were the intellectuals and writers shaping British cultural studies, overlapping with Marxist influenced, radical historians such as Christopher Hill and E.P. Thompson, whose study *The Making of the English Working Class* emphasised the political and cultural, as well as economic, generation of class consciousness and the self-organisation of popular movements. Of these figures, Raymond Williams left the most influential legacy on media and cultural studies in work that ranged across literary, cultural history and political economy studies, integrating humanities and social scientific research. Major works include *Culture and Society 1780–1950* (1958), *The Long Revolution* (1961) and *Culture* (1981).

A key impetus and theme for British cultural studies was to examine the cultural practices of working class communities formed in the rich historical interweaving of economic, political and cultural domination and conflict. Hoggart's (1957) work elevated working class experience yet, echoing Adorno, charted the perceived demise and displacement of working class culture and consciousness by the 'soft mass-hedonism' of an increasingly dominant commercial mass culture. The complexity and contradiction of popular culture were explored most extensively by Williams, a Welsh-born scholar and political activist, committed to working class education, who was professor of drama at Cambridge. Like Hoggart, Williams regarded commercialised culture as eroding authentic working class culture, but Williams traced this process back beyond post-war Britain to the commodification of literary work in the late eighteenth century. Also, in contrast to Hoggart and Adorno's pessimism, Williams (1981) highlighted an ongoing struggle to realise a democratic communication system in place of the authoritarian, paternal or commercial ones that existed.

In place of Adorno's contention that media industry innovation was a force for extending elite control, Williams 'harboured an optimistic reformism' (D. Schiller 1996: 109); he was more positive about the potential of new media for creative expression and, while critical of control, saw state-supported media such as the BBC as a site of struggle between undemocratic and democratic forces. Williams (1974: 151) wrote:

> Over a whole range from general television through commercial advertising to centralised information and data-processing systems, the technology that is now or is becoming available can be used to affect, to alter, and in some cases to control our whole social process.
>
> [...]
>
> We could have inexpensive, locally based yet internationally extended television systems, making possible communication and information-sharing on a scale that not long ago would have seemed utopian. These are the contemporary tools of the long revolution towards an educated and participatory democracy, and of the recovering of effective communications in complex urban and industrial societies. But they are also the tools of what would be, in context, a short and successful counter-revolution, in which, under the cover of talk about choice and competition, a few para-national corporations, with their attendant states and agencies, could reach farther into our lives, at every level from news to psychodrama, until individual and collective response to many different kinds of experience and problem became almost limited to choice between programmed possibilities.

In continental Europe key founding figures include Kaarle Nordenstreng (Finland), Armand Mattelart (Belgium) and Bernard Miège (France). Nordenstreng has been a leading academic and activist engaged in efforts to establish a New World Information and Communication Order (NWICO) in the 1970s and subsequent drives to establish more equitable communications exchange and people's communication rights in forums such as the World Summit on the Information Society (WSIS). He collaborated with Herbert Schiller (1979; 1993) and both were closely involved in developing the International Association for Media and Communication Research (IAMCR), which brought together political economists within the longest established international network for media scholars. Armand Mattelart was educated in France and worked as a professor at the University of Chile until the US-backed coup toppled the government of Salvatore Allende, when he took up a professorship at the University of Paris. The anthologies he edited with Seth Siegelaub (1979; 1983) presented and developed political economic work on *Communication and Class Struggle* with volumes on *Capitalism, Imperialism* and *Liberation, Socialism*. Bernard Miège's (1989) work on the capitalisation of cultural production rejected Adorno and Horkheimer's bleak and pessimistic account of industrialisation to offer a more nuanced, microanalysis of forms of commodification of culture. Miège's attention to the 'limited and incomplete nature of attempts to extend capitalism into the realm of culture' (Hesmondhalgh 2013: 25) informs a 'cultural industries' approach that highlights the ambivalent and contested process of commodification and seeks to incorporate a positive appreciation of the gains from industrialisation and new technologies.

Mapping differences between North American and European traditions

From the late 1960s into the 1970s when political economy work was developing in Europe, the US tradition remained 'primarily based' on the work of Schiller and Smythe (Mosco 2009: 88). Both were 'less interested' than European scholars in developing 'an explicit theoretical account of communication', argues Mosco (2009: 7), who identifies two main directions CPE research has taken. One, prominent in the work of Garnham, Golding and Murdock, has 'emphasized class power' while another stream (Mattelart) has examined class struggle (Mosco 2009: 7). Mosco reads the first tradition as documenting and examining hegemonic power while the second foregrounds resistance. There are differences, certainly: the work of the British scholars tended to be more national in focus contrasting with Mattelart's internationalist engagement with national liberation movements. Some early British studies such as a pioneering analysis of demonstrations (Halloran et al. 1970: 31) focus on how news is selected and presented in dominant media rather than outline 'alternative value systems'. However, Mosco's division of work is overdrawn and cannot be sustained in respect of output and analysis. Hesmondhalgh (2013) goes even further in distinguishing between a North American tradition and a European 'cultural industries' approach in political economy, favouring the latter and critiquing the former. For Hesmondhalgh (2013: 35) the North American tradition, identified with Herbert Schiller and Robert McChesney, is centrally concerned with 'cataloguing and documenting the growth in wealth and power of the cultural industries and their links with political and business allies'. The European 'cultural industries' approach, associated with Bernard Miège, Garnham and others is better at addressing the specific economic conditions and organisation of production in cultural industries, tensions between production and consumption, and complexity and contradictions in cultural provision. The main charge is that the European tradition engages in more sophisticated cultural theory, which is lacking in the North American tradition, and consequently is better able to address the inherent 'complexity, contestation and ambivalence' in mass communications (Hesmondhalgh 2013: 45). As I hope to show, I share the analytical concerns to address complexity that Hesmondhalgh pursues. However, I find this mapping of work, like Mosco's, to be overdrawn and reliant on a partial, and dismissive, reading of the work of Schiller and McChesney. Hesmondhalgh finds little evidence of engagement with media and cultural theory, but ignores Schiller's powerful critique of revisionist cultural theory in *Culture Inc.* (1989) and McChesney's critical engagement with cultural theorists' work (2007; 2008). Several of the charges cannot be sustained, notably that the Schiller–McChesney tradition ignores symbol creators (work on journalism refutes this most strongly), downplays the processes of commodification (central to the work of Dan Schiller, Mosco and others) and fails to address both information and entertainment (again the extensive work on commodification, commercialisation and the integration of marketing by scholars like Wasko, Meehan and McAllister refutes this).

The stated divisions distort the historical record but also obscure the plurality of approaches and interconnection amongst scholars today. Mapping intellectual tendencies to geographical settings involves too many truncations to be sustainable. More importantly it distracts from two vital but differently constituted tasks, that of locating scholarship in its particular historical political and intellectual contexts, and the task of developing appropriately sophisticated analytical approaches through critique and revision.

Winseck (2012) offers another mapping, outlining four main perspectives in political economy.

1   'Conservative and liberal neoclassical economics'
2   'radical media political economy'
3   Schumpeterian institutional political economy (including creative industries and network political economy schools)
4   the cultural industries school.

We have so far discussed three. Schumpeterian political economy, emphasising technology and innovation as driving forces for change and 'creative destruction', is examined more fully in chapter five, together with arguments for a 'network' political economy. Within radical political economy, Winseck (2012: 3) argues there are two main versions: monopoly capital and digital capitalism schools. The monopoly capital approach is associated with McChesney's work; its main weakness is 'its view of the media industries as a giant pyramid, with power concentrated at the top and not enough attention paid to the details of key players, markets, and the dynamics and diversity that exists among all the elements that make up the media' (Winseck 2012: 23). The focus on big media 'embodies a static view of the world' that blots out 'standpoints of resistance, especially labor'. The other variant, digital capitalism associated with Dan Schiller and Mosco, stresses the underlying continuity of capitalist dynamics shaping 'information societies' as much as they did 'industrial societies' (Winseck 2012: 23). Winseck argues that neither of these strands of radical political economy pay sufficient attention to explaining the complexity of the media industries. The monopoly capital school 'overemphasises the tendency toward market concentration', the digital capitalism school 'overplays the ineluctable colonization of the lifeworld by market forces' and regards commodification as a pervasive process, incorporating all, even oppositional, cultural forms (Winseck 2012: 24). Like Hesmondhalgh, Winseck favours a 'cultural industries' approach. We will examine these debates more fully and readers can reach their own conclusions on the value of different approaches. My own criticism is twofold. First, while there are important differences and limitations, these mappings construct an inaccurate caricature of the disfavoured position. Second, the appeal for complexity and ambivalence is a vitally important one but it should not be applied in a generalist manner at the expense of the values of critical interrogation espoused. In both cases the framing of unsophisticated vs. sophisticated serves as code to warn students to follow favoured paths and in my view does not always encourage efforts to illuminate critical problems, which is the objective of CPE.

International origins and development

CPE developed in other regions both through the analysis of national media systems and as part of a wider critique of imperialism and dependency, including its cultural dimensions. Critical scholars in Latin America, one of the chief targets for US-led development projects, challenged the then dominant modernisation paradigm which supported models of development that favoured Western economic and political interests. Various writers shaped what became known as dependency theory (Amin 1976; Cardoso and Faletto 1979; Mosco 2009: 101). This proposed that transnational businesses, supported by their respective states in 'core' countries, exercised power over 'peripheral' countries and regions through their control of productive resources and labour. Dependency theorists were amongst the first to examine international cultural flows and the ways in which modernisation programmes in developing countries favoured the interests and expansion of Western media companies. A body of critical communications scholarship developed in the 1960s that influenced and anticipated work on media globalisation in subsequent decades. This work drew on an intellectual and research agenda shaped by anti-colonial movements and struggle for self-determination by radical intellectuals such as Frantz Fanon in Algeria and Paulo Freire in Brazil, who had emphasised the importance of mass communication for liberation movements.

Summary of CPE development

There are diverse traditions, strands and clusters (institutional and geocultural) that developed and continue to proliferate. The influence of political economy within the field of communications scholarship varies across time, subject area and region. However, a general contour can be outlined. CPE themes were framed against the backdrop of a resurgent Western Marxism, the rise of dissident social movements and anti-imperialist sentiments worldwide in the 1960s and 1970s. CPE emerged as an articulated set of claims and research priorities in the 1970s. This was a period of intellectual ascendency for neo-Marxist influence within the humanities and social sciences where media, communications and cultural studies were located. Critical political economy was never a uniform approach. Some strands have focused on ideology and subjectivity, others on the economy, capitalist production and class relations, labour and class struggle (see Schiller 1996: 132–84; Mosco 2009; Pietilä 2005: 221–44). The CPE approach that developed from the 1970s had at its core the recognition of media as industries which produce and distribute commodities (Murdock and Golding

1974). CPE became institutionalised on a wider scale during the 1980s. Yet, during this decade the Marxian influence waned across intellectual fields including communications, and political economy settled to an acknowledged but marginal place, with postmodernism and varieties of 'classic liberalism' dominant (Garnham 1990: 1; Curran 2002; McChesney 2007; D. Schiller 1996: 158–59). In the 1990s communications scholarship moved further from critical to more affirmative accounts based on the growth of digital media and reflecting a period of ascendant neoliberalism influencing Anglo-American and Australian academia in particular. Yet this was also a period in which the salience of CPE analysis of converging communications industries helped to increase the influence of a resurgent critical scholarship.

Notes

1 I have benefited enormously from the wisdom and generosity of scholars with whom I have discussed the book's themes in person and a great many more I know only through their writings. I would especially like to thank James Curran, Natalie Fenton, Des Freedman, David Hesmondhalgh, Matthew McAllister, Bob McChesney, Graham Murdock, John Nichols, Tom O'Malley, Julian Petley, John Sinclair, Joseph Turow, Janet Wasko, Granville Williams.

2 To resolve this 'interminable' debate requires, argues Peck (2006: 104), 'formulating a materialist conception of signification' that encompasses what Williams (1977: 80) terms 'the indissoluble connections between material production, political and cultural institutions and activity, and consciousness'.

3 Economism neglected what Williams emphasised throughout his writings, human agency in cultural processes and practices. Like Thompson (1978), Williams emphasised agency and lived experience against the structuralism of Althusser. However, Williams's alternative formulation of culture in terms of the social totality and 'structures of feeling' provided an uncertain and rather opaque legacy for cultural theory (Schiller 1996: 122–23).

4 Mosco (2009: 84) identifies several leading political economists influenced by Smythe's work at Simon Fraser University including William Melody, Robert Babe, Manjunath Pendakur, William Leiss, Sut Jhally, Robin Mansell and Rohan Smarajiva.

Chapter 2

Paradigms of media power

Liberal and radical perspectives on media processes

Introduction

The next two chapters introduce media political economy by considering problems that this critical tradition identifies and addresses. Chapter three discusses some of the concrete contemporary problems of the media. This chapter is broader and traces ways in which problems are identified within different theories of media and power. It begins with a division between liberal and radical approaches. This served as a heuristic device and teaching aid for courses in media studies in Britain from the mid 1970s. The liberal–radical division has too many limitations to be fully endorsed today, but it provides a useful starting point from which to expand outwards, to review key debates and consider their contemporary salience.

Forty years ago, the division between 'liberal pluralist' and radical Marxist approaches was used to structure the nascent field of media studies in Britain (Curran and Gurevitch 1977: 4–5):

> The pluralists see society as a complex of competing groups and interests, none of them predominant all of the time. Media organisations are seen as bounded organisational systems, enjoying an important degree of autonomy from the state, political parties and institutionalised pressure groups. Control of the media is said to be in the hands of an autonomous managerial elite who allow a considerable degree of flexibility to media professionals ...

> Marxists view capitalist society as being one of class domination; the media are seen as part of an ideological arena in which various class views are fought out, although within the context of the dominance of certain classes; ultimate control is increasingly concentrated in monopoly capital; media professionals, while enjoying the illusion of autonomy, are socialised into and internalise the norms of the dominant culture; the media taken as a whole, relay interpretative frameworks consonant with the interests of the dominant classes, ...

As Curran (2002: 108) explains, the liberal–radical divide was proposed, in part, as a pedagogic device to encourage students to 'think for themselves and decide in favour of one or other tradition or to consider whether there might be a more convincing intermediate position'. It was also an effort to foreground a Marxist tradition 'that had been marginalized in British academic life for much of the post-war period' (Curran 2002: 108). This radical strand also challenged the more long-standing tradition of liberal pluralist communication studies, then dominant in the United States.

In the liberal pluralist paradigm power, including media power, is dispersed; the relationship of power to media content and media discourse is contingent. In the Marxist account, media plays a key role in the management of society, the relationship between concentrated power and media discourse is one of determination. In the 1970s distinctive liberal and neo-Marxist approaches dominated and structured debates in Western media theory. Through the 1980s and 1990s such a division of the field became less tenable and less acceptable to all protagonists. Radical, neo-Marxist perspectives lost ground in the midst of a broader retreat from leftist ideas, towards more pluralistic accounts of media power and influence. Liberal perspectives were also strengthened by a variety of different, even incompatible, intellectual currents that shared opposition to the perceived rigidities, reductionism and determinism of neo-Marxist approaches. These included postmodernism, cultural studies approaches, liberal sociology, the 'process school' of semiotics (Fiske 1990) and emerging globalisation theories.

Is there value then in returning to a liberal–radical framework formulated more than a quarter of a century ago? The liberal–radical 'schism' structures a review of approaches to media (Goldsmiths Media Group 2000), yet it is clearly reductive to align and assign approaches towards media to two rival camps. As a binary, liberal–radical is ripe for deconstruction. So, we will try to interrogate rather than merely endorse the division and review both classical and contemporary arguments regarding its salience. Yet, the division between liberal and radical approaches connects to central issues in the political economy of media, concerning the relationship between media and other sources of power in societies, the nature and extent of 'autonomy' for media workers, the production and circulation of meanings in societies. How does the ordering of power in society relate to media providers in regard to their organisation, behaviour, content and output? To what extent are media organisations independent of powerful interests in society?

Not surprisingly the liberal–radical division has tended to be favoured by critical scholars, not least in challenging the taken-for-grantedness of mainstream (liberal) perspectives. Liberal scholars such as McQuail (2010: 11) propose an alternative division, between right (conservative) and left (progressive and liberal) that would tend to collapse the radical–liberal division. For perspectives on media power and in particular media policy a useful set of divisions is between neoliberal, liberal democratic, libertarian, postmodernism and critical political economic perspectives. Meyrowitz (2008) identifies three core 'narratives' of media influence: power, pleasure and patterns. We will draw upon these mappings but begin by reviewing the 'traditional' liberal–radical division and then tracing how accounts were modified in changed conditions.

Liberal pluralism

The core tenet of liberal pluralism is that power is distributed and dispersed across different groups and networks in society who can influence decision-making processes and institutions in allocating resources and taking decisions. While different groups pursue their own sectional interests to varying degrees, the political system is oriented to serving the needs of society as a whole. In contrast to domination theories of various kinds, including Marxism, power is pooled and shared; power is also contingent rather than ordered in a fixed distributional hierarchy. Liberal pluralism describes a political system that is relatively open to influences across society and this openness in turn legitimates its core principles of democratic accountability and fairness.

That is only a starting point. There are varieties of liberalism and these in turn privilege different 'jobs' for media, and different conceptions of how media and communications should be organised and regulated to serve democratic purposes. Baker (2002) describes elite, republican, pluralist democracy and his own 'complex', compound perspective. Modern liberal theorists have engaged with the evidence of conflict in society, and pluralists recognise that different groups and interests compete for power and influence, but the key characteristic of liberalism is that dominance is not pre-structured. In representative democracies most sections of society are represented by organised interest groups and parties who compete in institutionalised political forums so that political power is contingent and unpredictable.

In regard to media, the tenets of what Curran (2002: 127) calls 'liberal reflection theories' are that the media reflect rather than shape society. Media convey, circulate and enable the exchange of information, ideas and opinions across society. Different groups and interests in society can inform and influence society through the mediation of public media. Media systems are open to a sufficiently wide range of voices, ideas and opinions across society to legitimate public media's role on behalf of society. This vision has its origins in the hard-fought liberal claim to freedom of expression. In order to serve society, the media must have a high degree of autonomy. Within a libertarian perspective such autonomy is defined against 'interference' by states whereas other liberal traditions incorporate a role for the state as guarantor of communications against private interests. In general, liberalism promotes media autonomy from the instrumental interests of states, political groups, media owners and advertisers. In the twentieth century, liberalism faced imperatives to resolve for each medium the inherent tensions and contradictions between economic and political freedom, between 'market freedom' for the owners of media and ensuring that media supported democratic processes (Murdock 1992b; chapter three).

Liberal functionalism

Derived from Émile Durkheim (1858–1917), structural functionalism is associated with the US sociologist Talcott Parsons (1902–79). Functionalism proposes that human activities in societies or cultures can best be understood as complex, internally interdependent functioning systems; each part 'functions' by serving the successful working of the whole. Classic Parsonian functionalism has an inherently conservative political orientation, providing an account of the integration of social functions to produce a relatively stable social 'order'. Functionalism informed sociology and anthropology in the 1940s and 1950s, especially in the US, but is no longer influential in either field. It has, however, had a more lingering influence within media theory, including both liberal and radical variants.

Durkheim, in *The Division of Labour in Society* (1893), identifies a process of differentiation, whereby societal functions are divided up and undertaken by different, specialist social bodies. The notion that increasingly complex social systems require the functional differentiation of social roles and institutions is central to Parsons's evolutionist theory, describing a process whereby social functions initially conjoined, such as politics and religion, are separated and differentiated. Applied to media, such differentiation reaffirms media autonomy in two main ways. Media are differentiated both in their social function and in the maintenance of specialist rules and behaviours through professionalism. In the terms of a radical sociologist, Pierre Bourdieu, who challenged the conservativism of Parsons, journalism constitutes a field whose rules and practices seek to maintain, in always dynamic and unstable ways, its differentiation from other fields, such as politics.

For liberal functionalism, the media contribute in a variety of ways to the maintenance and reproduction of society. According to Harold Lasswell (1903–78) three media social functions are: surveillance (gathering information from the external environment), correlation (co-ordination between parts of society) and transmission (of social heritage and values from one generation to the next). Early twentieth century communication theories focused on information and persuasion, in print media and radio broadcasting. Harnessing the power of media and propaganda for the 'normal' management of complex societies was a theme developed by Harold Lasswell and Walter Lippman. However, challenges to the framework of strong media effects influenced what became known as the 'uses and gratifications' approach, focused on personal engagement with media and social benefits, a key strand of Meyrowitz's (2008) 'pleasure' narrative. This was also, in part, a shift from news and information to entertainment and fiction. Researchers identified various media gratifications including pleasure, relaxation, escape, identity formation and sense of belonging. Later theorists of communication (Carey) and of 'media events' (Dayan and Katz) identify media as agencies of social integration. For Dayan and Katz (1992), media events such as national sports or ceremonial state occasions serve to affirm a common shared identity. Similar arguments were made for the 'national' social integration of public service broadcasting (Cardiff and Scannell 1991). In a benign and inclusive formulation of liberal functionalism, Schudson (2005: 179) describes how ' ... both public and privately owned media in liberal societies carry out a wide variety of roles, cheer-leading the established order, alarming the citizenry about flaws in that order, providing a civic forum for political debate, acting as a battleground among contesting elites'. Media also convey messages from the people 'below' to those in power 'above' and thus have a role of 'moral amplification' in systems of representative democracy.

Radical traditions

A starting point for radical critique is to counter the claims that media are independent and autonomous institutions. Instead, radicals highlight the nature and extent of linkages between media and other sources of power. Liberal communication scholars readily concede that the media do not correspond to normative ideals of neutrality and autonomy. At issue is the degree to which the media's subjugation to authority undermines claims made for the way media systems perform and, in a related debate, the most suitable ways to organise and provide media services. A defining feature of radical approaches is to connect media to the production and maintenance of inequalities in the distribution of social power and resources. However, as we will explore, there are markedly different directions in which this is developed, leading to important divisions within the radical tradition, and different connections and alignments with other approaches. One direction is towards radical functionalism, which has been described as 'the mirror opposite of liberal functionalism' (Curran 2002: 137).

Radical functionalism

If there are underlying common interests in society then the integrative role of media can be regarded as beneficial and benign. If, however, social benefits and resources are unequally and unfairly shared out then the assertion of common interests may be regarded as misleading, if not mystifying. 'The media's projection of an idealized social cohesion may serve to conceal fundamental differences of interest' (Curran 2002: 137). The media serve to integrate individuals into the structures of society, as liberal functionalism claims; however, since that society is unequal and conflictual, to carry out the task of integration requires 'systematic propaganda'. That is the claim of Herman and Chomsky in what is perhaps the best known and most influential version of radical functionalism. Their book *Manufacturing Consent: the political economy of the media* was first published in 1988 and republished with updated contributions in 2002 and 2008. The book was not only a radical thesis, supported by detailed empirical work, but a radical intervention, provocatively and directly challenging cherished self-conceptions of democratic media in liberal systems, the United States in particular. The book came out in a period of still high regard for American news journalism, approximating, if not always realising, a watchdog role. If propaganda was all too evident in the state control of communist systems, the authors argued that the media systems of the so-called free world generated propaganda through different mechanisms of control, all the more insidious for these operations being disavowed by operatives and commentators right across the system. The book also took up and re-presented the work of elite democracy theorists of the early twentieth century including Lippman, Lasswell, Bernays and others, affirming that these provided unabashed and explicit blueprints of how the system works, written by its intellectual architects. Elite democratic theory conceives governance as the province of an expert cadre, and democracy as involving 'a problem of managing minds in mass society. For Herman and Chomsky, the media mobilise support for the special interests of the most powerful groups in society and in doing so purvey a systematic bias in coverage. This occurs not just in what is said and reported, but in what is omitted, distorted or marginalised:

> Leaders of the media claim that their news choices rest on unbiased professional and objective criteria … If, however, the powerful are able to fix the premises of discourse, to decide what the general populace is allowed to see, hear and think about, and to 'manage' public opinion by regular propaganda campaigns, the standard view of how the system works is seriously at odds with reality.
>
> (Herman and Chomsky 1988: xi)

Manufacturing Consent is presented in some media textbooks (Barlow and Mills 2012) as a synecdoche for the critical political economy of media tradition. This is misleading and problematic, as we will see, because it represents only one highly contested strand. Yet, Herman and Chomsky's account of the influences on mass media does engage with central and common features across the CPE tradition. In their metaphoric account of media processing, the 'raw material of the news must pass through successive filters, leaving only the cleansed residue fit for print … The elite domination of the media and marginalization of dissent … results from the operation of these filters' (Herman and Chomsky 1988: 2). Five main filters are identified:

1 the size, concentrated ownership, owner wealth and profit orientation of the major mass media firms aligns and integrates them with dominant interests; dominant media forms are 'closely interlocked, and have important common interests, with other major corporations, banks and government' (1988: 14)
2 advertising as the primary income source of the mass media
3 the reliance of the media on information provided by government, business and 'experts' funded and approved by these primary sources and agents of power
4 'flak', organised negative responses to media conduct, serves as a means of disciplining the media and 'trying to contain any deviations from the established line' (1988: 29)
5 anti-communism as a political control mechanism.

The first two filters address key political–economic factors of ownership and financing. The third filter addresses the media–source relationship in ways that connect with broader liberal scholarship but provides a critical account of media dependency on elite sources of information, such as governments, and resource-access inequalities, for instance between police and protestors. Herman and Chomsky (1988: 22) highlight the ability of state and corporate institutions to produce massive PR campaigns which far exceed the resources that opponents can muster:

> the large bureaucracies of the powerful subsidise the mass media, and gain special access by their contribution to reducing the media's costs of acquiring the raw materials of, and producing, news.

The fourth filter, using a term flak derived from anti-aircraft shells, includes the activities of governments, political parties, corporations and lobbying groups seeking to discipline media through criticism of output. The fifth filter is ideological; anti-communism, they argue, has been used to mobilise popular sentiment against those who threaten US state–corporate interests. While anti-communism remains a potent mobilisation by the Right, they acknowledge and address how, following the break-up of the Soviet Union and expansion of state-capitalism by China, the same function is realised by other mobilisations such as the neoliberal promotion of free markets, the 'war on terror' and 'humanitarian' interventions.

Their approach follows a tradition inspired by C. Wright Mills's work on the power elite, tracing the linkages between media owners, managers and senior personnel with the rest of an elite ruling class, through operational and ideological business and cultural associations (Mosco 2009: 190–91). For Chomsky (1989) the propaganda model (PM) makes predictions (about how the media function, how media performance will be discussed in society and how the model itself will be evaluated) whereby 'the needs of established power' will be asserted and predominate at each level. Focusing on 'the spectrum of opinion allowed expression' (Chomsky 1989: 59), their work is based predominantly on content analysis of news output and qualitative analysis of the dichotomous treatment of geopolitical, labour and social justice issues that generate 'systematic selectivity', 'worthy and unworthy victims' and propaganda campaigns on behalf of corporate–state interests, notably those of the United States and its allies. Herman (1986: 176) argues:

> The US mass media, for example, tend to focus often and indignantly on the trials and tribulations of dissidents in enemy states while ignoring equally or more severe victimisation in the 'colonies'. This dichotomous treatment extends not merely to isolated news items; there is also an observable tendency for enemy victims to be subject to intense coverage ... which are almost never applied to victims in friendly states.

Overall, Herman and Chomsky assert that 'the "societal purpose" of the media is to inculcate and defend the economic, social and political agenda of privileged groups that dominate the domestic economy and the state' (1988: 298). The propaganda model has been applied and defended by radical media scholars, particularly in studies of the mobilisation of support for war, government information campaigns and corporate PR (Source Watch 2013). Arguably, the key strength of this work is to trace, through media output, what Klaehn (2009: 44) calls 'the symbiotic relationship between journalists and agents of power', but this is also the grounds for its strongest critique.

Criticisms

The explanatory reach of the propaganda model is a common source of critique but also a useful and productive basis for rehabilitation. The PM proposes a strong, systemic and near totalistic account of media processes. Yet the empirical basis for the original study is almost exclusively coverage in influential, elite news media in the United States, predominantly addressing the foreign policy activities and interests of America during the Cold War. Even strong critics such as McNair (2006) acknowledge the salience of their account of a narrow, disciplined and conformist US media between the 1940s and the 1980s. The tendency to shift from this specific conjunction to make broader systemic claims is rightly criticised. It is questionable how far the PM is applicable to other areas of US news coverage, let alone news coverage from other media systems, and non-news media output. Beyond the important critiques of extrapolation (from specific media conjunction to general, and from content to influence) a more concretely situated analysis, alert to the particular political economic factors and other influences on media output, leaves open for examination how other media configurations relate to the ones Herman and Chomsky describe. How does the PM relate to systems with significant publicly owned as well as private media? For its advocates the propaganda model is international in 'scope and applicability' (Klaehn 2009: 49; Klaehn 2010), yet while some filters have wide applicability taken together they map, at best, multi-party liberal systems in advanced capitalist economies. Moreover, the actual application of the model to other media systems tends to overstate the degree of correspondence with the US corporate model that the propaganda model identifies and critiques.

A second area of criticism concerns what Schudson (2000: 180) calls 'flat-footed functionalism'. In partial defence, it is important to consider the ambition of the propaganda model. It seeks explanations for recurrent patterns of reporting identified through empirical research. It aims to offer a systematic theoretical account with predictive value for news content and reporting. There have been few attempts at such explanatory–predictive modelling across communications studies. The trade-off between such modelling and microanalysis is not just between reductiveness and sophistication, but also between connectedness and contingency. As predicted by Herman and Chomsky various forms of liberal criticism are predicated on a disavowal of the strong relationship between media and elite power that the PM advances. Schudson (1995: 5) concedes that US media limit diversity of opinion in ways that 'foreshorten the representation of views on the left' yet argues that these tendencies 'stop far short of uniformity'. Herman's (1999: 268) own reappraisal of the model concedes the latter point while reaffirming the salience of the model to explain and predict, 'mechanisms by which the powerful are able to dominate the flow of messages and limit the space of contesting parties'. Herman and Chomsky write in *Manufacturing Consent* (1988: 302) 'As we have stressed throughout this book, the U.S. media do not function in the manner of the propaganda system of a totalitarian state. Rather, they permit – indeed encourage – spirited debate, criticism and dissent, as long as these remain faithfully within the system of presuppositions and principles that constitute an elite consensus, a system so powerful as to be internalized largely without awareness'.

Yet the key charge from other radical scholars is that Herman and Chomsky's account is too deterministic. Functionalism confers a status of necessity on social phenomenon and in this radical functionalist account the media serve to reproduce social power hierarchies in systematic ways. Summarising a multifaceted critique Eldridge (1993: 25) writes:

> it is a highly deterministic version of how the media operate, linked to a functionalist conception of ideology.
>
> [...]
>
> Moreover ... the ways the messages are received are assumed. Yet it is one thing to recognize that there are inequalities of power, whether economic, political and cultural, but quite another to clarify how far the media modify or reinforce those inequalities. We continually need to ask questions about control through the whole process of production, content and reception. This is a conceptual, theoretical and empirical challenge.

For Murdock and Golding (2005: 62) the PM illustrates an instrumentalist approach, one that focuses on the deliberate and purposeful exercising of power, to affirm that private media are 'instruments of class domination'. This, they argue is 'partly right', however:

> by focusing solely on these kinds of strategic interventions they overlook the contradictions in the system. Owners, advertisers and key political personnel cannot always do as they would wish. They operate within structures that constrain as well as facilitate, imposing limits as well as offering opportunities. Analysing the nature and sources of these limits is a key task for a critical political economy of culture.
>
> (2005: 63)

Herman and Chomsky describe their approach as an 'institutional analysis' of a system that is decentralised and non-conspiratorial. For Herman (1999: 263), 'the media comprise numerous independent entities that operate on the basis of common outlooks, incentives and pressures from the market, government and internal organizational forces'. Yet, their account presumes a homology and fit between capitalist enterprises, state and parties, and mainstream media that are theoretically weak and empirically challenged. The PM is not conspiratorial, as some critics allege, yet it assumes that the most important influences on media all flow in one direction, towards supporting the status quo (Eldridge 1993; Schudson 2005; Curran 2002: 148), a deficiency acknowledged by Herman (1999). There is a further criticism which indicates important divisions within the radical tradition. Herman and Chomsky's account is dismissive of media work and workers. The vast majority accommodate to system requirements while a small minority challenge the status quo but are variously punished and marginalised for doing so. The process of filtration allows little consideration of agency or initiative on the part of media workers. By contrast, engaging with the organisation of media workers, their reflexivity on their own practice, and the tensions between creativity, autonomy, professionalism and control is the starting point for a radical media sociology that reintegrates aspects of the liberal–radical divide (Goldsmiths Media Group 2000; Hesmondhalgh 2010, 2013)

The propaganda model and similar accounts of the strategic use of power by political or corporate elites tend to underestimate contradictions in the system and the contending influences that help to explain the diversity or 'contradictions' of content and output (Murdock and Golding 2005: 74). Herman and Chomsky argued that beyond the main 'filters' were 'secondary effects', some of which support propagandist purposes while others, such as the professional integrity of journalists, could be countervailing influences. The revising tradition of critical scholarship goes further in identifying the range of contradictory forces that the media are subject to in capitalist democracies.

Contemporary radical functionalism

Work within a radical functionalist tradition includes that of the campaign group Media Lens, who apply the propaganda model to UK media. A central claim in David Edwards and David Cromwell's book, *Guardians of Power: The Myth of the Liberal Media*, is that 'the corporate mass media – not just the right-wing Tory press, but also the most highly respected "liberal" media-broadcasters like the BBC, and newspapers like the *Guardian*, the *Observer* and the *Independent* – constitute a propaganda system for elite interests' (Edwards and Cromwell 2006: 2). In fact, central to their claim of a systematic distorting lens is that faith in 'liberal' media to carry alternative perspectives is misplaced. The media function to maintain deception; elites require manipulation in order to mobilise public opinion behind actions such as the wars in Iraq, and 'humanitarian' interventions such as US–NATO military action in the Balkans in the 1990s. *Guardians of Power* amasses evidence to support the thesis of a compliant media that 'overwhelmingly promotes the views and interest of established power' (Edwards and

Cromwell 2006: 178). They argue that three major biases are built into 'neutral' professional journalism:

1 Reliance on official sources.
2 News hooks [and news values]. A dramatic event, official announcement, publication of a report is required to justify covering a story, favouring establishment interests and news management.
3 Carrot and stick pressures from advertisers, business associations and leading political parties have 'the effect of herding corporate journalists away from some issues and towards others'.

(Edwards and Cromwell 2006: 12)

However, there are numerous problems with this analysis. Radical functionalist accounts can demonstrate persuasively the selectivity in some media reporting, and the alignment between certain reporting and dominant power interests. But such accounts do not provide an adequate basis for totalising claims. The search for a systemic 'control' mechanism can only be sustained by an effort to fold the full range of mediated communications into a uniformity. To do so shifts from an evidence-based analysis to assertions of control, while conceding and down-playing dissent and disruptions. Schudson's (1995: 4) critique of the propaganda model is relevant here, finding it 'misleading and mischievous … in its conclusion that every apparent sign of debate or controversy is merely a cover for a deeper uniformity of views'.

Alternative expression within mainstream media is further diminished by casting it as a mechanism to sustain liberal myths: disagreement and dissent is tolerated, even promoted, to prove and perpetuate the 'myth' of media freedom. But a final variant of this approach is that it is overly reductive and dismissive in its account of 'mainstream' media and over-invests in the progressive capabilities of 'non-corporate', alternative media online. A totalistic critique of the 'corporate' mainstream can then only espouse 'alternative' media as a solution, in particular the power of Internet-enabled 'non-corporate journalism' (Edwards and Cromwell 2006: 202). A key problem with such analysis from a CPE perspective is that it conflates all major media as 'corporate' so that differences in ownership and financing are rendered insignificant. For Herman and Chomsky these factors do matter, but they follow common patterns in the overwhelmingly commercial US media system. Transferred to other media systems such as the UK, with a mix of strong public and private media, the adoption of this critique of 'corporate media' compounds a denial of salient differences across different institutional arrangements and their influence on content. Edwards and Cromwell explain the presence of a more liberal media in Britain, compared to the US, by reference to parliamentary opposition to state–corporate power, but this fails to acknowledge how public service structures from the BBC to Channel Four, or the trust-based management of *The Guardian* and the *Observer*, came about, or indeed the role played by anti-market factions within the Right in the development of media institutions and regulation.

By contrast, an analysis of media coverage before and during the Iraq War by Lewis and Brookes (2003) found important differences in reporting *within* public service media. The BBC, while fiercely attacked by Labour government flak, was broadly supportive towards the government and army sources. Channel Four news was more sceptical and critical towards official accounts. Propaganda model analyses focused on evidence of control are also poor at addressing exceptions and variations in mainstream media output. Freedman (2009) examines a moment of mainstream media disunity, when a Labour-supporting popular UK newspaper, *The Mirror*, came out strongly against the Iraq War in 2002. Explanations for this stance included a rebranding of the paper to respond to perceived demands for more serious analytical and international news coverage after 9/11. The paper signed up the radical former *Mirror* journalist John Pilger who described the United States, in a Fourth of July special, as 'the world's leading rogue state … out to control the world' (*The Mirror* 4 July 2002), generating critical 'flak' from a leading US investor in the paper, Tweedy Brown, who phoned to complain. The paper sustained a case against the war as counter-productive, reckless and likely to increase rather than reduce risks for the UK from terrorism. In doing so the paper also responded to a shift in popular sentiment culminating in the two-million-strong anti-war march in February 2003. The paper's political editor, David Seymour, said the anti-war position was 'over-whelmingly supported by the readers'. The paper's editorial stance shifted once the war began, maintaining opposition but focusing on supporting courageous British soldiers, with a broader retreat from critical, campaigning perspectives towards a resurgence of entertainment news. Yet Freedman argues that in the earlier moment of social crisis, with elite disagreement and a strong popular opposition movement, space for dissenting opinion was opened up in main-stream media. At the same time pressures to reproduce dominant perspectives were evident, from investors, shareholders, government and, as public opinion became more ambivalent, the paper was unwilling to align itself with a 'minority' anti-war position. Freedman (2009: 67) concludes 'Moments of social crisis can open up spaces for innovative and radical coverage but they sit uneasily with the market disciplines of a "free press" that privilege, above all, profitability and competitiveness'.

Edwards and Cromwell's attitude towards journalists working in the system is condescending. The understanding that informs these radical critics' own stance is variously described as 'unimaginable' or 'unthinkable' within the confines of mainstream media. Likewise for Herman and Chomsky (1988: 2) journalists work under constraints because 'the operation of these filters occurs so naturally … that alternative bases of news choices are hardly imaginable'. Such an account evades important political–economic, and labour, considerations. This tends to be a world of heroic dissidents, insiders who become enlightened outsiders, with occasional anomalous good reporting from insiders being acknowledged, but discounted. As a consequence, key considerations are flattened and ignored: how are hierarchical controls imposed? How and why do conditions of control differ, for instance under different institutional arrangements? How does media work differ across varying, and changing, environments? Such neglect is too high a price to pay for the clarity and impact of such totalising readings of media performance.

Influences within radical functionalism can be identified that help delineate different strands of critical political economic thinking. First, radical functionalism has tended to bear greater influence from the work of a 'later' Frankfurt School theorist Herbert Marcuse, notably his focus on psychologistic explanations for dominance and subordination, emphasising concepts such as false consciousness and the 'repressive tolerance' of dissent (Jay 1996). A left libertarian and often anarchist orientation articulates a strong suspicion of power centres as tools of ruling class interests that are inherently repressive. The socialist emphasis on harnessing such resources for socially progressive purposes tends to be collapsed into liberalism, and dismissed. Divisions over the state also influence divergent accounts of media reform and democratisation. Radical functionalism tends to favour anti-system initiatives including radical media, by viewing mainstream media as either wholly corporate instruments or irretrievably co-opted to serve establishment interests. By contrast, other CPE approaches identify a purposeful struggle to create and sustain public media with attention to democratising policy, and public service operations, in alliances with media workers (chapter nine).

Revisions and debates

If the 1970s saw a division between liberal and radical/Marxist being used for pedagogic purposes, scholarship in the 1980s and 1990s brought signs of convergence in media sociology. Part of this was revision within radical scholarship, part commonality with a more empirical mainstream media sociology. Underlying tenets informing radical critiques were challenged by research from media sociology, cultural studies, and by alternative approaches notably drawn from postmodernist theory. By the end of the 1990s the liberal–radical schism had given way to a partial synthesis in *radical pluralist* perspectives. This shift has been examined in some detail (Goldsmiths Media Group 2000; Curran 2002). We will briefly explore some key developments to trace how liberal and radical accounts were revised in three key areas: domination theory and ideology (post Marxism); media theory (new influences); news processes and sources (liberal and radical).

Domination theory and ideology

We now have many accounts of the shifts in 'radical' scholarship away from a pronounced Marxism to what has been called 'radical pluralism'. This involved shifts from a class-conflict model of society towards a more pluralist conception characterised by struggles – over identities, culture and meaning, as well as material resources – that were fluid, complex and contingent. Studies of subcultural formations found active resistance within working class subcultures that reworked aspects of commercial culture, fashioning 'contrary cultural definitions' (Clarke et al. 1976). Such work challenged the presumed homology and passivity of 'the masses' and highlighted problems in conceptions of 'false consciousness' and ideological indoctrination inherent in domination perspectives.

The concept of a 'dominant ideology' which informed radical accounts in the 1970s was also rejected as insufficient and reductionist, in favour of theories of the 'relative autonomy' of ideology and sociocultural identities. It was also challenged for its presumptions of intellectual coherence within 'ruling' ideologies, in place of attention to divisions, contradictions and tensions. These debates marked shifts within and beyond a Marxian tradition, focused in particular on theories of ideology. Althusser provided critical scholars with an account of the 'relative autonomy' of culture in place of the economism inherent in the base–superstructure model, although his account of media as Ideological State Apparatuses was itself narrowly functionalist (chapter one). A greater influence on radical culturalism was Gramsci's concept of hegemony. The Italian Marxist Antonio Gramsci (1891–1937), in the form his work was adopted, offered radical media theory a way out of rigid determinism by emphasising conflict and contestation. The concept of hegemony could help explain how dominant ideologies were constructed and suffused popular culture (involving processes of consent and construction of the popular) but also, crucially, how the inherent conflicts between different groups and interests were played out. For Gramsci *egemonia* denoted the taken-for-granted cultural frameworks and beliefs that enabled ruling class authority to remain generally unchallenged.

This paved the way for radical studies that were attendant to moments of crisis and division, when dominant ideologies were denaturalised and contested. However, Gramscianism offered 'a rather unstable basis for reformulation since it tended to mean different things to different analysts' (Goldsmiths Media Group 2000: 25). As Eagleton notes (2003: 212) '[t]his ardent Leninist has come by a devious process of editing to stand for a Marxism soft-focused enough to suit a post-radical age'; yet, as adopted, Gramsci influenced a 'non-reductive style of Marxism which takes cultural meanings seriously without denying their material determinants'. While a Gramscian influence remains evident, rallying to Gramsci proved short-lived and transitional, as Marxian influence declined in media and cultural studies during the 1980s and 1990s.

Postmodernism and power

Another important route was towards a postmodernist 'post-Marxist' reworking that used discourse theory to reject Marxist epistemology and critical realism (Laclau and Mouffe 1985). For Laclau, classical Marxism is determinist and essentialist, not only because it privileges the economic 'in the last instance' but also in proposing the proletariat as the subject of history. The collapse of belief in the organised working class underlies much revisionism in political and cultural theory from the mid twentieth century. Laclau's theoretical framework emphasises the fluidity and unfixity of social identities.

Postmodernism is a reaction against the notion that there are underlying rationalities that order social relationships and which can be identified and regarded as truths (Balnaves et al. 2009: 101). Foucault's analysis of power emphasises multiple forms and modalities of power maintained through discursive practices. In contrast to theories of power as an inherently repressive force, Foucault conceives power as productive and constitutive. One consequence of this is that emancipation can shift from tackling inequality to epistemic struggles over meaning. Such a move connects with broader shifts from class conflict politics towards more plural, identity-based struggles over incorporation/marginality/dissent. There is no singular politics or political orientation in postmodernism. However, influential versions offered an analysis that was congruent with liberal pluralism, marking a 'revival of pluralism in a new form' (Curran 2002: 141). For Baudrillard, postmodern societies generate simulations, where signs refer to themselves and not representations (where signs are taken as referring to external reality). Everything has become hyper-real where the real is irretrievable. According to this approach, cherished liberal readings of media are demolished. But so too are any radical emancipatory claims.

News and news sources

A critic of the PM as 'unidirectional' is Daniel Hallin. Influenced by Gramsci, Hallin adopted a modified account of elite domination. For Hallin (1994: 12) 'cultural institutions like the media are part of a process by which a world-view compatible with the existing structure of power in society is reproduced, a process which is decentralized, open to contradiction and conflict, but generally very effective'. In his classic study *The Uncensored War* (1986), Hallin found that critical news media coverage occurred only after sections of the Washington political elite had turned against the Vietnam war. Change in media coverage 'seems best explained as a reflection of and response to a collapse of consensus – especially of elite consensus – on foreign policy' (Hallin 1994: 53). Hallin put forward a model of overlapping spheres of media discourse: consensus, legitimate controversy and deviance. Media will often promote (elite) values and institutions but beyond this sphere of consensus is a sphere of legitimate controversy. This broadly corresponds to the bounded debate that the PM critiques, while a further sphere of deviance corresponds with communications outside mainstream media/politics that are excluded or 'denigrated. Hallin's model identifies gradations in each sphere and some dynamic movement of actors, institutions and the framing of topics between them. It also encourages focus on instances of change, crisis and the management and communication of dissent.

Gramsci also influenced a British alternative to the propaganda model by Stuart Hall et al. in *Policing the Crisis* (1978), which focused on processes by which consent was achieved and contested (see Hesmondhalgh 2006). The book advanced an influential theory of media–source relations in an avowed 'structural–culturalist' approach. Journalists operating within a professional framework of 'objectivity' and 'authoritative' reporting defer to institutional sources, already legitimated by their power and expertise, who serve as the 'primary definers' of news. Media-source relations are based on structured preferences for official sources. The authors (Hall et al. 1978: 58) found evidence of:

> a systematically structured over-accessing to the media of those in powerful and privileged institutional positions. The media, thus, tend faithfully and impartially, to reproduce symbolically the existing structure of power in society's institutional order.

'Primary definers' of news, including governing politicians, senior police, judges, business leaders and other establishment figures 'will almost always succeed in shaping news agendas and interpretative frameworks' (Manning 2001: 15). Suppliers of news played a key role in the maintenance of ideological hegemony.

This modified but maintained a domination or 'control' account which came under stronger attack in the 1980s and beyond. Another strand in radical–liberal revision concerned the analysis of media–source relationships and approaches to understanding source strategies and resources. Schlesinger (1990) criticised the mediacentrism of accounts such as Hall's that focused on media to the detriment of sources and argued that the concept of 'primary definers' overstated their cohesiveness and failed to deal with disagreements between them. Casting the media as 'secondary definers' presented too dependent and passive a role. Schlesinger argued that powerful groups must compete for control of the media agenda; dominance of any ideological position was an achievement of media–source engagement, rather than a wholly structurally determined outcome. Consequently Schlesinger and Tumber (1994: 21) assert the 'dynamic processes of contestation in a given field of discourse'. Another influence, and shift from Marxism, was that of radical sociologist Pierre Bourdieu whose concept of field has been discussed already. Bourdieu's concept of cultural capital was also influential; primary definers were not structurally predetermined, it was argued, but achieved and maintained their status through the expenditure of economic, political and cultural 'capital'. Non-elites could build up status (authority, reliability, routine availability, subsidy) while official sources could lose authority and legitimacy. From radical scholarship, then, revisionist arguments moved towards a radical pluralist synthesis (Goldsmiths Media Group 2000). From accounts emphasising elite control there were shifts towards pluralist accounts of elite source competition, and conditions of success for opposition and 'resource poor' groups to gain access (Davis 2013; Cottle 2003b). This convergence is best understood by identifying shifts in liberal scholarship as well.

Liberal revisionism

One strand of liberalism accepts the claims of operational autonomy and indepen-dence put forward by many practising journalists and media workers themselves, albeit predominantly those working in 'settled' liberal democratic political systems. A strong liberal version denies the influence of pressures from above on day-to-day work (see Goldsmiths Media Group 2000). However, mainstream liberal communication scholars came closer to acknowledging the salience of factors identified by the radical tradition, while falling short of accepting their conclusions.

Liberal pluralist media sociology, influenced by occupational sociological studies and the 'ethnographic turn', has provided necessary additions, as well as correctives, to political economy accounts. Commercial media institutions are driven by core economic interests to secure future profitability and expand market share. But in addition to market forces, organisations are subject to other influences. Studies of journalistic media (Gans 1980; Baker 1994; McNair 1998; Bennett 2011) identify these as:

- economic influences (including economic structure, levels of competition and ownership concentration, influence of advertising)
- political influences (governments, politicians, pressure groups and powerful interests as well as political–legal framework and wider political culture)
- sources' influences and media interaction with extra-media social actors
- technology
- management control, corporate policies and organisational dynamics
- professional culture and norms
- gender, ethnicity and the sociocultural backgrounds of professionals and actors
- consumer preferences and influences.

Liberal approaches to news are characterised by their emphasis on the individual autonomy of media workers. Reliance on dominant sources is explained as arising more from the organisational routines and professional values of news gatherers than from instrumentalist imposition. Yet source research acknowledges that the traditional liberal claim of media independence (the 'fourth estate') must be modified (Goldsmiths Media Group 2000). If there is some degree of source dependence (the radical claim), discussion shifts to consider how structured it is and how 'open' or 'closed' is the resulting mediated discursive space. Is dependence on elite sources evidence of the subversion of democracy, or proof of its functioning? Schudson (2005) presents reliance on official sources as a guarantee of media support for the 'democratic order'. Source dependence is also balanced by the imperative for media organisations to maintain their independence as a source of legitimation, allied to their market value, for users. Media are formally disconnected from other ruling agencies, Schudson argues, because they must attend as much to their own legitimation as to furthering the legitimation of the capitalist system as a whole.

What liberal accounts defend is the capability of media professionals operating under corporate ownership to continue to serve society. This position shifts when, as today, there is increased disquiet about the crisis for commercial news media and the loss of reach and resources for news journalism in the US and other media systems. Schudson's own work is illustrative. Having been a trenchant critic of radical scholarship by Chomsky, Herman and Bagdikian, Schudson shares their concerns about the damage to journalism from corporate disinvestment, stating 'Wall Street, whose collective devotion to an informed citizenry is nil, seems determined to eviscerate newspapers' (cited in McChesney 2007: 97).

Radical pluralism

The interweaving of critical political economy, sociology and critical cultural theory has produced synthesising accounts that are more open, contingent and less deterministic, while sharing a focus on the nature and effects of power imbalances in communication resources. These 'radical pluralist' accounts acknowledge the potentiality for creativity, agency and uncertainty within the production process, as well as its structuring limitations. In turn, structures are conceived as 'dynamic formations that are constantly reproduced and altered through practical action', so that 'analyzing the way that meaning is made and remade through the concrete activities of producers and consumers is equally essential' (Murdock and Golding 2005: 63). Curran (2002) reviews the various liberal and radical traditions in media sociology and puts forward a revising model identifying key forces that serve to sustain relations of power and countervailing forces. This is an effort to overcome the limitations of both liberal reflection theories and radical functionalism. A central weakness of liberal functionalism is its failure to adequately acknowledge the 'influences, pressures and constraints that encourage the media to gravitate towards the central orbit of power' (Curran 2002: 148). CPE retains an emphasis on the 'ascendancy' of influences, and of the structuring significance of capital and class. For example, a study of the Obama healthcare policy debate found that proposals for publicly funded insurance, strongly opposed by private insurance firms, were marginalised across US corporate media coverage, despite majority public support (FAIR 2009). Yet radical functionalists assert that the main influences on the media are system enhancing and supportive of the status quo. For Hallin (1994: 13) the propaganda model is 'perfectly unidirectional; no forces working in other directions are taken into account in any serious way'. Professional journalism is regarded as 'false consciousness' at the expense of understanding how this ideology provides resources, including the ability to assert professional values against pressure from managers, owners and advertisers. Instead, Curran, Golding and Murdock and others highlight the more varied configuration of media in liberal democracies (such as public service media), and the presence of 'countervailing influences that pull against the magnetic field of power' (Curran 2002: 148).

Elaborating a theoretical model of influences on media organisations Curran (2002: 148–55) identifies eleven factors that tend to encourage media to support dominant power interests:

- state censorship
- high entry costs (economic barriers to mass media production)
- media concentration
- corporate ownership
- mass market pressures (i.e. commercial incentive to maximise audiences)
- consumer inequalities (i.e. provision 'skewed' towards serving affluent consumers)
- advertising influence
- rise of public relations
- news routines and values
- unequal resources (unequal access to economic, social and 'cultural' capital)
- dominant discourses.

However a further list of countervailing influences is identified:

- cultural power (intra- and inter-group influences of alternative understandings/ values)
- state empowerment (for instance, press subsidy systems and forms of public broadcasting)
- media regulation
- source power (capabilities of groups, including 'resource poor' groups, to secure media exposure or access)
- consumer power
- producer power
- staff power.

This 'reconstituted radical perspective' (Curran 2002: 165) offers a valuable toolkit for analysis. It encourages analysis of the conditions that enable media debate to be more open and contested as well as those that explain elite influence. The approach informs an analysis of media coverage of the urban left who held power in local government in London and other UK cities in the 1980s (Curran et al. 2005). This describes how an adept and comparatively well-resourced left-wing administration at the Greater London Council (GLC) could contest critical accounts with alternative frames through media access, advertising and effective public relations – while individual councils were less organised and able to challenge stories about the 'loony left'. Vehement attacks on the GLC from right-wing national newspapers were not reproduced in reporting by local or national news on public service broadcasting (PSB), governed by rules on impartiality and with news agendas that were more focused on council provision. The authors argue that consideration of core political economic influences (media ownership and regulation) needs to be supplemented by consideration of media sources and cultural influences. The right-wing newspaper attack on the urban left was greatly facilitated by the hierarchical structure of power within the popular press, with journalistic output shaped by the influence of owners and senior editors. However, the different institutional organisation of PSB influenced different types of coverage and was responsive to the emerging sophistication of public relations (and marketing) strategies adopted by the left. Cultural power was another key force, as perspectives on anti-racism, feminism and lesbian and gay equality, which were ritually denounced in the right-wing media, moved to the mainstream as social attitudes shifted. Curran's (2002) model reaffirms radical insights while jettisoning an overly 'mechanical' radical functionalism. Yet this partial synthesis of radical and liberal analysis, for all its analytical value, cannot mark a point of resolution. Critical debates move on, so that today there is a revivified liberal pluralist orthodoxy, accompanied by a displacement of the terms of the liberal–radical debate traced in this chapter. Curran's model encompasses a pluralisation of modes of communication but focuses upon, and asserts, the centrality of mass media. Contemporary liberals are less likely to be found contesting the evidence of elite influences on major media, although that remains characteristically downplayed, but rather in finding evidence for new conditions across digital communications that diminishes such concerns about media power concentrations altogether.

Conclusion

The liberal–radical division provides a useful way to understand historical debates and retains some salience, not least with 'radical' serving as a positive term for scholars who challenge traditional liberal claims. In the form outlined at the beginning of this chapter, liberal and radical represent incompatible accounts. But we have traced some intermediate positions between the two – indeed a strong tradition of research dubbed 'radical pluralist' seeks to do just that. The unequal distribution of power in society undermines the liberal case. The significance of conflict and the influence of dissent across media weakens the radical account. Radicals are right to critique the tendency in liberal accounts to focus on political power influences while neglecting economic and corporate ones. Yet the fusion of a power elite in some radical functionalist accounts is disabling. Intra-capitalist competition, divisions and differences of interests and outlook amongst powerful agents are important factors influencing public communications. One firm conclusion is the need to investigate media arrangements carefully, critically and empirically. Radical pluralism advocates more open, exploratory investigations of the relationship between media and the social, investigating how successfully different groups mobilise available resources to influence media agendas or to intervene in public communications. More open, empirical investigations illustrate the debt to pluralism by radical accounts, which nevertheless continue to argue that the material and symbolic resources that shape media discources are highly unequally distributed. Where these more synthesising, radical pluralist perspectives are most distinct is not in their methods, or even their local findings, but in the way they conceive and address problems of the media.

Chapter 3

Media cultures, media economics and media problems

Critical political economy explores problems of the media. It investigates problems arising from the manner in which media services are organised and provided, and problems concerning content, conduct, consumption, usage and influence. This chapter offers an overview of critical concerns that have shaped the tradition and introduces contemporary debates, themes and topics that are examined in more detail in parts two and three. While broad, it focuses on key issues concerning the organisation of communication resources and hence on questions of control, markets and states.

Addressing 'problems': some preliminaries

Lazarsfeld (1941) distinguished critical research from administrative research carried out on behalf of public or private sponsors; '[c]ritical theory seeks to expose underlying problems and faults of media practice and to relate them in a comprehensive way to social issues, guided by certain values' (McQuail 2010: 11). Critical scholarship is evaluative. It brings values to bear on the analysis of phenomena and the formulation of problems. Such problems may be long-standing and general, even elemental, but the enunciation of problems is itself always located, in time and space, in sets of values and presumptions. Critical political economy has a prescriptive mission (McChesney 1998). This normativity, however, is associated with problems of its own. First, historical accounts of problems in the critical tradition are challenged in regard to their salience for contemporary media. Second, much prescriptive work has addressed problems in specific media systems and this must be reviewed in efforts to provide more internationalist and comparative perspectives. Third, problems are not only per-spectival but also unstable formulations in language. As De Certeau (1974: 189) cautions, 'Any talk about cultural problems advances on the grounds of unstable words; it is impossible to determine the conceptual definition of these terms: their meanings depend on their functioning in ideologies and disparate systems'. One does not need to adopt the anti-foundationalism advanced in much postmodern theory to agree with a critique of positivism, and recognise that understanding the material world is mediated through language and meaning construction.

Problems in the media: marketisation

CPE is associated most of all with a critique of *marketisation*. For Murdock and Golding (1999: 118; Murdock 2003), marketisation means 'all those policy interventions designed to increase the freedom of action of private corporations and to institute corporate goals and organizational procedures as the yardsticks against which the performance of all forms of cultural enterprise are judged'. Among the main processes of 'marketisation' have been *privatisation*, 'the sale of public communication assets to private investors'. In Europe, this occurred across the telecommunications and broadcasting sectors, for example in the controversial privatisation of the French public channel TF1 in 1986 (Kuhn 1995: 185–98). Another feature has been *liberalisation*, the introduction or extension of competition in media markets by 'opening up previously monopoly or restricted markets to new entrants' (Murdock and Wasko 2007: 2). This occurred across Europe in broadcasting (Humphreys 1996; Hardy 2008). A third process is known as *deregulation* but is better described as liberalising re-regulation. This refers to shifts in regulatory regimes towards relaxation of rules and greater reliance on industry self-regulation, resulting in a shift from the defence of 'public interest' objectives to the promotion of corporate interests (Murdock 2003: 20). A fourth process is *corporatisation*, pressurising public organisations to emulate profit-oriented businesses by seeking new sources of income and maximising their market value. The pursuit of marketisation worldwide over recent decades has 'involved a concerted institutional and ideological attack on the established organization of public culture' (Murdock and Wasko 2007: 2).

The critique of marketisation highlights the deficiencies of media markets to provide the range of information and cultural resources to serve citizens and users. This highlights problems arising from corporate ownership of the media; concentration of ownership, the range of content produced and the values promoted by capitalistic market provision of media services (Thomas and Nain 2004). There are many dimensions of the critique but key tenets are that the provision of media under market conditions does not and cannot realise the full potential of media to serve democracy, citizens and the common good.

There are classical arguments in defence of market provision of media, but also contemporary perspectives that refute the diagnosis as well as the proposed treatments that CPE advocates. In summary these argue that problems of control, scarcity of supply, limitations in the quality and diversity of information and cultural expression, and lack of access, have been or are being overcome. Consequently, 'critical' political economy is no longer accurate, appropriate or salient. A critique of corporate concentration made sense in the latter half of the twentieth century, it is argued, but contemporary media and communications are more diverse, independent, open and critical than ever before. We'll examine these claims through the rest of the book. The aim of this chapter is to take a brief tour through the main perspectives and debates, in order to identify underlying issues, perspectives and problems.

Neoliberalism

New liberalism, neoliberalism, marks a reassertion of individualism animated by a modern notion of consumer sovereignty. It is a political philosophy 'rooted in a claim that the market is more rational than the state in the redistribution of public resources' (Chakravartty and Zhao 2008: 4). The neoliberal argument that the media are best organised according to free-market principles rests on various claims. Central is a belief in the efficacy of market competition to provide the best and most desirable mechanism for satisfying consumer wants. For Adam Smith (1776), competition ensures that the best quality goods are produced at the lowest prices. The search for market share ensures that producers adopt the most economically efficient means of production and deployment of labour. The marketplace is conceived as a space in which individuals enter into voluntary transactions, and where the inherently conflicting interests of producers and consumers are resolved to the benefit of both parties. In neoclassical economic theory '[u]nder perfect competition economic resources are allocated between different goods and services in precisely the quantities which consumers wish (their desires expressed by the price they are prepared to pay on the market)' (Whish 1989: 4).[1]

Real markets only ever approximate to perfect conditions, as even mainstream economists readily concede, but the principles and desirability of market mechanisms are strongly upheld by neoliberals, not least in regard to communications. A free-market environment in communications, they argue, allows for the greatest circulation of ideas, information and expression. In competitive markets, media firms must be responsive to what the public wants in order to remain viable. Accordingly, competition ensures that the media are subject to popular control. Moreover, markets serve popular tastes and interests, which may be blocked by restrictions on supply imposed by regulation or state action. For free marketeers, the media should be 'free' from state 'interference', the role for government should be the minimum necessary; media regulation should be strictly limited and directed towards facilitating the profitable production and exchange of goods in national and international markets.

Such market liberalism has long been the province of the neoliberal right (Adam Smith Institute 1984), but support has grown in other quarters influential in contemporary media debates and in academia. Some versions of left-wing thought share a deep opposition to the capitalist state and associate media regulation with social and cultural control and authoritarianism. Left and right libertarianism thus opposes interference with the freedom of economic transactions carried out between individuals. Support is also found amongst cultural theorists whose principal target is the distorting interference of cultural elites on media provision. In market-based media it is the consumer who is sovereign. Media must give the people, or at least economically viable market segments, what they want. This is contrasted with regulation by elites or cultural commissars who 'interfere' in markets to impose what they think is best. Media regulation is criticised for impeding innovation, creating stifling bureaucracy and imposing cultural paternalism.

Social market critiques

In order to understand neoliberalism we need to understand welfarism. Liberal democratic systems in the twentieth century expanded the provision of public services so that non-market provision coexisted with private exchange within market economies. Such systems organised the provision of utilities (water, telephony, healthcare) as public services, provided either directly by government or through agencies overseen by government. State intervention, which is anathema to the libertarian wing of economic liberalism, finds justification in 'social market' approaches developed in the twentieth century. For Maynard Keynes and later advocates of social market policies, market failure necessitates state intervention. From this tradition of economic thinking, which influenced the post-1945 democratic states in Western Europe, the state may intervene in the exercising of property rights in the economy in order to support public policy objectives. There are three main types of market failure recognised by modern neo-Keynesians: externalities, public goods and monopolies.

Externalities are costs associated with market transactions that neither buyers nor sellers assume, but for which society pays, a classic example being car pollution. Externality is a useful concept through which to consider the social and cultural consequences arising from media. US critical scholar McChesney (2003: 131) comments:

> Media have enormous externalities. If the market generates a lousy journalism that keeps the citizens poorly informed, the entire society suffers – not just the consumers of particular media – because the resulting political governance will be shoddy. ... Conversely, if the market generates a splendid journalism that leads to wise policies, everyone benefits, even those who are not purchasing specific media products.

Public goods are those whose use is non-rivalrous. Many media products are, in economic terms, public goods. Whereas private goods, such as a sandwich, are exhausted in the act of consumption, public goods such as free-to-air (FTA) broadcasting are not: my consumption does not prevent another consuming the same good. As Chan-Olmsted and Chang (2003: 217) put it, 'most media content products are nonexcludable and nondepletable public goods whose consumption by one individual does not interfere with its availability to another but adds to the scale economies in production'. Why are public goods a form of 'market failure'? The general presumption of competitive markets is that they result in economically efficient outcomes. The level of output and the price at which output is traded are set by equating supply with demand. Further, the value to the individual who purchases a good and the social value, the value to society as a whole, are regarded as equal. However, when social value and individual value diverge markets will usually not produce efficient outcomes. For 'non-rivalrous' goods their social value is the sum of everyone's willingness to pay, for instance:

> The social value of a TV programme is not represented by my individual valuation, but by the aggregate valuation of all those people who might watch the programme. There is no reason why consumption should be restricted to the person (or the group of persons) with the highest willingness to pay, because their 'consumption' does not reduce the amount of the good that is available for others. A market mechanism which excludes consumers who are not willing to pay a certain price would not, therefore, lead to an efficient outcome.
>
> (Koboldt et al. 1999: 56)

This has underpinned the rationale for a shared tax on users (licence fee) in public service systems (Graham et al. 1999). It also highlights efforts in commercial media to find ways to create scarcity in order to realise value. In a celebrated essay on media political economy Garnham (1979) describes the main mechanisms used by businesses to manage the public good character of cultural and informational good. These include making content scarce by enforcement of intellectual property rights; controlling access through box-office or other restrictions on distribution; creating built-in obsolescence through the manipulation of time (such as daily news); and creating value by selling audiences to advertisers.

The third kind of market failure is monopoly. In competitive markets, new firms will be encouraged to enter to capture a share of profits. According to the theory of imperfect competition, however, cost advantages associated with size will dictate that an industry should be an oligopoly unless either some form of market intervention or government regulation prevents firms from growing to their most efficient size. Under conditions of oligopoly, where a few firms dominate a market, these firms will tend to raise prices, enjoy supra-normal profits and may be reluctant to invest in innovation. Media markets tend towards concentration (chapter five).

In addition to the market failure problems of concentration, public goods, and externalities, Garnham (2000: 54, 59–62) highlights problems arising from the network character of media. Media are organised around technologies of reproduction and systems of distribution. Such networks present a problem for the model of market competition amongst suppliers of discrete, substitutable products or services on which neoclassical economics is based. Networks work best when resources are shared and pooled for the benefit of both providers and users (positive externalities). Yet this can mean that a monopoly service is both more efficient and more welfare maximising than a fragmented market of competing suppliers. A classical example is a nationwide postal service based on fixed price stamps and deliveries to all households. Concentration, public goods and network characteristics are all forms of 'market failure' in that they challenge the effective working of a neoclassical model of market competition, but the consequences and proposed remedies vary for each according to different paradigms.

For neo-Keynesians and social market economists, the state may use a variety of measures including those affecting the price and availability of goods, such as subsidies and fines. The other main mechanisms are forms of regulation, including the control of licensing and the application of rule-based standards, notably competition regulation, that can be legally enforced. A critique of market provision has been developed particularly effectively by neo-Keynesians in Britain, influencing New Labour's media policies. In a BBC-commissioned book, co-written with Gavyn Davies (later BBC Chairman), economist Andrew Graham (1997, revised 1999) challenged claims that the broadcasting market alone could either adequately satisfy consumer wants or serve citizens. A market system would tend towards concentration of ownership owing to the economies of scale and scope in broadcasting. Commercial broadcasting would produce 'market failure' in consumption as well as production. In a purely market system consumers would fragment more than they really wished, buy fewer good pro-grammes than was collectively desirable and under-invest in so-called 'merit goods', goods or services beneficial to society and individuals' own long-term development. Broadcasting could give rise to negative externalities (adverse effects arising from such things as the promotion of violence) as well as positive externalities, such as cultivating new knowledge, interests and skills (education being one such 'merit good'). Media concentration might be economically desirable but democratically undesirable by allowing dangerous accumulations of media power. What could offset these various market failures, Graham argued, was public service broadcasting, a 'highly effective form of intervention' (Graham et al. 1999: 20).

Radical critiques

The social market approach gained salience partly because it adopted the dominant language of market economics to present a social and cultural case.[2] Critical political economy goes further in offering a deep-rooted critique of market provision. A starting point is to challenge the supposed 'neutrality' of the market. Markets are not natural, independent mechanisms, they reflect the outcome of political and legal struggles concerning how firms can behave and so are open to alternative paths of decision-making. Second, market mechanisms influence what kinds of media are made available to whom; they 'regulate' the supply and consumption of media and, according to this tradition, do so in ways which are often detrimental.

Against market liberalism, critical political economists argue that unregulated markets cannot satisfactorily serve the needs of citizens or satisfy the wishes of audiences (Baker 2002). The market system is inherently exclusive and inegalitarian, in tension with principles of democracy and justice (Calabrese 2004; Venturelli 1998). A market-oriented media system does not provide adequate means to distinguish between people's private and individual role as consumers and their public and collective role as citizens (Baker 2002). Competitive market pressures may not consistently promote diversity and fairness in media content. Media conglomeration diminishes competition (McChesney 1999, 2013). Rising capitalisation restricts entry to the market, creating a zone of influence where 'dominant economic forces have a privileged position' (Curran 1996: 94). Access to capital functions as a 'powerful exclusionary mechanism' (Manning 2001: 102). This leads to market censorship. Increased capitalisation 'has introduced an invisible system of ideological control by preventing groups with limited financial resources from competing in the market, and it has restricted consumer power by narrowing the range of choice' (Curran 2001: 218).

The idealised notion of market democracy ignores the structuring influence of advertising in commercial broadcasting and press, which Curran (1996) describes as a 'licensing' power (chapter six). The skewing of media finance, notably advertising, to favour certain kinds of audiences and disfavour others, results in certain ideas being privileged while others may be rendered invisible by lack of user exposure. Consumer demand is only partially effective in oligopolistic, commercially driven systems, financed by advertising. The concept of 'consumer sovereignty' ignores the variety and complexity of influences which shape media content, notably in large, bureaucratised, advertising-dependent, media organisations. This tradition, then, challenges the belief that 'the free market produces a media system which responds to and expresses the views of the people', arguing that 'market dominance by oligopolies has reduced media diversity, audience choice and public control' (Curran 1996: 92, 95). The increasing power of private economic interests over the political process undermines democracy and further removes the market and economic agents from democratic control. However, the radical democratic approach also challenges the limitations of statist alternatives to market provision and acknowledges the value of markets in meeting market-expressed preferences, as well as benefits arising from market competition and innovation. For instance, Lee (2000: 131) describes a broadening of political discourse in the post-dictatorship period in Taiwan, where media market competition contributed to 'the fostering of diverse media accounts that complement and check one another', marking an 'emancipatory alternative to aristocratic, oligarchic or authoritarian dictatorship'.

The market as media regulator

The concept of the market as regulator is deployed by contending sides but in very different ways. In pro-market rhetoric, it means allowing normal market processes to occur without regulatory interference. For CPE critics, this masks a selective call for only certain kinds of regulation, or indeed state-sanctioned benefits, to be diminished. As many scholars have noted, the rhetoric of 'deregulation' is misleading since marketisation has involved a reorientation of regulatory tools, not merely a diminution of regulation (Humphreys 1996; Leys 2001). In critical rhetoric, the concept of the market as regulator serves to challenge the identification of the market with neutrality on three main grounds. First, even the most 'free' markets have been shaped by and continue to be governed by law and public policy. The opposition between 'free markets' and state intervention, used to justify pro-market 'deregulation', is thus seriously misleading since actual media markets are invariably the result of government policies, subsidies, regulations and a variety of other conferred benefits. Second, 'market regulation' (liberalisation) is itself a policy outcome, not merely the absence of policy. Third, market forces are regulatory mechanisms. Market mechanisms shape the availability, nature and range of content. In this way, market forces generate outcomes that are akin to those that might be achieved through other kinds of regulatory intervention. Concerns about censorship, restrictions on the supply of content or diversity losses are thus directed towards market controls, rather than being perceived as arising only from state controls (see Keane 1991). The broader critical charge is that the outcome of market forces need not be accepted as 'natural' and unalterable but should instead be subservient to securing broader social and cultural benefits from communications media.

An underlying division then is between free-market and anti-market positions with a spectrum of intermediate liberal and radical tending perspectives. We can also distinguish between criticisms arising from deficiencies in how media markets actually work, and more fundamental challenges to the suitability of market mechanisms for the provision of media services. The latter are characteristic of the radical democratic tradition of critical political economy.

The state

The problems of media markets and marketisation have been a dominant theme of CPE analysis, especially in Euro-American studies. This has involved a critique of states for their promotion of corporate business interests and their rolling back of public provision and public regulation. There are, though, plenty of divisions amongst radicals regarding the state, which reflect concerns across the spectrum of democratic theory, and attention to the complex variations in states in comparative analysis.

Any global mapping of *problems* of the media might justifiably begin with the state. The power to control and restrict media can be exercised most fully and directly by states. In any account of media control, violence against journalists and media workers must rank as amongst the most severe and objectionable forms. Authoritarian states may authorise restrictions or use extra-judicial means to silence or intimidate journalists. According to the International Federation of Journalists more than 2,000 journalists and media staff have been killed in the line of duty over the last 20 years, 121 by targeted killings in 2012 alone, many carried out by state or para-state actors (International Federation of Journalists 2012). The reports and various rankings by Reporters without Borders, Index on Censorship, Freedom House, IFEX and others demonstrate the repressive power

of states exercised over and through media. Media worldwide have been harnessed to repressive, sectarian and anti-democratic purposes. The classic liberal
concern to protect media from state interference remains both salient and shared
by radical democratic media theory. However, classical liberal theory of the
media has provided a complex and problematic legacy. Liberal theory of the
press holds that the primary democratic role of the media is to oversee the state.
This task requires that the media are 'free' from state interference. The theory
supports a free-market economic model particularly powerful in the United
States and encapsulated in the 'marketplace of ideas' formulation of the
US Supreme Court (Baker 1989; Stein 2008). The libertarian model of press
freedom was formed through the political struggles against authoritarian rule
(McQuail 1992; Hardy 2008). A key problem was that it came to be applied in
the twentieth century to the quite different conditions of private ownership of
powerful media (Keane 1991).

Liberalism has, from its inception, grappled with the problems of speech and
speech rights (Barendt 2005; Hardy 2008) and from the late nineteenth century
confronted problems of corporate media ownership, monopolisation and
market-driven pressures for sensationalism. Different political systems favoured
different solutions depending on the leading values requiring protection, market
conditions and power interests shaping policy at any one time. The two main
responses came to be recognised as 'social responsibility' and 'social market'.
The 'social responsibility' model was best articulated by the Hutchins Commission
on Freedom of the Press in 1947 in the United States (Siebert et al. 1963). This
in turn influenced the 1947–49 Royal Commission on the Press in Britain
(O'Malley 1997; Curran 2000). Both combined a critique of market failure in
the press with promotion of media professionalism, involving 'the adoption of
certain procedures for verifying facts, drawing on different sources, presenting
rival interpretations' whereby 'the pluralism of opinion and information, once
secured through the clash of adversaries in the free market, could be recreated
through the "internal pluralism" of monopolistic media' (Curran 1996: 99).

This 'Anglo-American' concept of *social responsibility* rejected a purely libertarian
view of the press as unrestricted freedom for publishers. Addressing the growing
criticisms of concentrated ownership and the narrow business control of editorial
agendas in the US press, the Hutchins Commission proposed that the press
should become more like 'common carriers' for diverse opinions (drawing on the
model of European public service broadcasting), and should be subject to an
industry code of practice, overseen by a new independent agency. The Commission thus accepted a role for government in supplementing privately owned
media, but its defining boundary was that no economic restrictions should be
placed on private enterprise. The alternative *social market* model, developed in
several European countries, justified state intervention in markets on behalf of
democratic objectives, in particular pluralism of voice and, later, cultural diversity.
This engaged a more positive assessment of democratic states' capacity to
advance social benefits (Christians et al. 2009). In addition to public service

broadcasting, the main forms of social market intervention have been press subsidies and grants and subsidies for other media and cultural industries.

In classical liberalism, private property rights are generally upheld but they are not deemed to be the most beneficial way of organising all resources and activities. There is a role for the state to protect the welfare of citizens, through investing in defence for instance. The state should also provide various resources for the wider public good, such as roads and transportation facilities. Of course, such services may well be shaped to benefit private interests, from imperialist armies to railway networks, but in principle they are organised to serve the common good. Twentieth century welfarism built on this. Western European democracies responding to the rise of socialist and communist movements, financial crises and world wars, developed welfare states that included social and welfare support, active labour market policies, and a significant role for the state as actor and manager in market economies. The public provision of utilities, based on 'natural monopolies' informed the provision of telecommunications and other universal services. In Western Europe, for example, the notion of public service broadcasting was developed from the 1920s, provided by 'specially mandated, non-commercially driven, publicly owned and funded and publicly accountable' organisations (Brants and De Bens 2000: 9). There has been a profound change in the media policy landscape since the 1970s. The ascension of policies of marketisation has been part of a paradigmatic policy shift whereby Western European nation-states moved away from the Keynesian consensus of the post-war years and began to adopt market-oriented strategies and policies (chapters seven and eight).

Radical perspectives on state and media

Liberalism asserts the autonomy of the political and its separation from the economic; classical Marxism insists on their integration. However, how the state is understood in relation to the political sphere and the economic sphere has been a major source of contention within Marxist thought, and between Marxism and other state theories (Jessop 2008; Hill 1997; Dunleavy and O'Leary 1987). Within Marxism the state is an instrument of class rule. State capitalism describes a relationship in which the state promotes and serves the interests of the dominant economic class, who own the means of production. The key differences are between Marxist accounts that privilege economic relations of production and see the state as a superstructural phenomenon serving capital (economism), and approaches that seek to theorise the relative autonomy of the state and the political sphere. In the 1970s and 1980s economist Marxists such as Clarke and Holloway accused Poulatzas and others of 'politicism', according primacy in theory and practice to the state and politics without grounding this in the 'capital relation' and associated class struggle. This, they argued, took for granted the 'bourgeois' separation of the economic and political institutional order of modern societies.

The problem of offering a satisfactory account of the relationship between the political and economic sphere is an ongoing challenge. In general, critical political economists have moved from economism towards an appreciation of the relative autonomy, and complexity, of the state. In democratic political systems, states are susceptible to democratic pressures to create socially beneficial outcomes, even while aligned with serving capital and political and economic elites. Any state theory must deal not only with international variations but also with globalisation processes and the reconfiguration of state power (chapter seven). The contribution of CPE analysis within the internationalising of media studies (Curran and Park 2000a; Thussu 2009; Hardy 2012a) has included analysing the various interconnections of state and market power (Sparks 2008; Chakravartty and Zhao 2008). For Sparks (2000b: 47):

> The experience of Central and Eastern Europe highlights the fact that, in most of the world, there is a close relationship, and often interpenetration, between capital and politics. The belief that these two terms are polarized into the states of (desirable) complete separation and (undesirable) complete fusion is to mistake extreme cases for the norm.

In China, Winfield and Peng (2005) conclude 'there appears to be a convolution of the Party line and the bottom line, a Chinese media system moving from totalitarianism to market authoritarianism', while Lee et al. (2007: 24) propose 'party-market corporatism' as a concept to explain both the interlocking of the state and capital in China, and 'the management of the state-media-capital tripartite relationship'.

Perspectives on the state and media tend to draw on a mixture of theoretical, historical and empirical analysis, although this is not always explicitly acknowledged, as in Althusser's account of Ideological State Apparatuses (chapter one). A highly negative assessment of the state comes from libertarian strains that conceive the state as an essentially repressive force on individual freedom. However, this can lead to an analysis in close alignment with neoliberalism by disfavouring state action yet tacitly justifying corporate rule and the freedom of powerful economic actors. Another, radical democratic, perspective argues that democratic institutions and processes can be used to develop policies that serve wider social and cultural goals. There is then a historical debate between revolutionary strategies to capture and overthrow the state or reformism, establishing social welfare policies through 'parliamentary socialism'. Connected to these more general conceptions of the state, economy and democracy are specific debates concerning the role of the state in communications.

Media and the public sphere

Jürgen Habermas's *Structural Transformation of the Public Sphere*, first published in 1962, has had an enormous impact on Western media scholarship, especially following its translation from German into English in 1989. Habermas argued that the eighteenth century bourgeoisie in Britain, France and Germany engaged in critical discussion through face-to-face communication, in coffee houses and other shared spaces, and mediated communication, especially through newspapers and periodicals. For Habermas, this early bourgeois public sphere provided a space for collective will-formation in which an autonomous public opinion was created that influenced the conduct of emergent democratic governance based on multi-party political systems. For Habermas (1989: 36):

> Les hommes, private gentlemen, or die Privatleute made up the public not just in the sense that power and prestige of public office were held in suspense; economic dependencies also in principle had no influence. Laws of the market were suspended as were laws of the state. Not that this idea of the public was actually realised in earnest in the coffee houses, the salons, and the societies; but as an idea it had become institutionalised and thereby stated as an objective claim. If not realised, it was at least consequential.

Habermas's own account has been described as a 'melancholic historical narrative in two acts' (Dahlgren 1995: 7). The public sphere was destroyed by the very forces that brought it into existence, undermined by corporate *and* state power, as commercially driven media came to dominate and the state, political parties and business organisations 'used their control of social resources and political power, as well as the techniques of public relations, to dominate the process of public communication' (Hallin and Mancini 2004: 81). For Murdock and Golding (2005: 77) '[t]his general ideal of a communications system as a public cultural space that is open, diverse and accessible, provides the basic yardstick against which critical political economy measures the performance of existing systems and formulates alternatives'.

Garnham (1990, 1992) provided an influential 'reinterpretation' of Habermas (Curran 2004: 18), extracting from the public sphere ideal, and the emphasis on the material conditions for mediated democratic communication, a principled defence of public service broadcasting. A model of media citizenship was thus derived from Habermas's original account of the public sphere and adopted in arguments to oppose market dominance and justify expansion of non-commodified public media. Croteau and Hoynes (2006: 39) organise their critical account of US media by contrasting a 'market model' and public sphere model. The market model conceptualises media as private companies selling products, success is measured by profits, the media encourage people to 'enjoy themselves, view ads and buy products', media are ultimately accountable to owners and shareholders and regulation is perceived as interference in market processes. In the public sphere model, media are conceptualised as public resources, success is measured by serving the public interest, the media encourage people to 'learn about their world and be active citizens', media are ultimately accountable to the public and government, and regulation is regarded as a useful tool to protect the public interest.

Habermas's original account of the public sphere has been highly influential in Euro-American scholarship and is also subject to extensive critiques ranging from historical accuracy and the neglect of plebeian spheres to the privileging of rational discourse and the positing of a centred, rational subject as the agent of communicative exchange (Calhoun 1992; Keane 1998: 157–89). The Habermassian public sphere privileges the exchange of information and opinion and neglects the entertainment activities of media on the untenable grounds that these are not part of rational exchange and not concerned with public issues (Curran 2002: 237–39; McGuigan 1996, 1998). Political theorists, communication, and feminist scholars have challenged and deconstructed information/entertainment and public/domestic divisions, addressing, for instance, how politics is engaged through entertainment (Calhoun 1992; Curran 2010a; Street 2011).

While CPE has shared these deficiencies it also provides resources to overcome them. There are three principal features. First, a critique of market liberalism, as described above. Second, an expanded conception of cultural citizenship and of communication rights for all. Murdock (1992b) argues that, in addition to access to the full range of information, citizens must have scope to engage with the greatest range of contemporary experience, both personal and collective; to excavate the historical roots of present conditions; to have access to the broadest range of viewpoints, expressed in the widest range of possible voices and forms. Here, the informational, political speech role of media is privileged, but this argument connects a much broader range of media provision and mediated communication to underlying values of citizenship. The third feature is a pluralistic model of media organisation. This multidimensional assessment of state and market informs radical democratic models of how the media should be organised that draw on another key argument, namely that there are different tasks required of media in a democratic system that can best be served by having a combination of media sectors differentially organised and financed, generating different communication spaces and styles. Curran (2002: 240–47) provides the best exposition of such a normative model, proposing a core public service sector encircled by private, social market, professional and civil media sectors. For Baker (2002), this compound model is best able to serve a 'complex democratic perspective', one that combines and goes beyond elite, republican (participatory) and liberal-pluralist democratic theories. It seeks to ensure that the media system is not controlled by either the state or the market, while incorporating both state regulation and private media. There are dynamic disequilibria in the system: the various sectors not only provide different purposes but also ways of influencing the performance of other sectors to strengthen media independence, enhance diversity and generate quality. Such normative models were constructed to address problems in Anglo-American media systems, and their authors would reject universalising them as a blueprint against the grain of diverse existing media systems.[3]

Critical political economy of media is concerned with how communication resources are cultivated, organised, allocated and used. Questions of communications are intimately linked with questions of governance. Considerable variation and evolving differences exist across critical political economy. Nevertheless, as it developed from the 1960s there are some common values that serve as an entry point, at least to consider how problems have been addressed. CPE is concerned with a vision of a good society based on values of social justice, quality of life, mutual responsibilities, democratic accountability and environmental sustainability. Any political economic system should be assessed on how, within all ecological and geopolitical constraints and affordances, it hopes to create a good society and cultivate the good life for all, one that sustains and provides for public goods as well as private consumption.

Problems of the media

The problems of the media can be approached in media-centric terms or in terms that start with values for sustainable life on earth. To what extent do systems of media and communications, or any particular communication operations and exchanges, serve to promote good living for sustainable life as a whole? How do communication systems and operations serve to sustain or contest dominant power relations? Another central question is 'whether, on balance, the media system serves to promote or undermine democratic institutions and practice' (McChesney 2008: 12). What follows is a listing of key problem areas, organised around media structures, behaviours and outcomes.

Communications regulation and the policy process

- communications policies that serve corporate media or state interests over the wider public interest
- policies (or non-decisions) that threaten or limit people's communication rights
- how the communication policy process operates
- democratic participation and oversight.

Organisation of media services: private; public service media; community and alternative media institutions

- the form and consequences of commercial organisation of media
- subsidies and support for public service media systems
- support for alternative media institutions and systems.

Financing of media services

- the influence of advertising in shaping media markets, content and communications services
- state and public financing; subsidies and levies.

Organisation and social relations of labour in media and communications

- working conditions, pay, protection, equality, protection for editorial independence and for artistic integrity
- access and opportunities for employment and training
- industrial democracy and worker participation in decision-making.

Content and outcomes

- the range and quality of information, ideas and imagery
- the nature of journalism and its relationship to democratic practices
- depoliticisation of society, knowledge gaps
- media representation
- voice and access to public communications
- the relationship of media to racial, gender and socio-economic inequality
- the relationship of media to national government policies, foreign policy and militarism
- the relationship of media to transnational governance
- the nature of commercialism and its impact on culture.

Holistic and integrated concerns

- the relationship of communication to global and contemporary capitalism
- the relationship of technology to media, and to politics and society
- the relationship of media to the distribution of power in societies
- the relationship of media to popular social movements.

Communication problems and twenty-first century media

For some critics the critical political economy of media tradition is fixed in the problematics of mass media that informed its creation in the 1960s and 1970s. The tradition is unable, or in milder versions ill-equipped, to serve as a basis for understanding changes that have transformed media and communications systems. In its late twentieth century versions CPE is associated with the critique that media systems in advanced economies are dominated by a handful of corporate providers. A central problem is the lack of plurality of voice and diversity of ownership under a market system. This account is challenged for its neglect of more recent or pressing problems that fall outside of the 'mass media' provision problematic. Online privacy, state and corporate control over data, Internet controls, intellectual property and data management all involve the kinds of relationships that CPE has examined between states, major corporate actors and consumers. But they all involve relationships between various kinds of communication users and producers, hybrid identities and relationships with and between networks. A 'mass media'-oriented political economy tradition has astigmatism along with problems of ageing. Yet a more fundamental critique is that the communication problems CPE has addressed have been largely overcome by changes in media, so as to render the critiques redundant and obsolete. In particular scarcity of supply has been overcome through digitalisation. The model of mass media provision, and its attendant concerns about control and influence, is much less salient as communication resources have been distributed throughout society. Central claims are that media and communications systems, transformed by technological innovation, are progressing from scarcity to abundance, from control to chaos, and from producer power to consumer power. The rest of this book examines these claims in various ways and the attendant gains and losses accompanying changes in media. Here I will just introduce and summarise, drawing on Flew (2011) and other accounts, a model of change from a paradigm of mass media to one of convergent media.

Table 1

	Mass communications	*Convergent media*
Media production	Hierarchical/complex division of labour 'Critical role of media content gatekeepers and professionals' (Flew 2011)	New technologies (Web 2.0 etc.) 'give scope for individuals/small teams to be producers, editors and distributors of media content'
Media distribution	Large-scale distribution High barriers to market entry	Internet 'dramatically lowers barriers to entry based on distribution' Greater choice of media outlets, content and services
Media power	Asymmetrical power relationship between producers and consumers One-way communication flow	Greater empowerment of users/audiences Multiple communication flows Interactivity
Communication	One-to-many Predominant model mass communication	Many-to-many Mix includes mass self-communication (Castells 2009)
Media content	Tendencies towards standardisation and mass appeal; content designed to maximise audiences; limited scope for market segmentation	'Long tail' economics; demassification, segmentation and niche media content markets
Producer/consumer relationships	Mostly impersonal, anonymous and commoditised Audience as target	Personalisation Driven by user communities and user-generated content (UGC)

Table 2

Control	Chaos
Information scarcity	Information surplus
Sealed (closed)	Leaky (open)
Opacity	Transparency
Exclusivity	Accessibility
Homogeneity	Heterogeneity (diversity)
Hierarchy	Network
Passive	(Inter)activity
Dominance	Competition

An overlapping model of change but one that is more explicitly critical of radical accounts of media is proposed by McNair (2006), who argues that there has been a paradigm shift from a mass media 'control' paradigm to a chaos paradigm. McNair (2006: 199) summarises the paradigm shift as seen in Table 2.

McNair's central claim is that the 'vastly expanded supply and availability of information' has resulted in a 'power-shift from the traditionally information-rich elite to the no-longer so information-poor mass' (2006: 199). Both of the above mappings display common characteristics. First, they are stagist. Change is regarded in evolutionist terms as a progression from one stage to the next, even though this may be qualified by some unevenness and acknowledgement of co-mingling. Second, they tend to conflate changes which need to be distinguished analytically. For instance, these are sets of claims concerning changes in industries, markets (supply and demand), media forms and processes, political, economic and social and cultural changes. Conflating these tends to naturalise processes of change and render them self-acting and self-generating, characteristics of technological determinist thinking which tends to suffuse such accounts. A third feature, very evident in McNair's model, is to crudely position positive over negative value-terms. These are mappings that stack the deck in their favour. One consequence is that even if we might agree about the salience of shifts they identify, the alignment with positive terms tends to bracket out considerations of gains and losses in such changes. There is also very compelling evidence to indicate that in place of a stagist transition from one state of affairs to another, there are contradictory tendencies at work across media: concentration and disaggregation; convergence and deconvergence; control alongside chaos; disempowerment as well as empowerment. The mobilisation of values is clearer still if we contrast these positive accounts of communications with Croteau and Hoynes's mapping of market versus public sphere models. Affirmative maps, such as McNair's tend to equate private provision with openness. Notwithstanding these critiques, media political economy must engage with the claims and arguments put forward by McNair and others. These include:

- Scarcity and supply. Does the evident proliferation of sources of supply resolve, or significantly diminish, concerns about provision whether informational or cultural? (chapters four and five)
- Cultural convergence. Is there a mutually beneficial alignment of corporate provision with user choice such that problems of media provision have diminished?

The critical tradition has to reflect on changing conditions, the salience of its theoretical positions and on the manner in which it identifies and addresses problems. Its capacity to do so is questioned by critics of the approach. On the contrary I will argue that CPE's focus on resources raises the most salient critical questions about contemporary media and connects these with broader concerns about human life and human flourishing. Critical political economy is concerned with the production, distribution and consumption of resources used to sustain human existence. It is concerned with the manner in which resources are distributed and shared, but also how they are created and cultivated. The CPE tradition has certainly generated highly pessimistic accounts of media cultures and processes and it is right that the grounds for optimism are continually assessed at every point. Yet such evaluation should arise from analysis and be judged on the quality of that analysis. The CPE tradition is sceptical about tendencies to presentism and smooth evolutionary transition. At their best CPE scholars insist on examining tensions, contradiction, the co-presence of antinomies and gradations between them.

Any analysis needs to have regard for its explanatory limits. This applies when selecting a broad approach such as CPE, as well as at the micro level of selection of topics and research design. US political economist McChesney (1999: 31) argues that the core 'structural factors' influencing the nature of media content (including the overall pursuit of profit, size of firm, levels of media concentration and competition, advertiser influence, 'the specific interests of owners, managers and, to a lesser extent, employees') provide a 'context (and a trajectory)' for understanding media content, but 'can only rarely provide a detailed under-standing of specific media content'. I have described this reflexive appreciation of explanatory limits as humility (Hardy 2008). Acknowledging explanatory limits helps to promote the more open, eclectic and synthesising perspectives required for the vitality of critical media studies. CPE analysis benefits from recognising and drawing on specialist tools and approaches, such as textual analysis and semiosis, pyscho-social and psychological studies. Yet, in advocating intellectual humility, I do not advocate a self-limiting (ontological) account of political economic analysis. Throughout this book I aim to demonstrate that CPE analysis does not fit the reductive caricature of a mechanistic Marxist account of 'production'. There is no aspect of communications processes that does not connect to communication resources and so have a political economic dimension, even if a great many other aspects rightly command our attention too. CPE analysis engages with content, audiences and use, labour and sociology. To the extent that it has neglected concerns or offered poor explanations, these are matters that should continue to engage all those who draw on and develop CPE as a practice.

Doing political economy research

Part one has introduced media political economy and part two examines thematic topics. As a bridge this section briefly considers key resources, practical issues and methods used in political economic research. For the analysis of media industries, key sources include corporate documents in the public domain such as annual reports, financial statements, policy submissions, legal documents and communications with key publics such as investors, financial markets, regulators and consumers. Media content businesses have consumer-facing websites but large firms have sections or linked sites for other publics identified under terms such as 'investor relations'. Larger firms and some SMEs have a corporate public relations operation, variously identified as media relations or corporate affairs. Other key sources include trade and industry bodies, market analysts, ratings and media monitoring organisations. Trade bodies that market particular media platforms to advertisers are invaluable sources (Hardy 2013b). Other key sources are trade journals and online resources (aimed at those working in different trade sectors) that provide news and analysis for media sectors or specialised activities, and news media reporting across business, law, entertainment and technology.

Governments, supranational bodies (such as UNESCO and the International Telecommunications Union) and national regulatory agencies are important sources. Policy submissions to consultations and enquiries provide rich resources, and topics, for research, but access varies; policy-makers may accept companies' claims for commercial confidentiality and exclude material from the public record (Winseck 2012: 7). Problems can be even greater in countries where public discussion on issues such as ownership and control has been restricted by authoritarian governments (Mastrini and Becerra 2012: 7). There are also media and civil society organisations, many of which are non-profit making, providing a rich source of information. These include organisations that specialise in human rights and freedom of expression (IFEX, Reporters without Borders), media reform groups (*Free Press*, CPBF), trades unions and labour movement bodies. The sources discussed above are used to examine the structure and operations of cultural industries, and examine policy networks and communications governance.

Media work has been a 'surprisingly neglected topic' (Hesmondhalgh 2010: 157), including within political economy, but has received renewed attention in recent years (Murdock 2003; Hesmondhalgh 2010; Mosco and McKercher 2008; Mosco 2011). This includes studies addressing the increasing complexity and uncertainty of cultural labour, conditions of precarity and uncertainties concerning status, professionalism and purpose (Deuze 2007, 2011). There has been a distinguished if thinly populated tradition of participant observation of media workers, mostly conducted by liberal scholars (Gans 1980) but with others pursuing more critical themes such as Born's (2004) fieldwork in different departments of the BBC during a period from 1996 to 2001 when corporatisation and new managerialism coexisted uncomfortably with a 'counter discourse' of public service values. CPE research is not limited methodologically and draws on the range of methods from the social sciences and humanities. These include historical and archival research, documentation analysis; quantitative and qualitative content analysis, textual and discourse analysis; surveys, interviews and focus groups.

Notes

1 Under perfect competition four conditions pertain: first, together with allocative efficiency, described above, there is productive efficiency; second, goods will be produced at the lowest possible cost. Third, price will not rise above marginal cost, the cost of supplying one extra consumer (in contrast to monopolists' ability to retain high prices) and fourth, competitive markets will encourage innovation and product development, thus maximising consumer benefits.

2 Such arguments influenced the Davies Committee report on BBC funding and were reflected in speeches and policy by successive Labour Culture Secretaries (Hardy 2004).

3 For a more comparative-normative perspective responsive to the diversity of media systems see Buckley et al. 2008; for theoretical elaboration see Christians et al. 2009.

Part II

Critical investigations in political economy

Chapter 4

Concentration, conglomeration, commercialisation

Introduction

If advocates of free markets are correct, where commercial media predominate we should discover a diversity of media firms catering to the widest range of interests, demand should drive supply, and competition amongst suppliers should benefit consumers with falling prices, greater innovation and increasing quality. Instead, in many instances, a growing multiplicity of outlets coexists with monopolisation in services and lack of diversity in sources. Instead of power over supply being in the hands of sovereign consumers it is concentrated within media conglomerates and advertisers. Critical scholars contest the suitability of relying on market forces alone to provide media services, but they also examine how far patterns of concentrated media ownership, and firms' efforts to minimise competition, depart from free-market nostrums.

Media ownership and control are probably the most readily identified concerns of critical political economy. Yet this is a heavily contested and congested area of enquiry. At its broadest are efforts to understand the changing nature of media businesses. For critical scholars this analytical task is linked to considerations of consequences: how do different ways of organising media influence what kinds of content are provided and how services are used? How do organisational arrangements affect communication services and environments? Such questions are relevant both for a 'mass media' paradigm of content supply and a contemporary paradigm of communication services and resources.

Investigating media ownership was routinely disparaged by mainstream media scholars and culturalists in the 1990s, regarded as a tired, predictable and anachronistic topic. Attitudes have since shifted somewhat when understanding the *business* of contemporary communications became unavoidable for serious enquiry, and as global media corporations continued to grow years after their predicted extinction in a new Internet era. Yet, there is nothing rigid or static about media business strategies and growth, about the complex shifts in market power as media industries adapt to change, or about the patterns of concentration, convergence and deconvergence that arise. Nor are the issues of ownership any less salient in today's multimedia-rich media systems. A starting point is to explore and explain the coexistence of restrictions along media supply chains alongside market openings and expanded provision. The issues of media ownership have particular weight because governments in most market economies have, over the last thirty years, moved to liberalise media ownership rules to facilitate the creation of large media firms and argue that market expansion of itself can better achieve goals formerly justifying regulatory intervention, such as media plurality. Media regulation is examined further (chapter eight) but the market patterns examined in this chapter and the next are vital considerations in assessing such policies.

Today, media concentration of ownership coexists with 'flexible', increasingly non-unionised, production, decentralisation of corporate decision-making and niche marketing, yet it remains of central concern because ownership concentration 'can restrict the flow of communication and information by limiting the diversity of producers and distributors' (Mosco 2009: 162). Here, CPE enquiry pursues three overlapping concerns:

1   Media ownership: how does the specific character of ownership and control influence the organisation of labour, media production, strategies and operations of media institutions?
2   Concentration of ownership: the tendency across converging media sectors for a small number of firms to control the majority of output.
3   Corporate dominance: concern about the media being privately owned and organised according to a market-based system driven by imperatives of profits (commercialism) and commodity exchange (commodification).

Another strand of analysis pursued by Herbert Schiller (1989), Naomi Klein (2000) and others examines how processes of commodification have extended into places and practices once organised according to a different social logic based on universality, access, social participation and citizenship – what Schiller calls the corporate takeover of public space – processes analysed in very many quarters such as universities, the Olympics, shopping malls and city streets, as well as media 'spaces' such as the Internet.

The first part of this chapter considers the processes and dynamics of media concentration and conglomeration but also assesses evidence of counter-trends and reconfiguration of media firms. This account is then used to review critical debates and reassess arguments about concentration and problems of media ownership. Those critical debates include the following questions: Is there media concentration? What is the evidence? What are the appropriate ways to measure concentration and media plurality? Does media concentration have detrimental or beneficial effects in regard to the following?

•   information, opinion and perspectives
•   the range of media products and services available to consumers at competitive prices
•   cultural expression and diversity.

PART 1: KEY TRENDS AND PROCESSES

The media are businesses, predominantly, that operate according to business logic and capitalist economic processes. The same key trends that have affected and altered businesses across advanced economies have reshaped media operations. In their analysis of structural trends in the US media industry, Croteau and Hoynes (2006: 77–115) identify four broad developments: growth of corporations; integration; globalisation; concentration of ownership. For Castells (2009: 71) the major trends have been globalisation, digitisation, networking and deregulation. Castells (2009: 56) offers a useful summary of changes to the organisational and institutional structure of communications over the last two decades:

- widespread commercialization of the media in most of the world;
- globalization and concentration of media business through conglomeration and networking;
- the segmentation, customization, and diversification of media markets, with emphasis on the cultural identification of the audience;
- the formation of multimedia business groups that reach out to all forms of communication, including, of course, the Internet;
- and increasing business convergence between telecommunication companies, computer companies, Internet companies, and media companies.

For Castells, these organisational changes form part of a communication revolution that includes technological transformations but also transformations in cultural identifications and practices, the latter including opposition to the consumerist branded culture of the global entertainment industry. This serves as a timely reminder that cultural changes must be examined, not inferred from an account of organisational change, yet understanding the business organisation of media is a foundation for investigating other questions about the scope and range of services provided, and their reception, use and appropriation.

Corporate growth and integration

Over the last thirty years the major business trend has been the growth of large media corporations that have exploited new opportunities to establish multiple media ownership nationally and to transcend national boundaries in ownership and operations. Transnational corporations (TNCs) grew in size and market share especially after 1945. In the cultural industries the post-war period was characterised by national mono-media firms with only a handful of firms dominant in transnational markets, of which most operated only regionally or in specific media sectors such as the film or music industries. Larger media conglomerates formed in the 1960s and 1970s but it was the 1980s that saw an intensifying process of mergers and acquisitions in cultural industries. Media mergers and acquisition activity reflected wider trends across industries. For instance, 1986, the 'year of the deal', saw 3,300 corporate acquisitions in the US. A further wave of consolidation took place in the US in the mid 1990s, surrounding the passage of the deregulatory Telecommunications Act 1996. The World Trade Organization's Basic Tele-communications Agreement (1996) contributed to global consolidation trends. In 1999, for instance, 72 per cent of media companies operating in Europe were involved in some form of merger or acquisition activity. A sustained period of growth and consolidation in US media culminated in the AOL–Time Warner merger in 2000. Valued at around $160 billion, this was nearly 500 times larger than any previous media deal and, at the time, the largest in business history. Growth and consolidation patterns may be illustrated by a selective record of merger activity

1985   Murdoch's News Corporation buys 20th Century Fox
1986   Matsushita acquires RCA for $6.4bn (then the largest non-oil acquisition in history)
1989   Sony acquires Columbia Pictures (and Tristar) (Japanese electronic hardware company buying entertainment software)
1990   Time and Warner merge
1991   Matsushita acquires MCA
1994   Viacom acquires Paramount ($8bn) and Blockbuster ($8.5bn)
1995   Westinghouse acquires CBS ($5.4bn)
1995   Disney acquires ABC/Capital Cities ($19bn) (Vertical integration)
1995   Seagram acquires Universal Studios
1996   Time Warner acquires Turner Broadcasting ($7.4bn)
1998   AT&T acquires TCI (inc. Liberty) (Telecoms–media convergence)
1999   Viacom and Columbia Broadcasting System (CBS) merge ($80bn)
2000   Vivendi acquires Seagram/Universal ($35bn)
2000   AOL and Time Warner merge ($166bn) (ISP – media conglomerate)
2002   Comcast acquires AT&T Broadband ($47.5bn)
2003   News Corporation buys a controlling interest in Hughes Electronics (DirectTV) ($6.6bn) (US satellite/global satellite TV)
2003   Sony and Bertelsmann merge music units into Sony BMG ($5bn)
2004   General Electric (NBC) buys Vivendi Universal Entertainment ($5.2bn)
2006   Disney acquires Pixar ($7.4bn)
2006   AT&T (owned by SBC) acquires BellSouth Corp ($67bn)
2006   Google acquires YouTube ($1.65bn)
2006   Comcast acquires Adelphia Cable (consolidating US cable broadcasting industry) ($17.6bn)
2007   News Corporation acquires Dow Jones and Company (whose assets include *The Wall Street Journal*) ($5.6bn)
2008   Google acquires DoubleClick (Internet advertising company) ($3.1bn)
2008   Vivendi acquires Activision (games publisher)
2010   Comcast acquires NBC Universal ($13.75bn)
2010   Disney acquires Marvel (comics and brands) ($4.24bn).

The Asian Financial Crisis of 1997 damaged the global economy but it was in the period 2000–2002 that a series of shocks particularly affected Euro-American corporate media growth, notably the collapse in Internet stock value, a short world-wide advertising recession and the impact of the 9/11 terrorist attacks. The dotcom stock collapses of 2001 revealed AOL Time Warner's over-inflated value (Cassidy 2002). The company reported heavy losses in 2002 for AOL, whose dial-up Internet 'walled garden' service was obsolescent, and reverted to 'Time Warner' the following year (Motavalli 2002). The year 2001 marked a general slowing in corporate growth and some spectacular failures (including several of the early developers of digital television services in Europe), although this shakeout itself gave rise to subsequent consolidation and acquisitions. In the early 2000s growth picked up with the expanding market for digital devices and the corporate rush to occupy new spaces of communication and congregation, such as social networking sites MySpace.com, purchased by News Corporation in 2005 for $580 million, and YouTube, acquired by Google in 2006 for $1.65 billion. Another surge of mergers occurred in the period 2003–7, followed by the financial crash of 2008 and subsequent Great Recession, affecting the US and Europe in particular.

After the 2008 crash, marketing spending was reduced, resulting in a cyclical crisis in ad-dependent media sectors such as television, and marketing itself, but adding to the structural crisis for newspaper publishing. The 2000s saw an increasing presence of IT firms acquiring media content businesses but also businesses that deliver and manage information about communications use by consumers, for advertising purposes. Illustrating this trend was Google's acquisition of DoubleClick and Microsoft's purchase of aQuantive, both indicative of the long-heralded convergence between telecoms, IT and cultural industries (Hesmondhalgh 2013: 189).

Multinational communications conglomerates have developed in conjunction with three key trends: deregulation, corporatisation and digitalisation (Arsenault 2012: 104). The liberalisation of (cross-)ownership accompanied and facilitated a wider trend towards privatisation, monetisation and corporatisation of communications infrastructure and content. State-owned telecommunication systems were privatised or part-privatised. Public service media faced pressures to operate under market processes and disciplines (corporatisation) and release or monetise assets. Digitalisation and technological convergence have increased the strategic importance of connections between and across businesses formerly organised around distinct market sectors and services. Rather than leading to more egalitarian ownership and control, convergence 'has empowered an ever-shrinking pool of consolidated companies that have the ability to influence and control the deployment of multiple communication platforms' (Arsenault 2012: 105).

Globalisation and growth

A common factor reshaping media systems has been the growth and influence of transnational media corporations in national markets. A transnational corporation

(TNC) 'is one that maintains facilities in more than one country and plans its operations and investments in a multi-country perspective' (Herman and McChesney 1997: 13). Such firms tend to internationalise both products and production processes which in turn contribute to the dissemination and adoption of professional practices and media forms and formats.

Capital's inexhaustible search for new markets is eloquently described by Marx and Engels (2013 [1848]). The search for the investment of capital in media technologies and services, combined with the imperatives on firms to compete in increasingly liberalised international markets, has encouraged the expansion of multinational media corporations. The industrial and manufacturing base of post-war prosperity in Western nations suffered shocks in the 1970s precipitated by the OPEC oil crisis, stagnation combined with rampant inflation (stagflation) and collapsing profits, especially in heavy manufacturing industries. Firms attempted to restore profits through foreign investments and expansion into new markets. The shift from manufacturing to IT industries and services lies at the heart of what has been dubbed a 'knowledge economy' and analysed more critically as digital capitalism (Schiller 2007) or informational capitalism (Fuchs 2011) (chapter five). Informatisation, data processing and international communications became core requirements for capital growth. The various drives for capacity in information and communication systems also contributed to reshaping media and cultural industries. Finally, merger and acquisition activity in media has also partly resulted from the expansion of the financial sector and assets relative to other sectors of the economy, especially from the mid 1990s. Financialisation is intimately connected with the slowing rates of growth of the so-called triad economies of the United States, Europe and Japan since the 1970s (Foster and McChesney 2012). The financialisation of capital accumulation was analysed by the Marxist economist Sweezy, who regarded the growth of the financial sector as a response to the stagnation tendencies of monopoly capitalist economics. Deepening stagnation of production led to a shift from 'production to speculative finance as the main stimulus to growth; high levels of unused productive capacity in manu-facturing encouraged industrial corporations to 'pursue the immediate, sure-fire gains available through merger, acquisition, and enhanced monopoly power than to commit their capital to the uncertain exigencies associated with the expansion of productive activity' (Foster and McChesney 2012: 13, 17). Corporations have them-selves become financialised entities, operating like banks in managing capital flows and engaging in speculation on futures and other 'fictitious capital', as well as currencies and commodities. Media, telecoms and the Internet sector have been in the forefront of the financialisation of capitalist economies (Winseck 2012).

The expansion of multinational corporations, developing global production and distribution networks, has been uneven but ongoing, with strong foreign direct investment (FDI) from the mid 1980s. Growth has been driven by efforts to open and expand markets or to make production more cost-efficient by accessing lower labour costs, resources, infrastructure, production facilities or advantageous tax regimes. Overseas expansion is also connected to domestic market and regulatory conditions. As one report puts it (Council of Europe 2004: 10):

> Media firms move into other countries when their home market is saturated, to attain critical mass, to pool resources and to share risks. In several cases firms have turned to other countries because the competition authorities refused to let them go ahead with a national merger for fear that it would create a dominant position or a monopoly.

The largest US firms expanded operations significantly from the 1980s out of a well-developed market. In Europe, regional and international expansion had occurred as firms rebuilt after 1945 but the main phase of internationalisation began later, in the 1990s.

Global media companies

Following a sustained phase of merger activity since 1986, a handful of major global multimedia companies now dominate media production. These firms have responded to the dynamics and imperatives of capitalist accumulation and economic, institutional and market conditions, forcing them to become larger, integrated and increasingly global. Bagdikian, in his preface to the 1997 edition of *The Media Monopoly*, noted:

> Only fifteen years ago, it was possible to cite specific corporations dominant in one communications medium, with only a minority of those corporations similarly dominant in a second medium.
>
> (1997: xxv)

Herman and McChesney (1997: 104) describe a global media market dominated by 'ten or so vertically integrated media conglomerates'. By 2002 the top tier comprised nine companies: General Electric (owner of NBC), AT&T/Liberty Media, Disney, Time Warner (then 'AOL Time Warner'), Sony, News Corporation, Viacom, Vivendi, Bertelsmann. Between them, these firms owned '[m]ajor US film studios; US television networks; 80–85 per cent of the global music market; the majority of satellite broadcasting world-wide; all or part of a majority of cable broadcasting systems; a significant percentage of book publishing and commercial magazine publishing; commercial cable TV; European terrestrial television' (McChesney 2002: 151). The list of 'top tier' global media giants has been reduced in recent accounts to seven (Castells 2009; Hesmondhalgh 2013: 193). The list changes too as lines of demarcation blur between media content-producing firms and other digital giants dominant in communication services but with little content production. Where the traditional telecommunications and IT firms on the one hand and hardware firms (Samsung) on the other tended to be treated separately from media and cultural (content) industries, converged firms such as Google and Apple combine all three while remaining principally media content distributors rather than content creators.

The seven largest global conglomerates by media content origination are Vivendi, Walt Disney, Comcast, News Corporation [from 2013 two separate conglomerates], Time Warner, Sony, Bertelsmann. In 2010 Comcast was the largest media group (dominant in the US cable market) with revenues of $35.6bn, followed by Google ($29.3bn) and Disney ($27.3bn), the third largest company. By 2011, Google was the largest firm, according to Zenith Optimedia (2013), whose listing of the top ten global media companies (by revenues derived from activities that support advertising) was:

Google $37.9bn
Direct TV Group $27.2bn
News Corporation $26.4bn
Walt Disney $19.7bn
Comcast $16.2bn
Time Warner $15.6bn
Bertelsmann $11.3bn
Cox Enterprises $11.1bn
CBS Corporation $10.8bn
BSkyB $10.2bn.

In fact, the increasingly networked relations between mega-corporations are best captured by examining linkages between multimedia companies, telecommunications firms, converged communications infrastructure firms, Internet content companies, gaming and entertainment and leisure businesses (Winseck and Jin 2012).

Another key ranking by revenue ($ millions), the Fortune Global 500 (2013), based on figures from July 2012, places the highest ranking communications company, Nippon Telegraph and Telephone (NTT), at 29 (133,077), followed by AT&T at 32 (126,723) with Verizon at 50 (110,875), Apple at 55 (108,249), China Mobile Communications at 81 (87,544), Sony at 87 (82,237), Microsoft at 119 (69,943), Amazon 206 (48,077), Walt Disney 249 (40,893), Vivendi 257 (40,063), Google 277 (37,905), News Corp 332 (33,405), Time Warner 381 (28,974), Direct TV 406 (27,226) and Bertelsmann 492 (22,427). Other telecommunications companies include Telecom Italia 244 (42,070) and BT group 358 (30,734). As this listing shows, Japan's NTT is the world's largest telecommunications company, with powerful players from China rising up the rankings. Yet a critical charge remains salient, that conglomerates with US headquarters also dominate the 'global oligopoly'. Of the top fifty audiovisual companies in 2010, with total revenues of $470.5 billion, half were based in the United States, followed by companies with headquarters in Japan (7) and the UK (5). France and Germany each had three top tier companies, Italy two and the remainder were single entries Luxembourg, Brazil, Mexico, China and Canada (Wescott 2011). The top fifty transnational media conglomerates (TNMCs) without headquarters in the US are located in Japan (Sony, NHK, TV Asahi, Nippon TV, Tokyo Broadcasting System, TV Tokyo, Fuji Television), the United Kingdom (BBC, Pearson, ITV), France (Vivendi), Germany (Bertelsmann), Canada (BCE-CTV, Rogers Communication, Shaw Communication, Quebecor), Italy (Mediaset), India (Bennet Coleman, Zee), Brazil (RedeGlobo, Abril), Mexico (Grupo Televisa, TV Azteca) and China (CCTV, Shanghai Media Group, Phoenix TV) (Arsenault and Castells 2008).

McChesney (2002: 154) argues that many media systems are dominated by a combination of first tier global firms and a 'second tier' of large regional operators. Thousands of smaller companies remain, but for Herman and McChesney (1997), the emerging system is a tiered one in which a second tier of some eighty national or regional companies, with extensive ties to the top firms, operates within a system of structural dependency that acts upon the third tier of smaller firms. The emerging 'global media system' includes 'an unprecedented array of (mainly new) regional and local producers and distributors ... but [is] dominated by a handful of giant enterprises – diversified entertainment conglomerates' (Schiller 2006: 140). The cultural implications of TNC activities is considered further (chapter seven), but our focus here is on ownership and integration. Examples of such corporate alliances include News Corporation's partnership with Globo in Brazil and Mexico's Grupo Televisa's links with North American firms such as Univision (although limited by US law to a 25 per cent share), as well as with News Corporation, through the loss-making pay-TV venture Innova. However, other corporate networks show geocultural linkages of language, history, trade, conquest and colonialism. For instance, Angolan capital investment in Portuguese media illustrates a reverse corporate colonialism (Figueiras and Ribeiro 2013). Second tier firms such as Televisa and Grupo Clarín (Argentina) hold dominant shares of national, regional and geocultural media markets. Another driver has been the financialisation of capital, as investors have looked for profits in foreign markets. There has been a close relationship between finance capital and the US film industry since its inception but overseas activity has increased, with US financial institutions buying foreign theatres and film distribution companies, sharing risks and profit with local capital. US banks seeking profits overseas assisted efforts by Hollywood to invest widely (Miller et al. 2005: 124).

Concentration of ownership

Concentration of media ownership is not a new phenomenon, as is evident from studies of press industrialisation in the nineteenth century (Baldasty 1992; Curran and Seaton 2010), or the 1920s Hollywood studio system (Schatz 1997), but neither has it gone away in a supposed era of digital proliferation. On the contrary, the recent phase of megamergers between traditional media companies, telecommunications and cable operators, and Internet businesses, has been driven by the economic logic of market expansion and facilitated by novel digital communication technologies (De Bens 2007). According to Bagdikian (2004: 3) five 'global-dimension' conglomerates, Time Warner, Disney, News Corporation, Viacom and Bertelsmann own most of the newspapers, magazines, book publishers, film studios and radio and TV networks, controlling programme production, broadcast networks, cable systems and channels. In the first edition of his book *The Media Monopoly*, Bagdikian identified which companies held the largest shares, up to 50 per cent of total, in each market and calculated that fifty firms dominated across the media as a whole in the US. The total fell in each subsequent edition of the book. According to McChesney (2004b: 178) the major media markets of television networks, cable TV, music, film, newspapers, magazines and book publishing are 'almost all classic oligopolies with only a handful of significant players in each market'. The two largest firms in US radio broadcasting, Infinity (owned by Viacom) and Clear Channel, have a greater market share than the firms ranked 3–25 combined. Clear Channel Communications run by Randy Michaels, a former ultra right-wing 'shock-jock' DJ, embarked on an acquisitions spree after radio ownership restrictions were lifted by the Tele-communications Act 1996. By 2002 Clear owned 1,225 stations. In a formerly diverse cable TV industry six companies now control over 80 per cent of the market. Four firms sell almost 90 per cent of US recorded music, while six companies account for the same share of industry revenues (McChesney 2004b).

The national press in Britain has been highly concentrated for several decades. In 2006 the top five companies had a combined share of 87 per cent. In 2013, the top three newspaper publishers held a 68.43 per cent share of the daily and Sunday newspaper markets. The number of national newspaper titles, and ownership patterns, have remained largely unchanged in the last decade. New entrant gains from the successive waves of technological innovation have been modest because significant market barriers remain, notably content creation costs, marketing and benefits of scale. Between 1945 and 1995 the only long-term entrant to the group of dominant newspaper companies was News Inter-national (Kuhn 2007: 7). News International (which owns *The Times*, the *Sunday Times* and the *Sun*) continues to command the highest share of circulation, with 31.21 per cent share, followed by Daily Mail and General Trust (inc. Lebedev) 22.11 per cent and Trinity Mirror 15.11 per cent (Press Gazette 2013). Existing firms have also sought to restrict competition. News International's decision to drop the cover price of *The Times* from 35p to 20p in 1993 was widely condemned as a form of 'predatory' price-cutting designed to weaken market competitors and attempt to drive the only new national entrant, *The Independent*, out of business. Regional newspaper titles increased from 1,295 in 2003 to 1,324 in 2005, mostly due to the emergence of free weeklies. Yet, by December 2005, the largest five publishers by circulation covered 84 per cent of regional newspaper circulation, up from 79 per cent in 2003 (Ofcom 2006). Given these concentra-tion trends the next section explores the processes leading to concentration in more detail, but we will also consider de-concentration trends before returning to assess arguments about the significance of media concentration and corporate media ownership.

Economic analysis

Several economic characteristics of media markets encourage concentration and consolidation and it is the intensification of this market 'logic' that prevails in commercial media systems today. In particular, the benefits of economies of scale and scope are often considerable. Economies of scale occur when the cost of providing an extra unit (of a good or service) falls as the scale of output expands. Economists refer to average cost (AC) as the total costs involved in providing a particular product or service divided by the total number of consumers. Marginal costs (MC) refer to the cost of supplying a product or service to one extra consumer. Economies of scale exist where the marginal costs are lower than the average costs. Such economies are prevalent because many media industries have high initial costs of production combined with low marginal reproduction and distribution costs (Doyle 2002b: 13–14; Picard 1989: 62–72). Film, broadcasting and publishing are all characterised by high 'first copy costs', while the cost of bringing additional copies to market is low, falling to zero. When the gap between first copy and second copy costs is large there tend to be economies of scale. Beyond 'break-even point', the volume of sales at which total revenues equal total costs, the profits made from selling additional units can be immense. In addition, where fixed costs of production are high, firms need to achieve significant sales to spread the costs across a large number of consumers. This explains the strong orientation towards 'audience maximization' strategies. Economies of scope occur when activities in one area either decrease costs or increase revenues in a second area. Such economies drive the integration of firms, the repurposing of content across different platforms and media, as well as tie-in merchandising.

As in other industries, large media companies enjoy scale benefits when long-run average costs (LRAC) decline as output and plant size increase (Picard 1989: 122). Existing firms with high volume will usually operate at lower cost per unit than a new firm entering the market, creating a 'barrier' to market entry. Of course new competitors may have other advantages, but where entry to market is difficult there tends to be concentration. Historically this has fuelled concerns that the major means of communication would tend to be owned by the powerful and wealthy – because the strategies for profitability have required huge capital investment in resources, such as printing presses. What resource barriers persist today is at the heart of debate on the Internet (chapter five), but while some production and circulation costs have fallen dramatically with digitalisation, labour costs and marketing costs tend to remain significant barriers.

Corporate consolidation has also been driven by the benefits of horizontal and vertical integration. *Horizontal integration* refers to the process of acquiring competitors in the same industry or sector. This process is evident in the 'chain' ownership of

US newspapers in the late nineteenth century. There is no necessary connection between horizontal expansion and market concentration. However, when a firm attempts to secure as large a market share as possible the usual, 'successful' outcome is greater concentration. *Vertical integration* refers to the acquisition or control of companies in different stages of the 'value chain' leading from production to circulation, sales and consumption. Again, the process is not new. The Hollywood studio system in the 1920s is the classic example, notable also as a system dismantled in part through regulatory pressure when the US Supreme Court ruled in 1948 that the studios must give up their exhibition operations, and then subsequently reconstructed from the 1970s (Schatz 1997; Miller et al. 2005). However, vertical integration was a leading feature of changes in corporate organisation and business strategy from the 1980s. Older terms such as 'diagonal', 'multisectoral' indicate patterns of integration across product sectors as firms diversify into new businesses, but such industry-based distinctions are becoming less tenable with accelerating convergence. All the major multimedia corporations are vertically and horizontally integrated and pursue diversification to occupy strategic positions across platforms and services. BSkyB, part owned by 21st Century Fox, produces audiovisual content and sells 'triple-play' bundles of phone, TV and broadband subscriptions. Games companies such as Sony, EA and Nintendo have invested heavily in online and mobile platforms, and diversified revenues through micro sales transactions and advergaming (in-game advertising).

Corporate synergy

Achieving economies of scope has been another important driver of corporate merger activity. This took various forms including the integration of hardware manufacturers and software operations (Negus 1997). Another form was integration of telecoms and IT companies with media businesses involved in content creation, exemplified by the merger, but effectively acquisition, of Time Warner by AOL. Such economies usually arise 'when there are some shared overheads or other efficiency gains available that make it more cost effective for two or more related products to be produced and sold jointly, rather than separately' (Doyle 2002b: 14). Savings can be made if the creative and other inputs gathered to make one product can be re-used in another (repurposing). In addition, product and brand extensions can increase the scope for profits. The Scandinavian Broadcasting System (SBS), for instance, cut production costs through the simultaneous production of a variety of programming formats targeted at different national markets (Iosifides et al. 2005: 84). The US-owned SBS broadcasting group, based in Luxembourg, has expanded from its Nordic market base and now controls channels in Northern and South-Eastern Europe. Firms use other means to achieve scope benefits including licences, alliances and joint agreements. Where first copy costs are high, there are incentives to sell the product or associated products in as many formats or 'windows' of opportunity as possible. This underlies the dynamics of branding and merchandising and the more recent developments of content repurposing that the Internet and digitalisation have greatly facilitated. Herman and McChesney (1997: 54) identify two main kinds of 'profit potential' driving merger activity. The first is cost savings arising from 'fuller utilization of existing personnel, facilities and "content" resources'. The second is the combined benefits of synergy, 'the exploitation of new opportunities for cross-selling, cross-promotion, and privileged access'. Synergy, like convergence, was presented (especially during the 1980s and 1990s) as an imperative to justify liberalisation of communications policy, and like 'convergence' it provided a more palatable description for monopolisation and concentration.

The chief reasons for conglomeration and corporate synergy have been the ability to achieve economies of scale and scope, combined with a desire to limit risks from investment or competition (Winseck 2008: 42; Kunz 2007: 10–13). Synergy 'includes the ability of a corporation to successfully merge cultural customs, machine code, methods of operation, and external network associations across multiple holdings' (Arsenault 2012: 111). Combining cross-media, cross-platform assets has also been driven by marketing and promotion. Conglomerates can offer advertisers packages that keeps ad finance within the corporate family and help to move it across a portfolio of publishing opportunities (see chapter six). As well as cross-selling advertising another key purpose is cross-promotion of media firms' own and allied content and services. With the expansion of digital platforms and services, bringing together users with services and purchasing opportunities has placed a premium on the ability of firms to cross-promote (Hardy 2010a, 2013a).

Complexity and counter-trends

So far I have outlined trends and processes of media conglomeration and concentration. However, changes across media industries have been more varied, complex and uncertain; to understand this we need to incorporate other factors and influences affecting media firms across different sectors. If tendencies towards integration are clear, corporate strategies and market processes have also involved disintegration, demergers, fragmentation and the creation of new kinds of networks and interdependencies between firms. All these processes must also be understood in the context of uncertainties and risks, the unpredictability and high levels of failure of ideas, products, firms and operations. This is essential in order to understand market dynamics and corporate strategies as well as to account for their highly varied performance and outcomes in the face of competition for audiences and resources (Hesmondhalgh 2013; Croteau and Hoynes 2006).

Uncertainty and risk

The media mergers of the 1980s and 1990s have been described as largely defensive moves (Curran 2002), and as 'bulking up for digital' (Tunstall and Machin 1999) – attempts to manage the costs and risks associated with establishing and maintaining strong market positions. Financing is another source of risk. Financing growth through 'retained earnings', revenue derived from sales, generally enables control over media organisations to remain with those who currently have it. However, increased need for investment has necessitated greater use of debt financing whereby firms risk control passing to banks or financial institutions if they are unable to manage repayment of borrowing. With equity investment (selling tradeable shares in the company) there are risks of shareholders launching a takeover bid (Flew 2007: 10). More generally, firms need to manage the demands of investors; those institutions and individuals who hold shares in the company.

Financing and servicing debt increases the influence of bankers and financiers and their presence on company boards. There has been a marked increase in the proportion of directors of media companies representing banking, finance or equity interest; their presence has increased while that of representatives allied to the state has declined (Winseck 2008). Financial markets favour low-risk, short-term, high-return investments. In the 1980s and 1990s this tended to favour vertically integrated multimedia conglomerates that possessed a large library of media content. For Miège (1989: 43) to highlight uncertainty here is not to argue that producers necessarily lack capacity to shape the market but that they face 'great difficulty in mastering the conditions of valorization for all [their] products'. Miège argues control can only be achieved over a series of products, hence the need for a catalogue or repertoire. Yet the expansive logic of synergy fuelling debt-laden corporate expansion met the counter-pressure from investors for low-risk, short-term, high returns. In the terminology of network analysis, global firms organised around networks jettisoned unprofitable nodes in efforts to maintain profit margins.

Reassessing synergy

Synergy was a corporate buzzword in the 1990s but much touted benefits were unevenly realised. The lustre and hype surrounding synergy has diminished somewhat, as claimed benefits failed to materialise, different work cultures failed to mesh, or 'megabrands' flopped. Some firms that merged during the 1990s found it difficult to achieve profitable synergies (Baker 2007) leading to demergers and sell-offs. Time Warner had promoted synergies across its film, publishing, music and online divisions but the collapse of AOL contributed to a major shift in strategy. Time Warner sold off its Warner Music Group in 2003, book publishing in 2006 and demerged AOL in 2008. Spectacular corporate failures such as Vivendi in 2002 prompted something of a reversal of synergy hype. Yet neither the hype nor declarations that the phase was over were substitutes for a careful grasp of corporate reconfigurations. Acquisitions and integration continue apace; media mergers and acquisitions reached 1,351 transactions in 2012, twice the number reached in 2011, valued at almost $75 billion (BtoB Media Business 2013). Integration, though, occurs alongside demergers (below). The collapse of major media players such as Kirsch, Adelphi, Knight Ridder and Can West had a variety of causes including overdependence on forms of production and delivery in struggling sectors, increased competition, as well as internal problems of over-indebtedness, over-expansion or poorly performing investments. News publishing businesses have faced the greatest decline as websites such as newspaperdeathwatch.com and papercuts.org report, while the music industry and advertising-financed FTA television have also suffered.

Deconvergence

The 1980s was a period in which many firms expanded operations through multisectoral growth and overseas trade and acquisitions. The 1990s saw leading firms diversify into digital infrastructure and services to manage risks and to position themselves for rapidly evolving and uncertain markets. The Time Warner–AOL merger in 2000 is emblematic of a transition between phases of convergence. From the 2000s a deconvergence trend has been evident, with companies consolidating activities in a few core activities and selling off operations in other areas. One driver has been investor impatience with problems in realising value from acquisitions and convergence, especially in heavily debt-laden conglomerates who are driven to package and sell off divisions and assets to serve the high levels of capital return demanded (Winseck 2012). Fitzgerald (2011) identifies increasing pressures from investors on media conglomerates to generate high returns for shareholders, with less support for the arguments regarding long-term positioning and investments used to justify the earlier phase of corporate convergence. Alongside still considerable merger activity, Jin (2012) identifies a rising trend of spin-offs and demergers, with a peak in 2005 (442). One example is News Corporation, which split its satellite TV and film businesses off as 21st Century Fox from its newspapers and other publishing businesses in 2013, the latter becoming the new News Corporation. The deconvergence of News Corp. was multicausal and complex, reactive to investors concerned about the underperformance of the newspapers (and the toxicity of a phone-hacking scandal) compared to the stronger growth prospects for the TV and audiovisual side. Murdoch carefully retained power as Chairman of both companies, although shoring up the family dynasty remains as uncertain as ever.

Patterns of ownership, then, have not simply been towards corporate integration and consolidation but also disaggregation, the creation of new kinds of networking and interdependencies between firms. Hollywood has adopted strategies described as 'decentralized accumulation' (Wayne 2003a: 84, 2003b) whereby the power and logic of domination by a small number of vast entities is achieved via a globalising network of sub-contracted firms and individuals, mediated through trade unions, employer associations, education and the state. 'Hollywood' production has been increasingly globalised within a 'new international division of cultural labour' (Miller et al. 2005). While the precise patterns vary across industries and genres, cultural industries have adopted strategies of sub-contracting, working with SMEs, globalising business processes to reduce manufacturing and labour costs but also to tap specialist resources and expertise in fast-developing digital services. This reflects broader processes whereby production has shifted to the global South, with TNCs developing supply chains from low-wage countries for goods aimed primarily at the global North, with 'the surplus seized in considerable part by the omnipresent multinational firms themselves' (Foster and McChesney 2012: 26). CPE scholars have foregrounded the appalling labour standards and exploitation, notably in merchandising manufacturing, that coexist with the glamorous creativity celebrated in business literature (Miller et al. 2005).

Networks, alliances and joint ventures

Media integration has been examined above as a form of corporate ownership, whereby subsidiary businesses are subject to control by parent companies. However, there are other ways in which firms manage production flows, services and relationships with other, legally separate organisations. This includes forms of sub-contracting with small firms but also joint ventures with other media conglomerates.

Such co-operative arrangements between firms have significance for many of the contemporary debates about media ownership. Alliances and joint ventures provide alternatives to establishing a controlling interest through mergers and acquisition, highlighting more complex patterns of control. It is also the focus of critical arguments that media markets can be dominated by interlocking interests that 'soften' competition and can increase cartel behaviour amongst dominant firms. The result, argues McChesney is far from 'text-book' accounts of economic competition and represents what is dubbed 'co-opetition'. Herman and McChesney (1997: 104) describe how the major global firms:

> operate in oligopolistic markets with substantial barriers to entry. They compete vigorously on a non-price basis, but their competition is softened not only by their common interests as oligopolists, but also by a vast array of joint ventures, strategic alliances, and cross-ownership among the leading firms.

Bagdikian (2004: 9) found a total of 1,441 joint ventures between the dominant five US media conglomerates. In the Harry Potter franchise, for instance, there are joint ventures such as the collaboration between Warner Bros and the Universal Orlando resort on the theme park, The Wizarding World of Harry Potter. At the other end of the spectrum there are sales between separate, competing firms, such as the telecasting of the Time Warner films on US cable networks including Disney, ABC Family, Cinemax and HBO and ABC (Nielsen 2007). Yet here too there is co-opetition for mutual benefit. Tom Zappala, a senior ABC executive, announced he would work with WB to help launch the theatrical release of *Harry Potter and the Half Blood Prince* (in July 2009) by running a marathon of the first four films. According to Dempsey (2008) '[t]hese cross-promotion strategies often draw more people into the multiplexes at the same time as they're adding to the Nielsen ratings of the older titles on the network'. Alliances and joint ventures usually refer to formal arrangements between firms to pool resources or otherwise collaborate. Paramount and 20th Century Fox collaborated in financing and producing *Titanic* (Croteau and Hoynes 2006). In 2006 Time Warner and Viacom closed their rival networks WB and UPN then launched their jointly owned CW network. Co-opetition between firms, at least its public forms, can be relatively easily catalogued as instances of softening of competition. However, there is no predictable outcome from joint ventures or alliances per se as to whether supplier interests predominate over consumer benefits.

As discussed, there have been efforts to distinguish a 'monopoly capitalism' analysis, associated with McChesney, from a 'network capitalism' approach (Winseck 2012). The division is overdrawn in my view but does serve to alert us to differences in explaining the tendencies and forms of capitalist organisation. For McChesney, joint ventures represent efforts by firms to seek to control and manage markets. Contrary to litanies for competition, such strategies are anti-competitive and provide a more accurate insight into firms' behaviour, combining competition and collusion according to particular business objectives. In other accounts, greater emphasis is placed on such network arrangements as defensive moves, responses to market uncertainty and volatility. Networking relations and 'alliance capitalism' for Castells (1996) are core features of modern business operations, present in high-tech sectors where research and development costs are huge. Alliances between media industries and Internet/IT companies increased in the 2000s (Arsenault and Castells 2008; Arsenault 2012). Rather than endorse these as alternative accounts, they serve to invite us to consider the impact of specific network arrangements on control and competition in the markets affected.

Another driver for alliances has been global expansion, as multinationals seek partnerships with foreign companies to secure governmental approval in their host market. Multinational expansion may be constrained by national rules on foreign media ownership and investment. This is one reason why firms may seek strategic alliances with local firms to 'integrate operational functions, share risks, and align corporate cultures to achieve a collective market advantage' (Albarran and Chan-Olmsted 1998: 334). Alliances can offer the best opportunity to capture an already developed customer base, or overcome barriers to market entry. Alliances are also driven by the need of TNCs to localise media content and services. TNMCs form strategic alliances with NMCs (national media conglomerates) to obtain assets such as a firm's position within and knowledge of the relevant market, distribution systems, regulatory arrangements and links with power sources. Such alliances can allow TNMCs to avoid the risks and heavy investment required to establish wholly owned subsidiaries and instead adopt more flexible, networking arrangements allowing them to spread risks and gain control of new markets (Mirrlees 2013). TNMCs also form joint ventures to create new companies, such as Walt Disney's joint venture with South Korea's SK Telecom

Corporation to launch a localised, Korean-language Disney TV channel. Licensing arrangements are another form, in which TNMCs authorise licensees to distribute their copyrighted products. A third variant is an equity alliance, formed when a TNMC acquires part-ownership of a national media corporation through investment. Like concentration, there is nothing new about joint ventures but this mode of operating increased significantly from the 1990s. Critical scholars have also focused on another forms of alliance, the corporate interlocking arising from participation in boards of management of 'competitor' media interests, marketers and other corporate media interests (Bagdikian 2004; Bettig and Hall 2012, chapter six).

Presence of small firms

Amongst the counter-tendencies to concentration, it has been argued, is a flourishing of small firms (Hesmondhalgh 2013: 209–12). The creative conception stage of the production of cultural products in some industries (music) remains small scale with low barriers to entry. Hesmondhalgh argues that CPE perspectives that focus on conglomeration and integration 'often underestimate the significance of small companies', which are vital in terms of the number of people they employ, the potential to foster innovation and the emphasis many place on 'institutional independence' (2013: 210), notably in indie cinema and significant parts of music making where there is resistance to commodification amongst producers, performers and audiences. Small firms can be sources of creativity, innovation and cultural diversity throughout their operations. We need a media political economy that is engaged with the totality of cultural production and whose account of problems is properly sensitive to the diversity of conditions for creativity. One requirement is to examine market relations and interdependencies between small and large firms. Small firms' institutional autonomy is often vulnerable to the market dominance and strategies of conglomeration. Large corporations increasingly sub-contract to SMEs. Interdependencies between large corporations and small firms have also featured heavily in various phases of development of commercial film, TV and recorded music industries, with production, licensing, finance and distribution deals between majors and 'independents'. This highlights the importance of identifying different kinds of organisation of firms and relations between these across the various cultural industries. In sectors like publishing and parts of the music industry, the conception stage can be small scale, 'relatively inexpensive' and take place under 'relatively autonomous conditions'. Other factors include market opportunities and barriers to entry, for instance in markets being shaken up by new digital technologies, greater access to venture capital for SMEs, as well as deconvergence and disintegration processes in some vertically integrated companies. Above all, the promise of digital abundance has masked continuing patterns of corporate dominance. Despite the proliferation of independent music distribution online, Vivendi (owner of Universal Music), Sony Entertainment, EMI Group and

Warner Music still accounted for 48 per cent of global music revenue in 2009 (IBISWorld 2010, cited in Arsenault 2012: 108).

PART 2: CRITICAL ISSUES AND DEBATES

There are complex patterns of convergence and deconvergence, integration and fragmentation, yet concentration of media ownership remains a strong feature and a pervasive critical issue, but why? For one prominent CPE scholar the critique of concentration is misplaced, along with presumptions of control. The CPE tradition, argues Garnham (2011: 41) tells a 'drearily familiar' story: 'The capitalist mass media are increasingly concentrated on a global scale under the control of corporations and media moguls leading to a decline in cultural diversity, the suppression of progressive political views, and the destruction of local cultures'. Garnham traces the concerns about corporate media control to presumptions in the 1960s that this contributed to a dominant, pro-capitalist ideology. He highlights various problems. There was a lack of evidence that capitalism required a dominant ideology or that dominant elites shared one. The notion of control 'in the sense of being able to produce planned outcomes through the employment of subordinate economic agents was very tenuous' (Garnham 2011: 45). The media concentration thesis failed to recognise that:

> as capitalist economies have grown, the associated lowering of the costs of material goods linked to the release of higher proportions of household expenditure for the satisfaction of immaterial wants, including cultural products and services, and the expansion of the commercial cultural sector to meet resulting demand, has clearly widened cultural diversity on both a national and international scale even if it continues to be unevenly spread.
>
> (Garnham 2011: 45)

Garnham thus rejects the critique of concentration he contributed to advancing and, claiming Marx's thesis of the dialectical nature of capitalist development, contents himself that capitalism 'produces the very culturally enriched and educated workers and citizens necessary for its own supercession' (Garnham 2011: 46). In his earlier work Garnham was less sanguine. Media markets tend towards concentration because economies of scale and scope favour large organisations; 'their economic survival under market conditions depends upon the exploitation of monopolies' (Garnham 2000: 58). Given this, regulation is needed in order to control or break up monopolies and prevent firms dominating market power and, for liberal and radical perspectives, halt media power abuses.

The trends outlined above help to explain tendencies towards corporate growth, concentration and the accumulation of market power that underlies critical arguments about media power. Yet the core political economic critique of media concentration has been challenged on numerous matters of fact and value, evidence and evaluation (Compaine and Gomery 2000). Are media markets (becoming more) concentrated? Does it matter? Is there greater corporate media ownership? Does it matter *who* owns the media? Does media concentration and integration restrict or enhance media content diversity? Do the activities of transnational corporations enhance or threaten cultural diversity and creative autonomy?

Concentration: evidence and analysis

There are standardised measures for market concentration, such as the HHI index used in US anti-trust law. This measures concentration by squaring each firm's percentage market share and then adding up the squares. However, judgements about the relevant market used for such calculations are rarely straightforward. The economist Benjamin Compaine challenged Bagdikian's account of increasing media concentration to argue that the media industry as a whole was very unconcentrated (with a HHI index of 268, where only scores of 1,000 or greater indicate concentrated markets). Compaine (2001) acknowledges growing concentration in some sectors (newspapers) but argues that across the media as a whole there has been an expansion of outlets. Noam (2009) examines the US information sector, defined broadly to include over a hundred industries. His analysis confirms increased concentration in the media sector following the Telecommunications Act 1996. The revenue share of the largest five companies increased from 13 per cent in 1984 to 29 per cent in 2004. Yet, Noam, like Compaine, argues that the sector remains unconcentrated by the standard measures of the US Antitrust regulations, with the exception of the Internet, which Noam found to be highly concentrated. However, Baker (2007: 54–87) identifies three main problems with the Chicago School antitrust approach adopted by Compaine. First, the media as a whole are not the relevant market. Delivery and content businesses should not be collapsed together since market share in one says nothing about market power in the other. Different media products are often not substitutable from the perspective of audiences or advertisers, so issues of geographic supply and availability, subject matter and style are all relevant in identifying what the relevant market to consider should be. Second, economic criteria are not suitable surrogates for socio-political critieria, such as political pluralism and democracy. Third, even more thoughtful approaches that incorporate 'socio-political' criteria into antitrust analysis, such as the FCC's much criticised Diversity Index, focus on commodities without adequately addressing 'the noncommodified values actually at stake, namely the quality of media serving participatory democracy' (59). For Baker (2007: 16–17) 'The widest possible dispersal of media power reduces the risk of the abuse of communicative power in choosing or controlling the government'; 'Any form of participatory democracy needs media that provide serious presentation, and then professional scrutiny, of alternative offerings' (17). Baker (2007) criticises the manner by which concentration in markets is calculated by Compaine and others, while Kunz (2007) provides a detailed account of growing concentration in the US film and television industries.

Concentration is one indicator of the ability of firms to exercise market power. However, it is the manner in which market power, and media power, can be exercised that matters, not merely the number operating in and across media markets. A commonly found pattern, consistent with the capitalist development of cultural industries is for the 'profit seeking sector' to be dominated by large conglomerates, alongside which are clustered small and medium enterprise (SME) creative industries, a two-tiered market structure in which there is a limited oligopoly of firms controlling between 75 and 90 per cent of revenue/market share together with a number of smaller firms on the other tier fighting for a small percentage of the remaining market share (Albarran 2004). Such market analysis cannot account for the cultural vitality and diversity *within* these markets, nor indeed offer any detailed account of content itself.

Analysts continue to disagree over the appropriate measures to identify concentration (Iosifides 1997; Baker 2007; Ofcom 2012), with media convergence making assessments of media plurality ever more challenging. How market size and share relate to influence needs investigation across the various ways in which firms' behaviour influences market actors, suppliers and traders, regulators, politicians, publics and consumers. Market dominance generally entails the ability to influence favourable terms and influence the behaviour of other businesses and the options for consumers, unless regulations intervene or significant market changes occur.

Concentration and control

Media concentration is perceived as a problem because it limits, or threatens to limit, the plurality of sources of information and opinion. Radical scholars go further in arguing that market pressures favour a right-wing tending media, limiting access to voices from the left. The arguments then shift to a variety of considerations: whether ownership influences editorial content and diversity, whether concentration may have beneficial effects in enabling firms to remain profitable or to invest cost-savings to improve quality, and arguments that such concentration matters less as alternative sources of supply increase and consumption patterns change. Radical functionalists have traditionally argued that media reinforce elite power because they are owned by the wealthy and powerful. Leftist concern about interventionist owners is misplaced, it is countered, because control resides with executives and senior managers. They operate to serve the business objectives of the company but do not act in politically motivated or partisan ways as media owners like the UK 'press barons' Lords Northcliffe and Beaverbrook did in the 1920s (Curran and Seaton 2010). The potential for owners to influence content has diminished significantly, it is claimed, due to the rise of modern corporations in which ownership is widely dispersed with control exercised mainly by expert managers, and with media workers relatively free to act within the limits of accepted business practice (Demers and Merskin 2000; Tunstall 1996).

Later accounts of post-Fordism (Aglietta 1979; Piore and Sabel 1984) complemented the 'managerial revolution' thesis highlighting the rise of decentralised networking within and between firms and increasing use of flexible, contract labour. In an influential essay Murdock (1982) challenged the thesis of the managerial revolution to argue that while managers exercised operational control, media owners shaped the strategic organisation of resources, exercising 'allocative' control. How precisely 'control' operates across different kinds of organisations remains contested and underexamined, with some calling for the presumptions of owner and corporate control to be abandoned (McNair 2006; Garnham 2011). Large media firms, it is argued, are owned by a mass of investors to whom managing executives are ultimately accountable; control has passed from single owners to networks of shareholders.[1] Power, accordingly, is dispersed widely. Noam (2009) found the media industries to be owned mainly by institutional investors, rising as a promotion from 40 per cent in 1984 to 57 per cent in 2008. The largest investors had stakes in a multitude of firms, yet investors rarely emulate the forms of editorial interference associated with interventionist owners and media 'barons'.

Ownership matters because owners influence firms' behaviour. So argues Baker (2007: 90–91), rejecting a 'market determination' thesis that the behaviour of enterprises is dictated by competitive market structures. On the contrary, 'monopolistic competition allows the owner to chose between profit maximization, ideology, product quality, and greater – even if unprofitable – circulation' (Baker 2007: 96). There are important objections to relying on anecdotal, impressionistic accounts of owner control, or in generalising from the behaviour of 'media moguls'. Critiques of media ownership need to be carefully delineated. Yet the CPE tradition has continued to amass evidence and develop a theoretically rich analysis of problems of corporate media ownership. Several authors following Murdock (1982) have revealed the persistence of forms of centralised control, with many of the leading media conglomerates remaining owner controlled: Rupert Murdoch and family at News Corporation, Sumner Redstone at Viacom, and Berlusconi, formerly Italy's longest serving Prime Minister, with a 38 per cent stake in Mediaset, Italy's largest commercial broadcaster, as well as publishing and other interests. In Canada eleven of the top twelve media firms are owner controlled and this pattern predominates in Latin America, Australia and elsewhere (Winseck 2008: 44; Mastrini and Becerra 2012).

The extent to which dispersal of ownership through institutional investors safeguards media also requires careful examination. Bettig and Hall (2012) show how tobacco firms used their positions as investors and board members, as well as advertisers, to influence how smoking was represented in the US media during the devastating promotions of the twentieth century, and before the same process was pursued in markets such as Eastern Europe and Asia. Even if such instrumental interventions on editorial remain rare, major investors usually exercise 'allocative' control through their representation on management boards, influencing firms' strategic decisions.

Corporate bias

Capitalist media enterprises owned by profit-driven corporations may be expected to favour the fundamentals of the market economy and to give editorial support to political parties that favour their business interests. A useful distinction is made, however, between instrumental and structural influences on media content (Murdock 1982; Manning 2001: 82–83). Media owners may intervene directly, instrumentally, in shaping editorial. Rupert Murdoch has a lengthy record of such proprietorial interference as a long list of former executives, editors, competitors, critics and biographers attest (see Neil 1997; Street 2011: 159–84; Curran and Seaton 2010). Murdoch told a House of Lords Communications Committee (2007) he was a 'traditional proprietor' exercising editorial control over his UK tabloid papers, but argued he did not instruct the editors of *The Times* or *Sunday Times*, complying with measures established when he bought the papers to protect editorial independence. Manning (2001) and others show that *The Times* and *Sunday Times* became more partisan in news reporting under Murdoch. A survey of editorial coverage in 2003 found that the most influential of the 175 newspapers owned by News Corporation worldwide unanimously supported the US-led invasion of Iraq (Greenslade 2003). However, overt intervention is less common than more subtle alignments between the outlook of editors and their internalised awareness of Murdoch's political and other interests (Neil 1997).

Other influences are more entirely structural. Advertising placement is not usually governed by the political prejudices of advertisers. Rather, the cumulative decisions made by advertisers tend to favour certain media outlets over others (Gandy 2000). The result is a largely structural influence but one with tremendous importance for advertising-dependent media markets (chapter six). In more deterministic accounts, the influences of ownership and advertising tend to be seen as acting in one direction, imposing control on content from above. However, radical sociologists have acknowledged the complexity and indeterminacy arising from the interplay of sources of power, while insisting on investigating patterns of dominance. For instance, market forces are capable of constraining political partisanship by owners and so limiting owner power. Large numbers of readers did not share the right-wing enthusiasm of UK press magnates in the 1980s and 1990s yet needed to be persuaded to buy their papers if these were to be profitable. Staff power and the upholding of principles of journalistic independence and professional integrity can also act as countervailing forces (Curran 2002). Yet, proprietors can influence editorial behaviour, especially through exercising 'allocative' control over senior appointments, policy and resources (Murdock 1982). Further, as Murdoch's interventionist record illustrates, the claim by liberal pluralists that 'media controllers subordinate their ideological commitments to the imperatives of the market is only partly true' (Curran 1996: 95).

The influence of owners over the behaviour of business units and employees remains a vital issue. Yet this needs to be broadened to examine the complexity of media work and labour relations, as well as shifts in the economic and cultural power of media professionals. CPE analysis must show the ways in which different organisational arrangements and cultures of media work influence activities. Such detailed attention to media work is needed since the accounts of media work that have emerged in recent years have not always pursued either the macro analytical frameworks or criticality of political economy.

Network analysis and control

There are tensions between instrumental and structural accounts of media ownership. Instrumentalist accounts focus on owner behaviour and pursue a critique of intervention, ideology and the consequences of the pursuit of political and commercial interests. Structuralist accounts relocate agency to the dynamics of market competition. In one the promotion of capitalism arises from ideological affiliation; in the other it arises from the market imperatives and networking of firms. Both accounts have salience and help identify processes. Yet they also replicate problems in conceptual formulations of structure and agency that are irresolvable. There have been efforts to overcome structure–agency problematics in network analysis. For actor–network theory (ANT) sociology should be redefined as the study of network associations (Latour 2005: 5). Arsenault (2012: 102) proposes a 'network political economy approach' whose 'primary focus of analysis is on the processes, programs, and structures that constitute a given network rather than capital or markets'. There are a number of valuable features of this approach. It shifts the focus from traditional 'global media' content businesses to examine how the core communications system comprises complex networking relationships between multinational companies. It brings greater attention to telecoms- and computing-based groups within the core communications system. It highlights that digitalisation aids the production of diverse content. It proposes that to understand power we must recognise not only the control of big corporations but also the 'creative capacity of new producers' (Mastrini and Becerra 2012: 69). Conceptions of structure and agency are recast. Network linkages may take many forms including interpersonal interactions, but also strategic corporate alliances and flows of information between and within groups. A focus on network relations also grants 'equal, if not greater, significance to the processes of collaboration between actors' (Arsenault 2012: 103) rather than traditional CPE focus on competition and consolidation. The network approach

> sees power as embedded in networks rather than something that is a function of corporate hierarchies.
>
> [...]
>
> Power is thus not necessarily concentrated within any single company but embedded in the processes of association between key nodes in the network.
>
> (Arsenault 2012: 103)

Attending to such network processes can help displace analyses that are too centred on individual companies or agents (including owners), and help to identify the interdependencies and processes of co-opetition discussed. They can also theorise power in productive ways as both distributed (unevenly) in networks and as structured by network characteristics. Yet, sophisticated accounts of the dispersal of power can offer a dissolution that many CPE scholars will reject. The analysis of capitalist economic processes and class relations tends to be supplanted, and in place of structured hierarchies of power a flatter, more open and porous account of network power is offered. There are undoubted benefits from such network analysis but the framework can be as limiting as those it seeks to supplant. Arsenault (2012: 102) proposes ANT as an approach that 'complements rather than replaces more traditional political economic approaches', yet the division between these can be overstated. Arsenault argues that to assess firms' dominance 'we must look beyond traditional measures of the political economic power of media, such as allocational, economic, and attention scarcity ... power is equally evidenced in an actor's ability to institute network program changes in the media and communications sector and its ability to influence and leverage connections to parallel networks' (119). Shorn of the network terminology it is inaccurate to suggest CPE has pursued the former at the expense of the latter. There are also problems when networks are ascribed agency, as in Arsenault's formulation of networks as 'the dominant social structure guiding the operations of contemporary communications businesses'. How are networks 'guiding' forces? If dominant, how do networks relate to economic processes of capitalism and how should their relationship be understood?

Global media industries involve practices that are highly damaging to the environment from energy use and waste. This relates to another key problem area, media representations of the ecological crisis and environmentalism. Maxwell (2009) proposes an agenda for research on media industrialisation that encompasses non-human biodiversity, the latter sharing actor–network theory's efforts to move beyond human-centric perspectives in favour of a broader appreciation of organic life incorporating non-human actants.

We have traced above a number of issues and concerns but the CPE critique of media concentration can be summarised as follows:

1 The concentration of market power can stifle competition.
2 The private concentration of symbolic power potentially distorts the democratic process by granting too much capacity for influence to private media owners (Curran 2002; Baker 2007).
3 The media power at the disposal of media moguls tends to be exerted in a one-sided way, promoting pro-capitalist interests.
4 Media groups drive policy – 'centralizing and globalizing firms need and seek political support for their advances' (Herman and McChesney 1997: 172).

Traditionally the critique of media concentration made by both liberals and radicals focused on the consequences for democracy. Ownership concentration threatens to amplify the values and interests of media owners, restrict the public role of journalists and limit the range of voices and opinions necessary for an informed citizenry and effective democracy. Yet cultural pluralism has been a growing concern. The diversity of ideas and imagery matter as well as diversity of information (Murdock 1992b; Andersen 2000). Such an expanded understanding of media pluralism informs European policy-making. The Council of Europe (CoE) understands media plurality as the scope for a wide range of social, political and cultural values, opinions, information and interests to find expression through the media. Media pluralism encompasses 'the diversity of media supply, use and distribution, in relation to 1) ownership and control, 2) media types and genres, 3) political viewpoints, 4) cultural expressions and 5) local and regional interests' (K.U. Leuven et al. 2009: 5). Understood in this way, plurality concerns include:

- content variety and cultural diversity
- media access (social, cultural and economic access for individuals and groups in society, especially marginalised groups)
- independence of creators, programmers and journalists
- owner influence affecting media content and performance in entertainment, fiction and factual programmes as well as 'news'
- plurality of sources of funding for media.

Citizenship has been a central discourse of liberal and radical reformers in the UK, the United States and elsewhere in response to trends of consolidation, commercialism and liberalising reregulation (McChesney 1999; Feintuck and Varney 2006). Yet the tendency to focus on news and information has left the case for tackling problems of ownership and control in entertainment and cultural expression weaker. This has been especially problematic where governments have relaxed media ownership rules to allow greater concentration and con- solidation across media businesses, while retaining limited protection for news. It has been understandable why the protection of plurality in news and information has been the uppermost demand for media campaigners, yet a much wider case for tackling media power and strengthening cultural pluralism is required (Hardy 2010a: 267–87).

Commercialism

An overlapping set of critical arguments concerns media commercialism, the profit-maximising production and circulation of symbolic content. Here again there are concerns about content diversity arising from corporate behaviour and the core tendency of commercial market systems to favour profitable consumer markets and underserve less profitable consumer markets. Advertising finance tends to favour commercially friendly media content, large aggregate audiences or affluent niche audiences, and disfavour less popular content and the pref- erences of those constituting poorer groups, or interests, in society (Gandy 2004;

Turow 1997, 2011). Commercial markets fail to register the full range of people's preferences, which include non-market values and preferences (Baker 2002). More fundamentally, commercial markets are considered an insufficient basis for all media provision because the principles of market provision are inherently in tension with principles of democratic participation, equality and universality (Murdock 1992b). Here critical concerns move beyond competition or concentration per se to address problems of commercialism.

In the US increasing corporate control has been associated with a shift to hypercommercialism (McChesney 1999). Private media have always been required to balance their civic or cultural purposes with the exigencies of economic viability. Hypercommercialism refers to a shift whereby the drive to profits is paramount, reshaping the priorities and operations of organisations. Such hypercommercialism, critics argue, has undermined the relative 'autonomy' of US journalists, weakening professional standards and eroding the divisions between serious and entertainment news, and between editorial and advertising. News, editorial quality and reporting are being undermined through cost cutting. In entertainment media, hypercommercialism has involved increasing advertiser integration and the production of programme genres like reality TV that are cheap to produce and attract large aggregate audiences to secure advertising finance (Croteau and Hoynes 2006; De Bens 2007).

We can understand the complex outcomes further by returning to consider economic dynamics. For instance, Van Cuilenberg (2007) identifies five trends reshaping media markets in Europe:

1 digitalisation, leading in particular to convergence between audiovisual and telecommunications industries
2 exponential growth in media and information supply
3 diversification in media products, content, platforms and outlets
4 stagnation in media consumption (for media types *except* the Internet), and
5 increasing segmentation in audiences.

Two of the five trends especially favour competition in content (diversification in supply and audience segmentation; involving the production of products for niche markets and special interest consumer groups, and increased sales opportunities). Accordingly, we might expect media diversity to increase with the growth of communication channels, with technology promoting access to a greater range of ideas. However, the other three trends – digitalisation, growing supply and stagnating demand – 'stimulate media competition on price rather than on content' (42). Numerous empirical studies confirm that increasing media competition does not automatically lead to greater content diversity. For European scholars, particular attention has been given to the changes in broadcasting whereby commercial channels and operators were encouraged to expand in formerly highly regulated systems dominated by public service broadcasters. By 2008 there were 2,024 private TV channels broadcasting national or regional services in the European Union, compared to 301 public ones. In her study of Belgian television De Bens (2007) shows that increased channel competition led to greater convergence rather than diversity in programme output, as do van der Wurff and van Cuilenberg (2001) in the Netherlands.

Schudson (2005: 175) asserts that 'it is not clear that [European] public and private broadcasters differ systematically in the ways they present political news and current affairs'. Certainly, public service media's future in an increasingly commercialised environment is uncertain and trends towards convergence in news and other programming can be found, but significant differences remain discernible. News and current affairs output is generally much higher on public than private channels (Hardy 2008). Private channels show a much higher proportion of non-national fiction (predominantly US) compared to public ones: in 2007, 76.7 per cent compared to 39.7 per cent (European Audiovisual Observatory 2009). Yet, Schudson is right that rigid distinctions between 'market' and 'state' organisation, or 'commercial' and 'private', mask important differences within each category. In Britain, a publicly funded BBC remains comparatively well resourced, maintaining the largest share of viewing by households, but the principal satellite broadcaster, BSkyB, was allowed to develop in a largely unregulated form, increasing competitive pressures across the system. ITV, a commercially funded broadcaster established with public service obligations, was auctioned, then permitted to consolidate; two companies dominated what had previously been a regionally owned service, then merged in 2004 to form ITV plc. Permitted 'lighter touch' regulation since 1990, ITV lobbied, with success, for its PSB obligations to be reduced as it managed declining advertising revenues and audiences, and the diminishing value of its analogue spectrum. These changes contributed to discernible shifts in programming, with reductions in local news, children's and arts programmes. ITV reduced its current affairs output by half in the decade to 1998, shifting what remained to predominantly domestic over foreign coverage, so that by 2005 its international factual programming was the lowest of all UK terrestrial broadcasters (Seymour and Barnett 2006; Curran et al. 2009).

Conclusion

Ownership matters for content, but neither media content nor behaviour can be derived from an account of corporate and market structures alone. Instead, *how* ownership matters requires careful analysis that includes micro studies of production and work, texts, and people's engagements with texts. Political economy has been condemned for 'reading off' consequences for cultural production from important, but rudimentary, categories like 'public' and 'private' ownership. But, as the best work demonstrates, while media diversity remains an underlying concern, researchers explore the complex, shifting patterns of marketisation and their consequences (Thomas and Nain 2004).

Here, we need an analysis sensitive not only to the range but also the contradictions of cultural production. One such is the commodification of anti-capitalism, the distribution and marketing of counter-cultural works such as Michael Moore's documentary films. For McNair (2006: 49) this demonstrates the success of market capitalism against socialist mutations, and the pertinence of a 'chaos' paradigm in place of a 'control' one (although control remains an 'aspiration' of elites). For McChesney (2003: 34), by contrast:

> [t]he global commercial media system is radical in that it respects no tradition, or custom, on balance, if it stands in the way of profits. But ultimately it is politically conservative, because the media giants are significant beneficiaries of the current social structure around the world, and any upheaval in property or social relations – particularly to the extent that it reduces the power of business – is not in their interest.

The best response, arguably, is not to deny the openness, and contradictions, within communication systems but rather to assess their tendencies and investigate their boundaries, both material and symbolic, for content creation and exchange. Diversity concerns are increasingly met by arguments that media diversity has increased; digital expansion overcomes scarcity, while new media represent a shift from corporate control to user empowerment. The next chapter considers these claims and their implications. Conclusions about the problems of ownership will be deferred until we have further considered arguments that the Internetisation of media and communications has fundamentally recast the problems of scarcity, ownership and concentration.

Note

1 This managerial thesis reinterpreted a more critical account of the separation of ownership and control by Berle and Means (1932); see Mizruchi (2004).

Chapter 5

Political economy of the Internet and digital media

Introduction

Does the expansion of Internet-enabled communications mean that the problems associated with twentieth century mass media will decrease? More narrowly, do the critiques that shaped CPE analysis of mass media still have salience for networked digital communications? The Internet is part of a wider transformation in communications in which microelectronics-based information and communication technologies provide the basis for the distribution and combination of digital data, ranging from traditional 'mass media' to interactive, social networked communication. The growth and diversification of the Internet has been phenomenal: around a quarter of the world's population, some 1.5 billion people, now have access. This has enormous significance for the social, cultural and economic life of contemporary societies. Yet, much writing about the Internet, both popular and academic, adopts a technologically deterministic perspective, assuming that the Internet's potential will be realised in essentially transformative ways, and that such outcomes are imminent in the technology. This was especially true of techno-utopian pronouncements in the early 1990s, but after the hiatus of the dot-com collapse in 2000–2001, technocentrism has re-emerged in influential accounts by marketers, pundits, politicians and academics alike. While these can help to illuminate emergent Internet practices, they tend to lack a necessary appreciation of how these practices are shaped and situated in social, economic and political contexts. That is the argument of CPE scholars who insist on the need to analyse the controls, social relations, politics and economics of the Internet in assessing what kinds of practices are enabled and constrained in any given situation.

The Internet is a 'decentralised, global communications network mediated by the convergence of information, computing and telecommunications' that links computer-based networks to permit the exchange of data; it makes possible the combination and distribution of all forms of mass communication 'in a digital, global, multimodal, and multichannel hypertext' (Castells 2009: 135). From email to weblogs and wikis, the Internet also enables interpersonal, intergroup and individual communications to large audiences, what Castells (2009) calls 'mass self-communication'.[1] The Internet refers to a variety of technologies, data and services that continue to change and diversify rapidly but amongst these the worldwide web remains most prominent. The web enables a wide range of applications from static web pages to blogs, wikis and 'social-software – mediated platforms for large-scale conversations' (Benkler 2006: 216). The Internet thus combines 'vertical' communication, the production and distribution of institutionally organised, one-to-many communications, with 'horizontal' communications, networks of interactive, interpersonal and intergroup communications (Castells 2009: 65).

My focus, below, is on the relationship of the Internet with the forms and organisation of mass media, and so primarily on 'vertically' organised public communications that produce and circulate messages. Later chapters explore in more detail 'horizontal' uses and capabilities in relation to democratic communication, media power and alternative media, as well as commercialism and convergence culture. However, how the vertical and horizontal intersect, merge and combine to transform communications is of concern throughout. This chapter begins by tracing the history and influence of various claims and counterclaims for the Internet and convergent media, commodification and information capitalism. Focusing on the implications for mass media, in particular news media, the chapter engages with contemporary debates on the reshaping of media businesses, markets, media power and participation. Political economy analysis was relatively marginal in early 'new media' studies. To counter the speculation that continues to shape the visions of Internet celebrants and sceptics alike we need CPE analysis of 'the overall social and economic dynamics of the production and the consumption of new media' (Mansell 2004: 96; McChesney 2013)

Reviewing claims and counterclaims

During the 1990s two starkly contrasting sets of claims were advanced. One described the Internet as a technology of freedom, with no centres of authority, providing open access to information, bypassing and subverting existing structures of control, bringing greater freedom to individuals, enabling new social identities and collectivities to form, and providing the basis for the renewal of citizen-based 'digital democracy'. The other vision was of an Internet dominated by business interests, in which a handful of giant multimedia corporations extended their reach over a market-driven, privatised, e-commerce and advertiser-financed system. Judged from the present, nearly two decades on, neither account will do. Both extrapolate from utopian or dystopian visions – and are often also markedly narrow – ignoring the heterogeneity and range of activities in cyberspace and across geographical space. It is easy to point out deficiencies in mid 1990s accounts and indeed any singular or unidirectional account of the Internet. While emancipatory visions continue to energise online activities these are by no means dominant, and for most Internet users are not expected to be. It is clear, too, that for all its intense commercialisation the Internet is not entirely won for business – let alone the global media giants – and involves uncertainty, risk, challenges and threats as well as opportunities. The 1990s critique of corporate dominance seems to many to have underestimated at least two major developments: the expansion of social media and what Castells calls 'mass self-communication', and the extent of the crisis for traditional media businesses.

To a large extent the rival claims can be viewed historically, as some of the utopianism that greeted the emergence of the Internet has been answered and modified by criticism of the way the net developed. After the dot-com crash of 2001–2, the belief that Internet technology had transformed the very nature of capitalism was replaced, for a time, by more sober assessment (Mosco 2005). The mainstreaming of the Internet as a tool for business shifted debate to 'real' economy issues – how businesses, like news content creators, audiovisual producers or the music industry, can survive and make money. During the same period, a welcome, parallel shift in academic work brought more empirical investigation of the Internet (Livingstone 2010). Yet, however modified and attenuated, the key debates of the 1990s still matter. They continue to influence contemporary discussions and policy, and help us assess claims against actual developments. It is conventional to treat some of the exuberant 1990s claims as historical curiosities, yet it is also conventional to argue that such claims are being realised in more sober, modified form (Küng et al. 2008).

A central mid 1990s claim was that the Internet would break the control and dominance of media conglomerates. In doing so it would help remedy a range of information problems, reinvigorate and extend the public sphere and replace information control and scarcity with communication abundance. Importantly this vision engaged with and 'resolved' problems of existing media power, while tending to promote deregulation of existing controls on public media. The Internet would enable a massive expansion of content to be produced and circulated by dramatically reducing the costs and barriers to publication. As distribution costs fell to zero and as distribution overcame barriers imposed by space (such as physical distribution) and time, the Internet would allow multimodal communication exchanges that overcame the limitations of the 'mass media' model of unidirectional, one-to-many communication. Old media like television would be replaced (Gilder 1994). For writers such as Nicholas Negroponte (1995), Mark Poster (1997) and others the claim is also based on the *disintermediated* nature of the Internet – as providing unfettered access for open and rapid exchange of opinion between individuals, without mediators such as the editors and journalists that select and shape content for publication. While the push and publishing model of the 1990s web did not fully realise such claims, Web 2.0 theorists in the 2000s argued that the spread of horizontal communications and the polycentric nature of the Internet was shrinking the space occupied by gatekeepers and intermediaries.

Allied to belief in the accessibility of the Internet was the notion of abundance – any idea (and any good) could find its market in the emerging digital economy. One consequence of this emancipatory account is that the Internet (together with other digital media) undermines a traditional, scarcity rationale for communications regulation. Gilder (1994) argued that the Internet would eliminate long-standing concerns about media concentration and obviate the need for policy-making. According to Negroponte (1995: 57) 'Guaranteed plurality might require less legislation than one would expect because the monolithic empires of mass media are dissolving into an array of cottage industries'. Regulation of media services and media ownership would become increasingly unnecessary in an expanding digital market. Alongside market-liberal visions of abundance, other accounts hoped for an enrichment of citizenship and civil engagement that drew upon disillusionment and disquiet about existing media systems' provision, as well as intractable problems of advanced societies, from the social atomisation of 'bowling alone' (Putnam 2001), to plunging levels of political engagement and representation. For Rheingold (1993) electronic communities pose a fundamental challenge to the existing political hierarchy's monopoly over communications and provide the basis on which to revitalise citizen-based democracy.

Claims made for changes in media and communications relate to broader claims that the Internet provides a dynamic open environment which favours innovative network operations that bring together supply and demand, so that forms of (relatively) more perfect competition can be realised. The advantages that favoured monopolists in the old economy now favour nimble, networked enterprises, 'start-ups' and SME market entrants. The evidence of new concentrations of market power in e-commerce enterprises might be expected to engender caution but these firms are often celebrated as innovators writ-large. Google has been described as 'the first post-media company' (Jarvis 2009: 4), whose key to success is openness, focusing on linking rather than owning (Tapscott and Williams 2006: 134). This portrayal is testament to digital myths and successful PR more than the reality of a company that owns a growing mass of server farms for Big Data. According to Leadbeater (2009: xix) the mass media 'boulders' of the pre-digital age 'have been drowned by a rising tide of pebbles' in a new 'organisational landscape' in which new media companies such as Wikipedia, Flickr and YouTube organise and aggregate individual pebbles. The Internet, through its expanding array of nodes, favours horizontal peer-to-peer exchanges over mass media's top-down modes of address and demonstrates an 'underlying culture of sharing, decentralization and democracy' (Leadbeater 2009: 7).

Critical arguments and analysis

The broader claims of techno-utopianism were challenged on grounds of mis-diagnosis through technological determinism, evasion of problems of accessibility (digital divides) and failure to appreciate how dominant political and economic forces would act to shape what appeared to be an inherently ungovernable environment. As media historians are obliged to reiterate, across the history of communications technical innovations have been accompanied by claims that they will bring about (or accelerate) radical social change. In an interesting engagement with digital myths, Mosco argues that in addition to recognising and unmasking the lies contained within them, it is productive to appreciate myths as expressions of hopes and desires. 'What made the dotcom boom a myth was not that it was false but that it was alive, sustained by the collective belief that cyberspace was opening a new world by transcending what we once knew about time, space, and economics' (Mosco 2005: 4). Changes of media and technologies have historically been connected to the emergence of certain one-sided techno-optimistic and techno-pessimistic myths. Many academics, then, would agree with Sonia Livingstone (2010) that such accounts have been limited and limiting. Such dissatisfaction informed shifts towards more empirically based research and analysis, in place of rampant punditry (Curran et al. 2012; Fuchs 2008, 2011; McChesney 2013).

Much early writing on the Internet has been replete with what John Dovey (1996: xiii) calls the 'utopian rhetoric of technological determinism', the notion that radical change arises from technology, that the direction of change is predetermined by an inner technical dynamic, and that the technology has necessary and determinate 'impacts' on social life. Technological determinism suffused the punditry and policy discourses of Western politicians, to the chagrin of social scientists who had successfully established the social shaping of technology as a governing academic account. In fact, Internet scholarship has advanced more sophisticated, dialectical and blended approaches. The work of CPE scholars such as Mansell (2004) shifts from either technological or social determinism in favour of examining how the Internet enables certain social possibilities and impedes others (Livingstone 2010: 125–26).

The major flaw in claims for the transformative potential of the Internet is that they were 'inferences derived from the Internet's technology' (Curran 2012: 3). Such techno-Internet-centrism also tended to obscure a key insight from political economy, that the wider external context affects the Internet's impact: that capitalism influenced the Internet more than vice versa (Curran et al. 2012; McChesney 2013).

CPE scholars have been especially engaged with issues of access, inequality and digital divides (van Dijk 2005), examining uneven patterns of access and use of communication technologies over the geopolitical levels of international, national, regional, and domestic households. Tracing the relationship between information inequality and other socio-economic and cultural inequalities, researchers have examined how gender, age, class, education and socio-economic resources stratify online access and use, and the implications this has for the distribution of other resources.

A criticism of early 1990s claims of digital abundance was that they functioned as compensatory fantasies, projecting onto technology the capacity to overcome deep-rooted social and economic problems, extrapolating from the experience of an affluent, North American subjectivity. Yet the exponential growth of the Internet has continued to generate complex patterns of diffusion and exclusion. By 2013, only around one-third of the world's population had Internet access, yet the Internet had grown from its 'English speaking' roots in North America's scientific community to become a global network, growing from an estimated

40 million users in 1995 to 1.4 billion in 2008 and over 2.7 billion in 2013 (ITU 2013). In 2000 one-third (154 million) of the estimated total 406 million users were American (Norris 2001: 47). Now Asia currently outstrips all other regions, with 44.8 per cent of total users in June 2012, yet only 27.5 per cent of the population had access, compared to penetration rates of 78.6 per cent in North America and 63.2 per cent in Europe (Internet World Stats 2013). According to the ITU (2013) 31 per cent of the developing world is online, compared to 77 per cent in the developed world.

For advocates of participative culture, barriers to access tend to be acknowledged but discounted. Benkler (2006) regards the digital divide as a transitional problem. By contrast, others highlight both absolute and relative digital divides. In absolute terms, although diffusion has continued to expand there are signs of take-up plateauing. In the UK, household Internet take-up (78 per cent) exceeded PC ownership (77 per cent) for the first time in 2010 as a small proportion of households went online using mobile phones only (Ofcom 2011). Those without access included some elderly households and others who expressed lack of interest, but Ofcom acknowledged that cost was a key barrier for many. Norris (2001) argues that Internet penetration serves to exacerbate rather than reduce inequalities. The costs and investment (including time) in leading edge technologies sustain socio-economic disparities. A richer account of 'access' not only questions the destinations invoked but also seeks to differentiate and examine access to technologies, time, influence and decision-making, which are influenced by gender relations, education, socio-economic and cultural relations. Hindman's (2009) study of US blogging and Internet search shows that the Internet does not just remove old forms of exclusivity, it generates new forms, and he stresses that we should assess not just the capacity to speak but the opportunity to be heard.

Mansell (2004: 97) finds 'a very substantial tendency in studies of new media to emphasize the abundance and variety of new media products and services, and to concentrate on promoting access with little regard for the associated structures and processes of power that are embedded within them'. Instead, she finds 'continuing evidence of scarcity in relation to new media production and consumption [that is ...] contributing to the maintenance of deeply-rooted inequalities in today's so-called "information" or "knowledge" societies'. She advocates a rights-based approach that focuses on the gaps between what people should be able to achieve in exercising their freedom to construct meaningful lives and what they can achieve in practice. This draws on the development economist Amartya Sen's (2001) work on capabilities to ask how do such resources as those of the Internet and ICTs variously enable or constrain how people can realise their capabilities.

Digital inequality forms part of broader critical agendas embracing the social relations of capitalism and the politics of transformation. Based on the insight that resources are highly unequally divided in contemporary society, Fuchs (2008, 2009) calls for a critical theory of Internet and society addressing issues of ownership, private property, resource distribution, social struggles, power, resource control, exploitation and domination. This links to another broad theme: the relationship between communications and democracy. The potential of information and communication technologies (ICTs) to facilitate 'strong democracy', participative democracy where people are fully involved in decision-making on all issues which affect them or are important to them, must be seriously questioned wherever people are denied access on the basis of economic status, gender, geographic location, or language. CPE scholars have been particularly engaged in shifting from a narrow focus on technological access to consider wider barriers to power and decision-making.

Against tendencies to posit the Internet as a year zero, a rupture that is radically discontinuous with what has gone before, CPE scholars emphasise the need to consider carefully the co-presence of old and new, continuities with discontinuities.

Murdock (2004: 20) argues that to fully understand the Internet and digitalisation we must ground analysis in 'the transformations currently taking place in the organization of capitalism and the contradictions it is generating'. Schiller (2007) describes a shift towards 'informationalized capitalism', whereby 'political and economic elites assigned mounting strategic importance to information beginning around 1970' (2007: xiv). The impetus for information and communication growth came from the 'systemic crisis' in Western capitalism in the 1970s, with information commodities becoming the prime site for capitalist expansion, a key growth area to redress the stagnation in profits elsewhere, notably in parts of Western manufacturing.

Internet history

Making sense of claims and understanding the relationship between the Internet and mass media is best done through an historical perspective. Many excellent accounts are available (see Curran et al. 2012: 34–65; McChesney 2013: 96–129) and so my aim here is to highlight only certain aspects relevant to the discussion of media below. First, from its origins in the US government-funded work of the US military in developing a university-based research network, ARPANET, in 1969, Internet history has been shaped by a diverse mix of actors who interacted and often struggled to extend their modes of operation and influence (Curran and Seaton 2010). In its early formation these included the US government and military; businesses (initially mainly in science, computing and telecommunications); academics and scientists; a counter-cultural influence of (mainly US) students and graduates (what Barbrook and Cameron (1995) call the 'Californian ideology'); and hackers, key advocates of the open architecture of the Internet (MacKinnon 2012). The commercialisation of the Internet in the early 1990s was resisted by some actors, notably from within the counter-cultural and libertarian anarchist-influenced communities that had rapidly populated 'cyberspace', but also within the scientific and academic non-profit culture of the National Science Foundation Network (NSFNet), which prohibited commercial uses until the ban was lifted in 1991 and the NSF was privatised in 1995. The first commercial email, sent across the Usenet bulletin board system generated furious reaction. Yet, resistance was limited and short-lived (D. Schiller 2000). Commercialisation was regarded by most commentators as the inevitable consequence of the Internet evolving into a mass medium. For Lister et al. (2009: 170): 'To put it simply: where a free and open system of communicative networks (the Internet) has developed within an economic system based on property and profits (capitalism) one has to come to an accommodation with the other'.

Others, however, stress the influence of policy decisions, highlighting how governments – particularly the US government – played an active part in establishing commercial dominance. Schiller (2007) offers one of the most comprehensive political-economic accounts, describing how corporations leading the expansion of information systems or services pressed new demands on governments, who responded by projecting their policy preferences domestically and internationally.

Government intervention, in particular by the United States, was pivotal and sustained – not only in procuring continued R&D funding, but also in advancing telecoms industry liberalisation; the privatisation of what had been public information, strengthening legal rights to private property in information and shifting global trade and investment rules to favour services. Each of these policy shifts contributed to the process of accelerated commodification. The Internet became a 'state sponsored commercial system' (Curran and Seaton 2010: 258).

The leading edge of policy has been neoliberal and deregulatory. However, policy is also organised under constraints, notably the expectations and obligations of serving the public interest, and tensions between the interests of different commercial actors, governmental and civil society interests. Policy is a site for conflicts over values and goals. However, one key factor in considering the Internet and mass media was that government policy in the United States required the Global Information Infrastructure to be constructed by private companies, telecommunications and computing companies, who were becoming increasingly integrated through joint ownership or alliances with media content businesses.

The Internetisation of mass media

The drive to tie the Internet to the existing media system is now so far advanced it is barely contested, even though it flatly confounds many of the predictions raised earlier – that old media would collapse and that the Internet would provide the means by which peripheral voices would move to the centre of media systems. But while it is depressingly easy to prove Negroponte wrong, and point to the durability of global media giants like Time Warner, Disney and Viacom, it is clearly wrong to maintain that media power relations remain unaffected. The Internet has generated challenges to market power, disrupting business models and patterns of consumption and use, and facilitated profound challenges to twentieth century forms of media power. To avoid merely reproducing an oscillation between techno-optimism versus pessimism we need to situate analysis and distinguish processes carefully including three key aspects:

1 Institutional change and adaption
   • How have old 'legacy' media companies expanded into online media?
   • How have institutions adapted or failed to adapt to new conditions?
2 Market conditions
   • How do the technical, operational and business models facilitated by the Internet affect media content industries?
3 Emergent market and non-market actors
   • How does the way the net has developed influence the space and opportunities for new media content services – including alternative media?

While businesses have reorganised in the face of real and predicted changes in consumers' use of digital media, consumption of traditional media has proved far more buoyant than many 1990s accounts predicted. For instance, while a majority of UK homes are now connected to the Internet (increasing from 25 per cent in 2000 to 76 per cent in 2011) and the use of smartphones and mobile devices has increased rapidly, broadcast TV remains the most popular medium, with viewing increasing by around eighteen minutes over the last decade to just over four hours a day (Ofcom 2011). A study of news consumption amongst the UK adult population found the main source for news to be Internet 6 per cent, TV 65 per cent and newspapers 15 per cent (Ofcom 2007). The Internet is becoming the main source of news for the young, but television remains the most used source (78 per cent of adults), with most news consumers accessing only three providers (78 per cent) (Ofcom 2013). By the end of 2006 three out of four US respondents listed television as the main source of news – a rate basically unchanged from 1991 levels. Digital media continued to see the greatest audience growth, with other platforms falling, yet television remains the main news source for most Americans (Pew Research Centre 2012, 2013).

Old media took to the web. In 1993 only 20 newspapers had electronic versions but by 1995 there were 496 newspapers online worldwide. By 1998, more than 2,700 newspapers internationally had online businesses, of which 60 per cent were US based. Today, almost all commercial newspapers have a web presence. Online audiences for national newspapers are generally considerably larger than offline. In the UK the Guardian newspaper is the most read news site with 11.3 million, followed by the MailOnline with 10.6 million (Guardian 2013). Küng et al. (2008: 126) identify a first phase of media business development from the mid 1990s to 2001 and a second phase following the dotcom crash of 2000–2001; the first phase was characterised by 'breathless enthusiasm and predictions of profound transformation', with the second 'quietly bringing the extreme changes promised by the first'. In phase one there were some spectacular failures for old media ventures online. New Century Network, a US-based website consisting of 140 newspapers run by nine newspaper chains closed in 1998. Time Warner's Pathfinder Website launched in 1994 incurred huge losses that contributed to AOL's acquisition of Time Warner in 2000. Bertelsmann's online businesses, including music retailers BOL.com in Europe and CDNow.com in the US, sustained losses of $248 million over four quarters in 2001–2, and the company sold its ailing 50 per cent stake in AOL Europe (Küng et al. 2008: 128–29). Disney launched successful consumer websites such as ESPN.com and Disney.com but its move into portals, purchasing a majority stake in Infoseek. com and then consolidating this into a new portal Go.com, ended with closure and losses of $862 million in 2001. The failure of the AOL Time Warner merger strategy led to the then largest recorded corporate loss, $98.7 billion in 2002.

News Corporation's notorious 'iblunders' are summarised by Shields (2010). Delphi Internet Services, an early ISP launched in 1993, lost subscribers and was sold in 1996. News Corporation's acquisition of MySpace in 2005 for $580 million was part of a wider effort to remedy weaknesses in the online portfolio, but failed to retain users when Facebook and other services flourished. MySpace reached 100 million users in 2006, two years before Facebook launched, but then declined, notably after the site shifted focus from social networking to entertainment in 2010. MySpace's traffic of 50.1 million visitors in December 2010 was down 27 per cent on the year before. The workforce of 1,000 was cut in half at the start of 2011 and was down to 200 when the company was sold in June 2011 to Specific Media and Justin Timberlake for approximately $35 million.

Media firms were motivated by a mixture of opportunity, fear and not a little confusion when trying to predict trends and lead technologies in rapidly changing markets. Firms feared being left behind by new systems of distribution and competition from new suppliers outside their established markets. Facing the prospect of fewer users accessing traditional media content by traditional means, firms adopted various strategies, including joint ventures and acquisitions, in efforts to occupy new gateways (such as portals) and content sites. For instance, in 1996 Microsoft and NBC launched MSNBC, an online and cable news service. The drives to corporate consolidation have been described already; another pressure was market investors' enthusiasm for the Internet sector. Firms that failed to develop expected Internet strategies were punished by financial markets with depressed share prices. Pressure to expand was fuelled by the belief that the Internet was characterised by significant order of entry advantages ('first mover' advantages). Yet firms were understandably reluctant to cannibalise their cash-flow-generating businesses, on top of debt-laden investments, by offering their media products free via the Internet, in the absence of effective strategies to monetise (Küng et al. 2008: 126–27).

The diffusion of higher capacity connectivity, broadband, fibre optic and mobile, is also critical in explaining how traditional media industries have been differentially affected. The low-bandwidth capacity of most dial-up modems in the 1990s meant that the music industry and text and graphical publishing were affected earlier than audiovisual content. The process of 'Internetization'

(Fortunati 2005) of mass media has been uneven and complex. Nevertheless, there is overwhelming evidence that far from fragmenting into cottage industries the major media conglomerates rapidly dominated the most used parts of the Internet for media content services. Although there are variations across each industry/medium, the common pattern remains one in which traditional media content companies retain significant market share and presence.

Within a few years of the Internet's massification, in 1998, more than three-quarters of the thirty-one most visited news and entertainment websites in the US were affiliated with large media firms. Most of the rest were connected to outfits like AOL and Microsoft. Traditional news suppliers still heavily dominate news consumption online. A global listing of the ten most visited news websites included four search engines (Yahoo and Google sites) the BBC, CNN, MSNBC, The Guardian and The New York Times (Alexa 2013). The top ten newspaper websites in 2010–11 were all leading news organisations with the exception of the Huffington Post, a formerly independent news organisation acquired in 2011 by AOL, which had spun off from Time Warner in 2009. Leading the field was The New York Times brand followed by the MailOnline, the Huffington Post, Tribune Newspapers, The Guardian, USA Today, The Wall Street Journal, Xinhua News Agency, The Washington Post, Advance Internet, the Internet division for Advance Publications' affiliated newspapers and magazines (Guardian 2011). In 2010, 80 per cent of Internet traffic to news and information sites was concentrated on the top 7 per cent of sites, the majority of which (67 per cent) were controlled by news organisations that predated the Internet era (Pew 2011). Of the remaining share, 13 per cent were content aggregators and only 14 per cent were new online operations generating original reportage. According to Pew (2010a) 'the websites of legacy news organizations – especially cable stations and newspapers – dominate the online space in traffic in loyalty'. Ofcom (2010) found that news consumption occupied a mere 2 per cent of UK users' total time online, but that the overwhelming share was from news sites run by traditional news providers.

Explanations: stagism and change

Some explanations adopt a stagist model of transition. In strong versions 'old media' are regarded as walking zombies, staggering on but already dead. The case for regarding them as such is stronger for print news media (considered below) than audiovisual content industries. However, 'transition' arguments, favoured in some business and policy forums, tend to posit unidirectional change with relatively distinct and uncontested outcomes. By contrast, academic accounts have described a more varied and uncertain process of adaption. For instance, Boczkowski (2004: 4) in *Digitizing the News* writes 'what we often find is a merging of existing socio-material infrastructures with novel technical capabilities'. Online newspapers merge print's existing institutionalised patterns with the web's potentials and technical novelty – an ongoing process and one shaped by different local conditions – resulting in different patterns of change that are not merely imminent in the technology. Digitalisation has connected media such as print to other media platforms making them less distinctive and less independent. In business practices too, Küng et al. (2008: 146) discern the abandonment of 'violent new strategic directions ... in favour of a gentler path of adaption, absorption and combination of old and new media activities'.

Innovation and entrants

According to Schumpeter, capitalism develops through a process of 'creative destruction' and this trope has been incessantly invoked to describe the disruptive nature of the Internet and allied digital technologies. For Schumpeter (1942: 83) technological innovation, not capitalism, is the key driver of business innovation, blowing 'a perennial gale of creative destruction' that 'incessantly revolutionizes the economic structure from within, incessantly destroying the old one, incessantly creating a new one'. This echoes, but narrows, the 'affirmative' part of Marx and Engels's critical analysis of capitalism's revolutionary dynamism whereby the '[c]onstant revolutionising of production, uninterrupted disturbance of all social conditions, everlasting uncertainty and agitation distinguish the bourgeois epoch from all earlier ones' (Marx and Engels 2013 [1848]).

Dynamic, expanding markets provide opportunities for new entrants to challenge incumbents. Superficially at least, this seems to offer the most accurate and per-suasive general account of the Internet today. With an advanced search engine, Google has overtaken other firms in that emergent market to become one of the most powerful information corporations, with Google's search advertising now accounting for half of US Internet advertising revenues. Facebook has grown from a bedroom start-up to become the most used social media service in the West. Digital service companies from ISPs and search engines to social media and data management, in China, Japan, India and elsewhere, have seen phenomenal growth. Yet, for all their persuasive authority and evidence, dynamic market openings do not provide a satisfactory account of developments. Competition between incumbents and newcomers is a staple of management literature, yet it is highly misleading when applied across all media sectors. It originates in man-agement theories that posit that incumbents will tend to be slow to innovate and instead seek to shore up existing markets, processes and advantages, including regulatory support. Newcomers are innovators who shake up markets and force changes amongst all market suppliers for the ultimate benefit of consumers. Incumbents who fail to adapt successfully are destined to exit the market. This account approximates to perceptions about the way media markets are being transformed but is a morality tale rather than a suitably accurate description. The presumptions of mass media decline in the first phase of Internet studies (1995–2000) have been challenged by actual developments. First mover advan-tages tended to be exaggerated by failing to account for the advantages existing firms enjoyed, for instance in migrating existing consumers to new services. This also illustrates the broader problem with incumbency/newcomer phraseology: it applies to some market conditions but downplays the way dominant market players adapt to sustain market share.

At the heart of claims for an emerging 'new economy' was a 'mystical core' positing that the Internet would diminish the advantages of incumbent, large firms and equalise the terms of competition between corporate giants and entrepreneurial start-ups (Curran et al. 2012). The Internet would initiate a powerful wave of dynamism driven by creativity and innovation. Ideas would have advantages over the lumbering edifices of bricks and mortar that dominant Fordist firms represented. The Internet lowers costs, creating global market opportunities for low-volume producers and serving niche demands that were neglected under the shelf-space and supply pressures of a shop-based retail model (Anderson 2004, 2009). Yet, the central claim of the new economy thesis failed to take sufficient account of the sustained advantages of corporate size and reach.

Media economics and business analysis

Economics, business and marketing analysis can help us understand both the challenges of digitalisation for mass media businesses and the advantages that explain continuing patterns of dominance in the provision of public media content.

The Internet and allied technologies profoundly challenged aspects of analogue processes of production and distribution of content, with far-reaching impact on business models of the established media firms. Those challenges are well documented (Sparks 2004; Freedman 2006; Curran et al. 2012; Hesmondhalgh 2013) and might be regarded as legacy concerns given that 'mass media' today are thoroughly digitalised. Yet the nature of those challenges remains critical to understanding the past, present and possible futures of digital media. Internet delivery eroded earlier patterns of media consumption. The Internet erodes advantages based on physical space and time, features that have sustained local monopolies in media markets such as newspapers, radio broadcasting and cinema exhibition. The Internet also erodes advantages of production and distribution based on time. The advantages of market dominance in the production of a morning newspaper or prime time news are eroded because Internet content can be published at any time and remain available. Internet services can compete as direct substitutes for 'mass media' content or services, but an even more profound challenge is competition for the resource of consumer/user time. While consumption patterns vary, time spent on search, messaging and other activities challenged media dependent on direct sales and also those dependent on advertising revenue where consumers fall within the relevant market. Consumer/user time is also intimately connected with the resource of advertising finance in so far as advertisers migrate from mass media to alternative spaces.

The Internet and advertising

The founders of Google, Larry Page and Sergey Brin, believed that good search engines would allow consumers to find what they wanted without the need for advertising. Rejecting advertising finance as late as 1998, they argued that it would make search engines 'inherently biased towards the advertisers and away from the needs of consumers' (cited in Pariser 2011: 31). The path to Internet advertising was neither smooth, assured nor uncontested, but with the commercialisation of the web in the 1990s, broadband-enabled rich media advertising, and the growth of website, search and social media advertising, Internet advertising grew faster than all other sectors.

Mass media products such as a general newspaper combine a diverse range of editorial content and information with display and classified advertising. One major break with the past is that content is now distributed in an unbundled way. Digitalisation has facilitated the disaggregation of content, so that specialist, targeted, customised content can be pushed at or pulled together by users. This challenges the manner in which content services are provided and creates advantages for those supplying content in valued packages and forms. The supply of disaggregated content to high-value users, such as business executives, can also divert advertising revenue away from more traditional aggregated sources. In the US classified advertising has migrated from newspapers to sites like Craigslist, with pages for housing and cars, formerly staples of local newspaper advertising revenue. In the US Internet advertising overtook newspapers in 2010 (Curran et al. 2012: 20), while the newspaper industry's share of Internet advertising fell to 10 per cent in 2011 (McChesney 2013: 185); in the UK the Internet's share of classified ad expenditure rose from 2 per cent to 44.5 per cent between 2000 and 2008 (Office of Fair Trading 2009). Such disaggregation is key to the crisis in some traditional media such as newspapers and FTA commercial television, whose business model relies on creating audiences to sell to advertising. In addition the production and distribution of physical goods to disseminate content is an expensive and increasingly uncompetitive way to create audiences (Cooper 2011: 335). These disruptions have certainly created conditions for market entrants. However, political-economic analysis has also helped to explain why barriers to market entry have been higher than advocates of digital abundance acknowledged.

The Internet lowers some costs of production and distribution. Accordingly it lowers the barriers to market entry. However, in media sectors such as news production and audiovisual production, content production costs remain high. In newspaper production paper, print and distribution takes an average one-third of costs and these are reduced enormously by the ability to aggregate audiences online. Yet the other two-thirds of costs remain, in particular the labour costs to produce high-quality news coverage. This is borne out by the cost breakdown of one major US newspaper chain, Knight Ridder, which follows a very similar pattern (Hindman 2009). The main characteristics of mass media industries – high initial costs of production, low marginal reproduction and distribution costs – are reproduced online. While reproduction and distribution costs plunge compared to costs such as paper, printing and physical distribution of newspapers, content creation costs remain a key barrier in certain markets. The Internet lowers reproduction costs but the costs to produce a first copy of various kinds of media content such as general news or filmed entertainment remains a high barrier. For instance, the average cost to make a US TV show is between $1.5 and $2 million, with Netflix in 2013 spending a minimum of $4.5 million per episode for *House of Cards* (Deadline Hollywood 2013). That barrier is eroded by producing and packaging specialist or niche content, but remains a high barrier for 'premium' entertainment content and for aggregated news content services. This helps explain the direct competition of online publishing but also the barrier in meeting the costs of 'quality' content.

The lowering of market entry barriers allows new players to challenge incumbents, yet where content creation costs remain high, significant barriers remain. In addition, the Internet provides benefits of scale and scope that benefit incumbent providers. The principal benefit arises from more flexible and cost-effective delivery of existing content. Where content production remains capital intensive, there are advantages of economy of scale where upfront investments can be averaged over the entire user base. Realising such economies of scale increases the advantages of larger players over market entrants. Technological advance has overcome monopolies arising from scarcity, but 'the natural monopoly of economies of scale' (Graham et al. 1999: 24) remains. A belief that new network enterprises would compete against old Fordist firms failed to take account of the cost-advantages of large-scale production.

As well as content production costs remaining high, another key problem has been the difficulties in recovering costs through selling content to audiences. Multimedia firms can benefit from economies of scope as well as scale, where content costs are recouped through different sales vehicles. By contrast, those reliant on the Internet alone have tended to struggle to recover high production costs. Rather than Internet-only ventures, new entrants in content services tend to be firms who could cross-subsidise and achieve cross-firm benefits. In media many 'insurgents' have come from established positions in other markets (and allied markets), for instance Handbag.com launched by a major retailer, Boots, and the Telegraph Group publishers. Market openings have often been short-lived and the costs of sustaining attractive, high profile content for repeat visits remains prohibitive; the provision of expensive 'professional' media content is still largely governed by the economics of scale and scope which favour dominant firms (Freedman 2006).

These economic dynamics help to explain the absence of new online content providers in highly capitalised markets such as national news and feature films. According to van der Wurff (2008), the Internet has increased the availability of existing professional media content rather than adding new content; the Internet increases publication (not production) of content (Sparks 2004). Yet such assessments of the relative paucity of new 'mass media' providers must be balanced by acknowledging the diversification of content creation today, the enormous expansion of publication and online communication by organisations, and professional–amateur content creation and communication (Fuchs 2008). As van der Wurff (2008) and Benkler (2006) examine, there has been an enormous expansion in content distributed free by non-media organisations and individuals, with motives ranging from informing existing or potential customers to advocating causes – but not with the aim of making money by selling content or advertisements. Yet the resources for publication are greater in the commercial sector, and government, than in civil society. The Internet has significantly advanced the erosion of boundaries between editorial, marketing communications and transaction activities. Conventions to separate editorial and advertising, telling and selling, speech and commerce have been established more weakly and unevenly online (Sparks 2004). This has been amongst the drivers for commercial organisations to invest in online publishing and communications, in order to engage directly with consumers without media intermediaries, or wholesalers and retailers.

Incumbent advantages and strategies

Media conglomerates pursue strategies to seek to maintain dominant market positions, through investment, branding, cross-promotion and advertiser relationships (McChesney 2004b, 2008), control over gateways to services, efforts to control intellectual property, and expanding sources of control through surveillance and data mining to track and target users (Turow 2006, 2011). Some of these strategies proved unsuccessful but others remain relevant advantages, in particular those of branding and marketing (Sinclair 2011). Established media brands have proved to be key assets in increasingly competitive and cluttered markets. Brands could be extended into new online properties and services. Conglomerates can use websites to cross-promote and sell their other products and services. Large media companies could exploit their relationships with advertisers, for instance offering (or requiring) cross-platform advertising packages. Large corporations have greater access to capital than smaller companies and can invest in online businesses as a form of research and development, and use their finance capacity to seek to outspend rivals and outlast competition. The costs of maintaining Murdoch's short-lived iPad-only publication *The Daily* were estimated at $2 million per year for running costs and promotion alone, requiring 2 per cent of total iPad users in the US to subscribe 99 cents per week in order to break even.

There is support for the 'new economy' model advanced in Chris Anderson's *Long Tail* (2004, 2009). Anderson argues that online inventory overcomes the physical and cost constraints of goods displayed on store shelves. Distribution costs for digital goods like music, video and information approach zero, allowing a long tail of marketable products. Instead of focusing on the 'head', the few, lucrative blockbuster hits produced by global media corporations, Anderson calls attention to the long tail, the expansion of low-volume transactions that are the source of greater, and more predictable, profitability. The Internet allows producers to exploit 'the millions of niche markets at the shallow end of the bitstream', making low-volume sales to specialist markets economically viable (Anderson 2004). Online shops can overcome the scarcity of shop inventories to satisfy consumer taste, but niche markets also involve a power shift from elite control of supply to a demand-driven environment of expressive consumption, whose market signals are celebrated as a form of 'democratisation'.

However, the long tail is better at explaining retailing than content creation and is irrelevant in markets where barriers to entry remain high (Hindman 2009). Media companies are also well placed to exploit their own 'long tail', their back catalogue inventory that could be marketed and digitally distributed at little cost (McChesney 2000). Digitalisation expands opportunities to repurpose entertainment and information, complementing strategies of multimedia consolidation and using a web platform 'perfectly matched' for the media conglomerates which have been assembled (D. Schiller 2000).

Large companies have greater economies of scale, reducing costs and enabling more competitive pricing. They can also embark on strategies to undermine competition by temporarily lowering prices and by exploiting marketing and other advantages to disable under-resourced competition. Large firms have greater economies of scope; they can optimise shared resources to reduce costs and can exploit advantages of multimedia holdings, notably cross-promotion (Hardy 2010a). Summing up, Küng et al. (2008: 133) identify the benefits stemming from:

> the additional use of existing content that creates scale economies and better average costs for their use, from transaction cost reductions arising from the simplification and reduction of the costs of the acquisition of content and other resources, and from economies of scope produced by leveraging the market recognition of established firms so that lower marketing expenses are required for new activities, by exploiting existing audience and advertiser relationships and by creating opportunities for additional revenue without the concurrent need for full resources required by independent creation and distribution.

The challenges of operating cross-media activities increase advantages for well-established content providers. Taken together these advantages help to explain the patterns of dominance of major media firms in general news publishing and high cost audiovisual content. That presence challenges myths not only of a new economics but also (pre-digital) myths of a dynamic, self-correcting capitalism, both of which ignore or underestimate market and political strategies to maintain dominance.

Challenges for mass media businesses

Based on the analysis above critical scholars predict the continuing dominance of major media firms. For Sparks (2004: 325)

The struggle to find a workable business model that will permit profitable online operation is likely to result in the continued, or even increased, domination of the supply of media artifacts by the same large corporations that dominate offline media.

However, this account needs revision and updating to address how challenges and risks for various media content businesses have increased. The Internet and digitalisation 'offers both significant advantages as well as challenges to traditional media interests' (Freedman 2006: 278).

Volatility and risk in markets

Formerly 'mature' media markets characterised by slow growth and competition between a known group of players have become 'emergent' strategic environments that are considerably more volatile and uncertain (Küng et al. 2008: 127). Market environments across digital media are characterised by high volatility in which industry boundaries are unclear, business models evolve rapidly, consumer preferences are uncertain and competition comes from hitherto unknown players.

Realising economic value

Described as the world's largest copying machine, the Internet reinforces the public good characteristics of information. Commercial strategies rely heavily, if to varying degrees, on monetising intellectual property by creating scarcity. This includes:

> the use of copyright, controlling access, promotion of obsolescence, creation and sale of audiences and by favouring some kinds of new media over others. In the case of the Internet, by bundling services and 'walling off' electronic spaces through the use of payment systems …
>
> (Mansell 2004: 98)

The culture of free and the enormous inventory of content available without direct charge have meant media firms have struggled to finance online activities in several markets. Internet advertising, while growing, tends to be insufficient to sustain media firms' online activities. Above all, advertising revenues have accrued to providers of search, online classified advertising and other services, notably social networking. These beneficiaries lack the capacity, or incentive, to reproduce the forms of content creation that are becoming unsustainable as advertising revenues fall. As a UK government report, *Digital Britain*, puts it:

> The increasingly easy and perfect digital replicability of content makes it harder to monetise creative rights. The growth of Internet aggregators [such

as Google and Yahoo] has been good for advertisers who find new cheap and direct routes to those they need to reach. It is also good for consumers, providing them with free search, email ... access to social networks, to create and enjoy user-generated content and multiple other applications. But what aggregators do not do in any quantity is fund the creation of long-form professional content.

(DCMS/BERR 2009: 16–17)

Online advertising is also very unequally distributed. According to the Internet Advertising Bureau in 2005, 72 per cent of web advertising flowed to the ten most popular sites on the web. In fact the top fifty sites grabbed 95 per cent of revenues, although the remaining 5 per cent share over which suppliers competed was worth half a billion dollars.

Consumption and use

Media content companies compete with other Internet services and activities. There is greater capacity to access media via personal mobile communications and there is increasingly complex multiscreen usage amongst online users. Consumption of traditional media, notably linear television, remains high. Yet the growth of online gaming, e-commerce and social media indicates shifts in consumer activity and time spent that pose challenges for 'mass media' content services based on selling products to consumers, or selling consumers to advertisers. The majority of adult time spend online is with social media. In 2012 American Internet users devoted more time to social media sites than any other category, roughly 20 per cent on PCs and 30 per cent via mobiles, with Facebook (152 million visitors via PC) far ahead of Blogger and Twitter as the most visited site (Nielsen 2012).

Alternative content supply

Profit-making media companies are variously challenged by competition from other supplies of 'professional' media, by 'amateur' content creation and by Pro-Am hybridisations mixing both. In Europe, broadcasters have embarked on different strategies to sustain public service media. These have been shaped by institutional traditions, by technological innovation market conditions and by policies. In Britain, a strong public service provider, the BBC, expanded online but has been challenged, with some success, by commercial players who argue the BBC's 'free' provision makes markets unviable for competitors.

There has been a significant expansion of 'horizontal' media content used for interpersonal and intergroup communication. This challenges and displaces 'old' media in various ways, most notably in time spent consuming professional, public 'vertical' media content. According to an Ofcom (2006: 11) survey 11 per cent of UK Internet users in June 2006 had a weblog or a web page, of whom 45 per cent used these as a means of publishing original material, although only 11 per cent published on matters concerning current affairs and politics. Another study found that 38 per cent of US teenagers regularly share content online, 21 per cent remix original content and 14 per cent post blogs (Purcell 2010: 4, cited in Freedman 2012: 76). This proliferation of communications activity has profound implications, but how far it mitigates concerns about the range and quality of supply of public media content is a central issue for debate.

In the 1990s media conglomerates seemed threatened with extinction as paths to profitability appeared blocked. As well as new entrants taking market share, easy digital reproduction undermined the means to create scarcity and monetise content through copyright, and advertising finance would fail, as users would not be compelled to stay in their seats to watch ads. These remain profoundly challenging areas, responsible for much of the uncertainty and volatility for content and communications businesses. Yet, as McChesney (2013: 124) summarises:

> The corporate media sector has spent much of the past fifteen years doing everything in its immense power to limit the openness and egalitarianism of the Internet. Its survival and prosperity hinge upon making the system as closed and proprietary as possible, encouraging corporate and state surreptitious monitoring of Internet users, and opening the floodgates of commercialism.

In entertainment media, the most significant breakthrough has been proprietary models to sell content that also place restrictions on reproduction and circulation by users. Apple's iTunes, Amazon's Kindle and e-book business, Netflix, LoveFilm and other legal streaming services have been commercially successful and have shifted a significant user base from pirate downloads to legal purchases. Their success does not confirm a smooth triumph for media giants but rather more complex inter-corporate competition. Apple and Amazon's dominance of retail, and linked software and hardware, has given them considerable power over pricing. New digital giants like Amazon, Google, Apple, as well as telecoms, ISPs, and manufacturers like Samsung and Sony, are also investing heavily in the struggle to realise future convergence, and competitive advantage, by capturing the potential sales and advertising income streams across the Internet, DTV smart screens and mobile devices. Google protests against the proprietary 'walled gardens' created by Apple and Facebook, while launching its own proprietary services such as Google+. Such volatility is far from the competitive markets envisioned by 'new economy' advocates, but the clashes between leading corporations in different sectors highlights the utility of a network analysis suggested by Arsenault. The new digital giants also demonstrate the significance of network effects, whereby, according to Metcalfe's law, the value of a network increases in proportion to the square of connections.

Network value increases as more users participate. This creates 'winner-takes-all' markets where the gap between the number one and number two players is typically large and growing, generating new concentrations. Apple's iTunes has some 70 per cent of the music download market; Google 70 per cent of search; YouTube 73 per cent of online video; Facebook 52 per cent of social networking traffic. Network effects result in demand-side economies of scale (capture of customers) a opposed to supply-side economies of scale prevalent in traditional media industries. What is most unclear is whether any of the emerging systems, proprietary tending or more open, can provide the revenue base to sustain a large amount of original cultural production. The entertainment and news sectors are different in many ways but some insights can be gained by focusing on a central topic for CPE: the crisis and future for news media.

The crises for news media

The Internet will revitalise journalism and democracy by shifting control from an elite cadre of gatekeepers to the dispersed interaction of bloggers, social networks and consumers, argues Rupert Murdoch (2006) and an array of left- and right-wing commentators. For some the vision has been one of replacing old forms of journalism with new, while others have highlighted collaboration between paid professional journalists and 'citizen journalist' amateurs (Deuze 2009; Beckett 2008; Allan and Thorsen 2009). Another view is that the Internet has precipitated a crisis for the still dominant commercial model without remedying the losses for public-facing journalism (McChesney 2013). To evaluate solutions requires analysis of the crisis for news. Financing news media through sales alone has become increasingly challenging:

> Hard news is perhaps the hardest to make profitable. It is increasingly instant, constant and commoditised … With rare exceptions, making money in news means publishing either the cheap kind that attracts a very large audience, and making money from ads, or the expensive kind that is critical to a small audience, and making money from subscription. Both are cut-throat businesses.
>
> (The Economist 2012)

That newspapers in many media systems are in crisis because of declining revenues is generally agreed. There is much less agreement about the causes. Printed newspapers have seen sales decline in most markets since the 1950s. It is therefore important not to presume or exaggerate the impacts that may be attributed to the Internet. The phenomenon is also far from worldwide; while newspaper sales have declined in Euro-American media systems, the paid newspapers market has grown more strongly in African and Asian markets, notably India, with an estimated 37 per cent of the world's adult population reading a newspaper on a regular basis (Winseck 2012: 4). We need to examine specific characteristics in each media system, even if common trends are evident.

For many critical scholars, the Internet precipitated but did not cause a crisis in US journalism. US failure is attributed to corporate greed involving short-termism, short-sightedness and hypercommercialism, traced to the drive for super profits embarked on from the 1970s. According to Cooper (2011) advertising revenue net of circulation increased dramatically from 1970 to 2000, faster than GDP. The resources were available to sustain quality journalism, he argues, but the commercial model adopted saw profits extracted by stockholders rather than reinvested in journalism. Yet, Hallin (2000) highlights that alongside a 'stock-holder' theory of corporate greed, must be added a 'readership' theory of falling demand. Newspapers have been described as 'imperilled media' as younger audiences desert them for the immediacy and interactivity of the Internet. In the UK the number of British adults reading a national daily paper fell by 19 per cent between 1992 and 2006 (House of Lords 2008: 11). Newspaper circulation fell by 22 per cent between 1995 and 2007, from 13.2 million to 11.1 million. However, critics respond that the corporate model has failed to invest to provide a sufficiently attractive product to retain readers (in offline and online formats). The Internet's crisis then involves the interaction of different factors and influences, chiefly the decline in revenue, the actions and responses of corporate owners, notably disinvestment, and demand-side changes. Yet, most analysts agree that the Internet's 'free' news inventory and the shift of advertising and audiences online have accelerated a deepening crisis for newspapers (Fenton 2009).

For many new competitors such as search engines, news is not core business and is offered for free as a means of attracting recurring visitors (Küng et al. 2008: 150). This has made it more difficult for newspapers to establish pay-models and most newspapers launched free online services despite the considerable risk that this would cannibalise print revenues. Papers like *The Guardian* justified their strategy as the best way to reach new, younger readers who would not climb over pay walls. Other firms have rolled out subscription and charging models, initially achieving the greatest success in reaching business consumers (time-sensitive financial information), or high-value services (*Times* crossword). In June 2011, News Corporation established a new pay-subscription service for *The Times* and the *Sunday Times*. To date, however, few publishers earn sufficient online revenues to cover online running expenses let alone to recover online investments or compensate for declining print revenues.

An important counter-trend to declining paid-circulation has been the growth of free (usually weekday) papers provided along commuter routes in urban areas, attracting advertisers to an upscale salaried readership. Their success has led newspaper groups to shift from paid to free circulation for titles, or to risk can-nibalising their offer by mixing paid, cheaper short-form papers and free print in the same market, alongside combinations of free and paid content for smartphones, tablets and other computing devices. However, while some free papers have been viable, the costs of producing online news have generally not been recouped through combined revenues from advertising, subscription or micro-payment methods. Most online ventures remain heavily cross-subsidised and parasitic on other profit-making activities, with no truly viable model for online news content established.

Debt-laden corporations, having run down journalistic resources through cost-cutting and other measures to maintain profits, are now increasingly abandoning newspaper operations altogether during the latest recession; the *Seattle Post-Intelligencer*, for instance, cut staff from 165 to the 20 retained for its future, online-only presence, contributing to the estimated 200,000 media jobs lost in the US between 2004 and 2009 (McChesney and Nichols 2010; Mosco 2009: 124). Journalistic media based on professional routines and deadlines have been particularly affected with many firms seeking 'productivity' gains to feed and compete with 24-hour news, which critics say leaves journalists more desk-bound and dependent on sources. According to one study:

> In many, but not all, EU countries this type of journalism is increasingly suppressed or replaced by less expensive freelancing, with journalists working under deteriorating or even degrading working conditions and having insufficient resources to pursue stories in depth. More and more news is provided by agencies.
>
> (European Commission 2013: 28)

The number of journalists employed in the US declined by 26 per cent between 2000 and 2009 (Pew 2011), with similar falls in the UK as fewer journalists were required to produce more content due to office cutbacks, the integration of news online, and the demands of a competitive 24-hour news cycle (Fenton 2010). In such conditions journalists tend to be desk-bound, formulaic and to have increased dependence on sources and on PR-originated material (Davies 2008). All this would matter less if content diversity were as rich and blossoming as envisioned. However, leading news brands have been helped in defending their oligopolies by the weakness of their challengers (Curran 2012: 19). No successful business model for independent online news has emerged. Subscription is difficult because of availability and the custom of accessing free content. Financing through advertising is challenged by the small size of audiences. Existing online revenues can sustain only the smallest web-based news organisations (Downie and Schudson 2011), with few online independents being 'profitable or even self-financing' (Pew 2009).

Internet users have ready access, in a technical sense, to richer sources of information, alternative ideas and imagery than at any time in history. Yet, studies have found that content aggregators' search results tend not to give prominence to alternative news sources. A study of Google's and Yahoo's listings in relation to five public affairs issues found that no alternative news sites featured in the first page of search results (Redden and Witschge 2010). News aggregators, like Yahoo and Google, provide little by way of original news material and instead rely heavily on the newsfeeds of the major news agencies. In a study of international news online, Chris Paterson (2006) found that Yahoo and AOL reproduced Reuters and Associated Press material 85 per cent of the time. Yahoo developed a strategic relationship with the Reuters news agency in the mid 1990s and their model was widely copied. The majority of international news is provided by the existing major players, resulting in news being repurposed from a very restricted number of sources. According to UK communications regulator Ofcom (2007: 3), 'news outlets of all kinds often tell the same stories, from the same perspective, using much the same material'. The Pew Centre's study tracking stories over a week of media coverage in Baltimore found that eight out of ten stories 'simply repeated or repackaged previously published information', with most original news stories produced by old media, notably the *Baltimore Sun*, whose origination of news stories had fallen by more than 30 per cent over the previous decade (Pew 2010b). Yet the professional journalism itself was still heavily dependent on official sources and press releases for 86 per cent of the news stories.

In Euro-American media systems, news provision remains largely in the hands of dominant providers. Commercial providers are seeking to manage their migration from the declining medium of printed newspapers to online provision. This process involves the evisceration of some newspapers, including profitable and viable ones. There is a lack of viable new sources of news to counter the collapsing commercial model. Newspapers are dying (losing readers and advertising revenue) but the Internet is not substituting for the loss. Yet to fix our gaze on the decaying old media may well miss vital new growth. The Internet, it is argued, has nurtured a far more radical shift in communications production and exchange.

Participation

The Internet and digital technologies are alleged to have distributed tools for creativity, communication and collaboration into the hands of users, a process commonly referred to as 'democratisation'. This is associated with various claims. User-generated content (UGC) and a more collaborative approach to content production are celebrated as a resurgence of 'an older, folk culture, which was extinguished by the mass-produced, industrial culture of the record and film industry of the 20th century' (Leadbeater 2009: 56). The production of commercials for Doritos crisps by 'amateurs' is celebrated as exemplifying such 'crowdsourced' production (Leadbeater 2009: 105). The language of political democracy and equality is thus applied to the (co-)creation of content and economic value. 'You can participate in the economy as an equal, co-creating value with your peers and favourite companies to meet your very personal needs, to engage in fulfilling communities, to change the world, or just to have fun!' proclaim Tapscott and Williams (2006: 150). For these commentators the benefits of digital communications can and should be realised through free-market capitalism. A minority tradition, inspired by communitarian values, criticises market fundamentalism and envisions the expansion of non-commercial social production and exchange. For Benkler (2006: 10–11) 'the networked public sphere enables many more individuals to communicate their observations and their viewpoints to many others, and to do so in a way that cannot be controlled by media owners and is not as easily corruptible by money as were the mass media'.

Fuchs (2008) identifies a shift in the primary focus of accumulation strategies from information to communication and co-operation. Where the 1990s is associated with 'static page' content and information provision, the post-2002 phase is associated with the growth and investment in social networking platforms, wikis, and folksonomies that facilitate creativity, co-creation and sharing between users. However, like many critical scholars, Fuchs is sceptical of the adoption of terms such as Web 2.0. The latter is traced to the promotional work of marketers, notably Tim O'Reilly, and regarded by Fuchs (2012) and others as a 'marketing strategy for boosting investment'.[2] Optimistic accounts of friction-free capitalism, stilled by the dotcom collapse, resurfaced amidst new claims for Web 2.0 as initiating a 'new mode of production' (Tapscott and Williams 2006: ix), a more innovative, creative, participatory and efficient form of capitalism (see Freedman 2012). This repudiates an opposing critical account of 'monopoly capitalism' as a system structured around sustaining the most dominant interests operating in the marketplace. Confronted with such contrasting accounts, navigating through various techno-optimist and techno-pessimist strains can be confusing as well as dispiriting. Yet there are critical approaches that offer ways to engage with the complexity and contradictory dynamics of networked communications. Murdock (2003: 29) identifies the struggle over 'three cultural economics and their associated modalities of exchange':

1   commercial transactions
2   'free' distribution of public cultural goods
3   gift relations ('based on the reciprocal exchange and pooling of services and information').

The three systems and practices of exchange coexist and compete. This dynamic account highlights contestation, but in doing so Murdock warns against repeating the errors of an earlier phase of cultural analysis, which overstated and romanticised possibilities for dissent. The architecture of Internet communications does enable the kinds of non-commodified, non-proprietary 'gift' exchanges celebrated by Benkler and others, as enthusiasts share knowledge, insights and creative expression with one another, but the realisation of such 'non-market' values is ultimately constrained by the dominant political-economic system in which they exist. This accords with a core Marxian critique: a recognition of the dynamism, innovation and achievements of capitalism, yet combined with a recognition that capitalism is systematically unable to realise the full potential of its achievements for the benefit of the many.

The peculiar qualities of information are sources of contradiction whereby the social character of information meets the privatised and proprietary organisation of the market. For Fuchs (2009: 77) 'Information networks aggravate the capitalist contradiction between the collective production and the individual appropriation of goods'. Gift exchanges can repudiate and challenge commodification but can also be harnessed by commodification processes. User-generated content (UGC) is 'expressive of the generative possibilities of the Internet but all too easily used as "free" content by media and information companies who, in previous years, would have expected to pay for such content' (Freedman 2012: 87). For Fuchs (2009) 'the gift form is subsumed under commodity form and can even be used directly for achieving profit'. This is evidence of the 'structural need of capitalism to monetize, and incorporate within a system of market exchange, even those practices – like blogging, commenting and reviewing – that spring from non-commercial urges' (Freedman 2012). Much UGC is incorporated into a system of commodity exchange in which economic value is appropriated by companies selling the content and engagements of consumers to marketers (chapter six). One illustrative clash of modalities occurred when some 9,000 bloggers brought a class action to sue Huffington Post for 'unjust enrichment' in an (unsuccessful) effort to seek retrospective payment for their unpaid contributions. The bloggers claimed around a third of the $315 million AOL paid to acquire Huffington Post.

Decentralised network communications can allow ideas and information to flow more freely. The networked public sphere (Benkler 2006) also greatly enhances opportunities for people to participate in 'non-market' based communications, and in public deliberations on a scale hitherto unknown. These affordances and the practices that arise need full consideration (and are discussed further in later chapters). Yet a key theme in critical Internet studies is that the opportunities to realise such communications fully are constrained by the dominance of corporate capitalism and by the persistence of 'undemocratic problems of concentration, centralization and surveillance' (Sylvian 2008: 8). The concept of network is used in part to capture the integration of what might be regarded as the 'vertical' flow of top-down mass media content and the 'horizontal' flow of communications between individuals and groups. Interactivity and co-mingling within network communications is of huge significance for communications and democracy. Yet, the concerns about 'vertical' content supply remain vitally important as long as these remain the main sources on which people rely. We must also not treat 'horizontal' communications as entirely autonomous of the corporate–governmental systems on which their connectivity and expression depend. This invites consideration of the resource-base to sustain the three modalities outlined by Murdock. Gift exchanges and 'free labour' certainly demonstrate the power of altruism, as well as other incentives for (self) promotion, but they also rely on the transfer of resources of money, time and network access which are unequally distributed, with consequences for the communications produced. There has been a huge expansion of intergroup communications but beyond free labour, and crucially, too, free or inexpensive software and hardware, resources are in proportion to the ability to monetise or cross-subsidise online activities.

Conclusion

Networked communications have transformed the capacity for messages to be exchanged. Critiques generated in response to twentieth century media power need to be revised accordingly. This is not because mechanisms of control and filtering no longer exist – far from it – but they cannot (and never could) provide a totalising account. Yet this chapter has shown that problems of scarcity and control remain evident. There is undeniably increased digital plenitude but claims for digital pluralism need to be carefully qualified and assessed in regard to public media provision and consumption. There has been a 'media explosion', an accelerating expansion in the capacity to distribute and access information, but myths of digital plenitude ignore real (and in some areas growing) scarcities, and continuing patterns of dominance. The myth of digital abundance is problematic less because it is overstated and more because it is mobilised to suggest that market mechanisms can alone secure the pluralism hitherto sought through public policy. A key theme for critical political economists is that the Internet is a vital resource which has been allowed to develop according to corporate interests as a commercial medium with minimal consideration of public interest, democratic accountability or supervision. The 'tremendous promise of the digital revolution has been compromised by capitalist appropriation and development of the Internet' (McChesney 2013: 97). The Internet remains a contested, and richly diverse, space. This marks a huge advance for expression and exchange amongst individuals and groups. But if we take the claims seriously – for digital pluralism, for a networked public sphere – then we must pay attention to vertical structures of power – not least the dominance of media and communications conglomerates that continue to structure and shape its development.

Notes

1 Castells's concept of mass self-communication is useful, but fails to distinguish public facing content creation from public and private communication exchange (Fuchs 2009).
2 O'Reilly acknowledged that the formulation of Web 2.0 was 'designed to restore confidence in an industry that had lost its way after the dotcom bust' (O'Reilly and Battelle 2009: 1).

Chapter 6

Marketing communications and media

Introduction

Political economists have tended to share broader critiques of advertising as the leading ideological agency for capitalism, of its role in promoting consumerism and possessive individualism, and of its regressive, stereotypical representations of gendered, racial and other identities. But CPE researchers developed a more distinctive contribution. They argued that to understand advertising required attention to its economic as well as its ideological importance, addressing the nature and implications of advertising as a support mechanism for media. Overwhelmingly, research into marketing communications pursues an agenda conducive to the needs and interests of advertisers and the advertising industry, focusing on the effectiveness and efficiency of marketing communications. Critical output has been tiny by contrast (Mattelart 1989: 200) yet has been remarkably influential at times and, like Naomi Klein's *No Logo* (2000), has connected with wider social concerns about marketing communications. Critical perspectives are also generated by campaigning organisations, critical–artistic interventions such as Adbusters and other civil society organisations that draw upon and resonate with public attitudes.

From the 1980s critical discourses of advertiser power were challenged and disfavoured by culturalist scholars (Nava 1997; McFall 2004; Cronin 2003). Analysis of control, domination and manipulation was replaced by appreciation of people's imbrication in branding and consumer culture. This work has offered significant advances in theory and empirical enquiry, into brand strategies, advertising work and user engagement. Yet the disavowal of advertiser power has also led to rather anaemic, descriptive accounts that chart and interrogate advertising practice and culture without systematic critique. This makes them poorly equipped to address the transformations in capitalism and communications that lead to unprecedented advertiser power and are the subject of a new wave of critical scholarship of digital profiling, tracking and targeting (Turow 2011; Pariser 2011). This chapter traces both 'classic' and 'contemporary' lines of enquiry. In doing so it seeks to outline key arguments but also to contribute to identifying the revision and renewal of the radical tradition and to invite an assessment of their value and contemporary relevance.

Processes: commodification and commercialisation

Commodification is the process of transforming objects, products and services into commodities, things that can be bought and sold for money. In Marxist terminology commodification is the process of transforming use value into exchange value, the process of transforming 'things valued for their use into marketable products that are valued for what they can bring in exchange' (Mosco 2009: 2). Once commodities circulate with a price they attain exchange value, with money serving as their universal equivalent (Marx 1983: 93). Marx famously begins his major work *Capital* with analysis of the commodity, which congeals but also conceals the labour and social relations of its production. A key task for Marxian analysis is to uncover these, to peel back the 'onion skin' of the commodity's manifest form in order to reveal the humanly engineered system of production that produced it and to challenge the expropriation and exploitation of labour that sustained it. For Marx, products take the form of commodities when their production is organised through principles of exchange. Under capitalism, labour also takes on the properties of a commodity as workers are induced to exchange their labour power for wages that do not fully compensate for the labour they sell. Capitalists purchase the commodities of labour power and other means of production but create surplus value by selling the total output for more than the original investment, generating capital.

Commercialism (or commercialisation) is the orientation of activities towards the goal of increasing commercial revenue for profit. Commercialism describes one of the most overt and widespread phenomena in modern media, yet its usage is problematic, fusing sedimented layers of normative evaluation and critical debates about privileging profit-making over artistic or other values. Some writers narrow commercialisation to the 'creation of a relationship between an audience and an advertiser' and favour commodification as the more encompassing term (Mosco 2009: 132). However, there are good grounds to reverse this. Commodification refers to the processes of incorporation into commodity form. Commercialisation includes all ways in which the pursuit of commercial transactions shapes communication content and behaviour. It is the diffusion of a commercial logic across media shaped historically by civic and non-market values that defines a shift to 'hypercommercialism' (McChesney 1999). CPE examines both the intensification of commercialism and the extension of commodification into activities influenced by a different social logic, such as public access or sharing, but does so best with a historically attuned analysis that avoids prelapsarian overtones.

Political economic approaches to advertising

A political economy of advertising explores advertising's 'funding, production, distribution and regulation' (Golding and Murdock 1979: 18). This requires study of 'economic' dimensions – how advertising and media sectors function in the production, circulation and consumption of goods and services – 'political' dimensions – how marketing and communications are organised and regulated – and 'symbolic' dimensions – meaning and ideology – to explore the contribution of advertising to the production of meanings, social relations and material practices. These can be distinguished analytically but are bound together in material processes of promotion (McFall 2004). Advertising has been examined as part of a system of communications that 'engineers consumption to match production and reproduces the ideological system that supports the prevailing status quo' (Faraone 2011: 189). This requires study of communication as a sector of the total economy and for its 'linking function in the production, circulation and consumption of goods and services and its strategic, symbolic role in maintaining and perpetuating political and economic control' (Faraone 2011: 189). As we will see there have been tensions and debates within CPE on adequate theorisation of the interplay between economic and symbolic dimensions of advertising.

Critiques of advertising from the 1960s and 1970s had fallen out of favour by the 1980s for their reliance on concepts of ideological manipulation, 'false' needs, and overgeneralised accounts of advertising's 'function(s)', 'effects' and influence. Some of the deficiencies of general critiques of the *advertising system* were addressed by analyses of the *advertising industry*, exploring the corporate organisation of marketing communications, and of *advertising work*, examining the practices and reflexivity of practitioners. A fourth area of focus has been the *governance and regulation of advertising*, where CPE scholars have emphasised both the importance of public regulation of advertising and the efforts of organised lobbying by marketers, marketing agencies and commercial media to extend commercial speech rights and the 'right to advertise'. The fifth main area of analysis has been the *relationship between media and advertising*, where I believe CPE has made its most distinctive contribution.

Political economy of advertising industries and practices

The advertising industry has experienced the same core processes of corporate reorganisation that have occurred in media businesses and more generally across advanced economies (Turow 2010, 2011). Advertising agency growth accompanied that of transnational corporations and their expansion into foreign markets. From the 1980s there was a drive amongst major advertisers to consolidate their advertising accounts, with agencies consolidating and reorganising to match the needs of TNCs (Herman and McChesney 1997: 39), although there have been deconvergence trends too with the break-up of 'full-service agencies' (Nixon 2011). By the early 1990s there were seven major global advertising holding companies, with a second tier of large firms dominating regions and a third tier of national and sub-national firms. Today, four major global groups dominate: WPP Group (British), Interpublic Group (US), Omnicom Group (US) and Publicis (France), the last two seeking a merger in 2013 to create the largest marketing agency.

Political economists insist on the need to examine interrelationships between corporate media, ad agencies and big business. The tobacco giant Philip Morris, for instance, held seats on News Corporation's board, while Rupert Murdoch remained on the Philip Morris board for twelve years. Pfizer, the pharmaceutical giant, had directors on the boards of Time Warner, Viacom and Dow Jones. Such corporate interlocks indicate the 'continuing symbiotic relationship between news, advertisers, and advertising' (Bettig and Hall 2012: 165; Bagdikian 2004). The ways in which executive boards influence operations and editorial decisions require situated analysis, yet the corporate integration of advertising and media raises profound issues for democracy, media and culture about the powers of commercial speech. The interrelationship between TNCs active in marketing communications and media with the corporate funding of political parties is examined by Mullen (2013: 181), who argues that such alliances 'blur the distinction between political advertising (i.e. persuasion) and PR (i.e. propaganda)'. Communications TNCs such as Aegis, Omnicom, WPP, Havas and Interpublic colonise media and political systems across the world (Sussman 2011).

MEDIA AND ADVERTISING

The most distinctive contribution of CPE analysis of advertising, I wish to argue, has concerned the implications of media dependence on advertising finance and advertiser influence on media. There are critical concerns about the increasing amount of advertising carried, the placement of advertising, invasiveness and reach, but a core critique has concerned the influence of advertising on non-advertising content. Privately owned commercial media that depend on advertising revenue must compete for advertiser attention, and must serve advertiser interests if they are to prosper, critics argue (Herman and McChesney 1997: 6–7). This section traces some of the classical perspectives and issues before examining how far changing media and advertising relationships require these to be revised.

Dallas Smythe and the audience commodity

The pioneer CPE scholar Dallas Smythe established a distinctive theory of media and advertising focused on the creation of audiences as commodities (1977). Smythe's analysis was advanced as part of a wider effort to develop a materialist analysis of communications. Critical scholarship, he argued, had been too focused on content and ideological effects, instead of addressing the economic role of mass media in advanced capitalism. For Smythe this was the 'blindspot' in the Western Marxist tradition, whereby an overriding focus on the production of ideological meaning ignored the production of surplus value for capital. Critical researchers were investigating 'secondary effects', at best, and ignoring the primary economic aspects that a materialist political economy of communications should examine (Meehan 1993). Taking commercial, free-to-air television as his focus Smythe argued that the commodity produced by media is an audience commodity. Media content is the 'free lunch' used to recruit potential members of the audience and to maintain their local attention in order to sell them to advertisers (1977: 5).

> The appropriateness of the analogy to the free lunch in the old-time saloon or cocktail bar is manifest: the free lunch consists of materials which whet the prospective audience members' appetites and thus (1) attract and keep them attending to the programme, newspaper or magazine, and (2) cultivate a mood conducive to favourable reaction to the explicit and implicit advertisers' messages.

The media manufacture audiences as a commodity that can be sold to advertisers for a profit derived from the surplus value created by audience 'labour'. Smythe applied Marxian labour theory to the 'work' of audiences, who produce themselves as the audience commodity. Audiences also labour for advertisers 'to learn to buy particular "brands" of consumer goods, and to spend their income accordingly' (1977: 6). Audiences 'work to market [...] things to themselves' (Smythe 1981: 4); they 'self-market' (Jhally 1990: 67). Mattelart (1989: 203) praises Smythe for offering 'one of the first analyses of the organic link between advertising and the way the media function'. Smythe's work inspired and influenced North American political economy analysis and debates (Jhally 1990; Meehan 1993, 2005), but was criticised by contemporaries on a variety of grounds.

Murdock (1978) challenged Smythe's dismissive account of the Western Marxist tradition (influenced by the latter's Maoist sympathies) but their exchange reflected a more enduring division between Smythe's structural-functionalism and Murdock's espousal of a cultural materialist tradition (chapter one).[1] Basing analysis on the 'function' of media necessitates an account of system-supporting 'success' that negates the scope for contestation and resistance, features that Smythe is elsewhere keen to acknowledge and promote. In *Dependency Road* (Smythe 1981: 270), he writes:

> True, people are subject to relentless pressures from Consciousness Industry; they are besieged with an avalanche of consumer goods and services; they are themselves produced as (audience) commodities; they reproduce their own lives and energies as damaged and in commodity form. But people are by no means passive or powerless. People do resist the powerful and manifold pressures of capital as best they can.

Yet this appeal to agency is undermined in the 'blindspot' essay by a functionalist explanatory framework which elides the system-supporting 'function' of advertising with its imputed success. The result is an overly smooth account whereby audiences 'complete' the marketing effort. Smythe's mass media paradigm presumes a close connection between messages sent and received by mass audiences. Later analysts stress the risks and uncertainties of advertising effectiveness, ranging from placement to the persuasiveness of messages, through to reaching target prospects.

The audience commodity concept has been critiqued but also modified and developed. For Jhally (1990: 72, 73) the time purchased by advertisers is 'communications-defined time'; 'Media sell *potential* audience-power watching time, but the only thing they can guarantee is the *watching activity* of the audience'. Jhally acknowledges the argument that characterising watching as 'labour' is problematic since watching television does not have the characteristics of compulsion, and exploitation, found in wage labour. However, Jhally contends that watching activity is indeed compelled and thus an alienated activity. However, others object that watching TV has no wage equivalent, not least as audiences cannot convert the 'salary' received (Fuchs 2012). These debates have recently been revived and updated in considerations on the 'free' labour of Internet users, discussed further below.

Another body of research starts from the observation that what is purchased is usually estimated audience time, combined with target audience valuation. The audience commodity is less the actual aggregations of people who consume ad-financed media, rather it is the audience constructed through ratings. This has informed research on the system of ratings and audience measurement and has also been a focus for feminist political economists examining the relationship between capitalism, gender and class. For Eileen Meehan (1993: 386), the 'naturalistic assumption' of the audience in Smythe's work 'deflected attention from research into the effects of market pressures on corporate definitions of the commodity audience and commercial measures of audience preferences'. This analysis informed a broader critique of the equation of media supply with consumer demand (Meehan 2005). Denaturalising the audience commodity encouraged attention to the manner in which audience blocks are constructed and valued within ratings systems. Meehan's work examined ratings as a commodity (1993, 2005) in a highly monopolistic industry dominated by firms such as A.C. Nielsen in the US. Meehan, together with Inger Stole and Ellen Riordan, examined the construction of the female viewer in US radio and television in the twentieth century, work also developed by more culturalist scholars such as Ang (1991). Meehan (2002: 216) describes how the most highly prized commodity audience in post-war US network television was upscale white men, aged 18–34; channels that lost this ratings contest chased 'niche' audiences (women, children, African Americans or Hispanic Americans). Into the 1980s, women remained marginalised as a niche audience despite their influence over domestic consumption and their growing economic equality with men, an outcome reflecting 'the sexism of patriarchy as surely as overvaluing upscale audiences reflects the classism of capitalism' (Meehan 2002: 220).

Digital media and 'free' labour

Smythe's audience commodity concept has renewed relevance in contemporary studies of digital labour. The activities of users in building social media profiles, uploading pictures, creating content and communicating can be regarded as work to create an audience commodity that is sold to advertisers. Yet, as Fuchs (2012: 711) highlights:

> The difference between the audience commodity on traditional mass media and on the Internet is that in the latter case the users are also content producers, there is user-generated content, the users engage in permanent creative activity, communication, community building and content-production.
>
> [...]
>
> Due to the permanent activity of the recipients and their status as prosumers, we can say that in the case of corporate social media the audience commodity is an Internet prosumer commodity ...

Drawing on autonomist Marxist conceptions of immaterial labour, Terranova (2000: 33) analyses the 'free labour' involved in Internet activities from content creation, reading and online communication as 'simultaneously voluntarily given and unwaged, enjoyed and exploited'. Fuchs draws on Marxian concepts of labour, value and exploitation in his analysis of the Internet prosumer commodity. Social media time is 'work time' (Fuchs 2012: 722), a form of exploited labour where the surplus value is created by labour but accrued by capital (corporations such as Facebook). Fuchs acknowledges that users benefit from services, but argues that this does not equate to wages for work. Rather social media users have a simultaneous dual character 'as consumers of technological services and producers of data, commodities, value and profit'.

The audience commodity concept fuses two propositions, one of which is largely accepted and the other hugely contentious. The accepted proposition is that audiences are 'sold' to advertisers. Traditionally, transactions occur between media and marketers based on estimates of audience value as measured by ratings agencies or other research; increasingly they take the form of real-time micro-payments between marketers and digital service providers tracking users. It remains vital to resist naturalising the audience commodity – audience profiles remain partial assemblages of information (McStay 2011) – yet the ability to track and monetise users' activity makes possible the measurement of actual online behaviour (though still functioning as proxies for measuring attention and influence).

The contentious proposition concerns audience labour, both in Smythe's original thesis and in contemporary studies. Scholars object to the presumptions of passivity, acquiescence, co-optation and incorporation of audiences advanced by Smythe. The notion that we are unknowingly exploited offers an unpalatably passive, fatalistic account of working class agency and subjectivity, argues

Caraway (2011). While some call for an expansive concept of labour and exploitation attentive to unpaid domestic labour (Jhally 1990; Fuchs 2012), others object to the application of Marxian labour theory to relatively unconstrained and voluntary leisure activities. Comparing my social media usage to labour exploitation risks flattening important distinctions in information capitalism, from the Congolese workers mining Coltan for mobile phones, to the healthsapping intensive labour by Chinese workers producing high-tech gadgets. A third criticism is that the critique of unpaid labour risks disparaging voluntary activities, non-commodified exchanges and other aspects of gift economies (Hesmondhalgh 2010). A fourth criticism is that the analysis of exploitation fails to have sufficient regard for the value and benefits to users of digital services. Unpaid work in producing content, building profiles and self-presentation may be a form of deferred wages to those subsequently hired for paid work. However what critical scholars highlight is the realisation of value by the businesses supplying digital services from the unpaid activities of users (McGuigan 2012). In doing so they advance a critique of a much more incontrovertible aspect of the 'audience commodity' process: the creation of value by monetising users' activities by selling data and access to marketers.

Information gathered from users' online activities is monetised by selling marketers information, access to consumers and opportunities to reach them with personalised, targeted communications (Turow 2011; Pariser 2011). The evolving business models for commercial social media firms involve the generation of income from marketers based on connection to the communications activity, time spend, as well as content produced by users. Information about users' uploaded data, social networks, their interests, demographic data, their browsing and interaction behaviour is sold to the advertisers as a commodity in increasingly sophisticated ways, including real-time bidding.

Facebook's business model is principally based on advertising finance, with subsidiary revenues from games and apps. Facebook offers advertisers targeted advertising based on 'demographic factors such as location, age, gender, education, work history and the interests people have chosen to share on Facebook'. A corporate spokesperson told a BBC reporter (Cellan-Jones 2012):

> Facebook offers the most targeted advertising of any medium. If your business is selling alloy wheels in Manchester, then you can deliver your adverts to men aged 20–30 who live within 10 miles of the city and like Top Gear and Max Power.

Facebook offers so-called sponsored stories, whereby marketers can purchase 'stories' created when someone likes or comments on a page, and send these to other people who are either their friends or connected to the page. Users cannot opt out of being featured in sponsored stories and can only act by restricting whom they share their activities with. Facebook distinguishes sponsored stories from advertising messages yet, while associated with peoples' own communication, 'stories' can be generated by corporate pages' activities and distributed to networks of friends to appear in news feeds. Sponsored stories have been described as a way in which Facebook 'turns users into spokespeople for companies and products in ads that are broadcast to their friends' (Hill 2012). In October 2012 Facebook offered $20 million to settle a class action privacy lawsuit challenging the legality of sponsored stories, offering up to $10 each to nearly 125 million users.[2]

For Mosco (2009: 137) Smythe's audience commodity concept must be updated for digital systems 'which measure and monitor precisely each information transaction' and represent 'a major refinement in the commodification of viewers over the earlier system of delivering mass audiences'. Behavioural advertising is based on web browsing activity conducted over a period of time, while contextual advertising is allied to particular content viewed online, and includes retargeting, when advertising is delivered based on website content that a user has just viewed (Internet Advertising Bureau 2009). In behavioural advertising the audience is a commodity in the precise sense of a product that is bought and sold. Yet instead of the aggregated, imprecise 'audience' of cost-per-thousand targeting, now the commodity is a selective profile of an individual user for which behavioural advertising opportunities are sold. Digital users have been mostly unaware of behavioural advertising as corporations have lobbied successfully for automatic opt-in mechanisms to be applied so 'to suggest users are willing collaborators in their own subjection is a difficult position to maintain in this particular regard' (McStay 2011: 316).

Andrejevic argues there is power imbalance between those who control the circuits of surveillance and ordinary users who trade personal information for customised offers and in doing so provide an invaluable source of labour in the form of market research. There is increased capacity for economic monitoring, that is tracking activities for commercial purposes. On platforms like Google or Facebook 'monitoring becomes an integral component of the online value chain both for sites that rely upon direct payment and for user-generated content sites that rely upon indirect payment (advertising)' so that 'user activity is redoubled on commercial platforms in the form of productive information about user activity' (Andrejevic 2012: 84).

There are numerous objections to basing an account of media *consumption* on Marxian theories of labour, value and exploitation alone. Alienation and social reproduction do not describe the totality of user engagement with social media, nor encompass the media literacies involved in navigating 'free' services and benefits, albeit in structurally disadvantaged ways. Yet, for a critical study of advertising, the concept of Internet prosumer *commodification* addresses key aspects of advertising processes and the consequences arising from different forms of monetisation.

Many media operate in what economists call a 'dual product market', selling goods ('content') to consumers but also selling media audiences to advertisers (Doyle 2002b: 12). One consequence is that ad-financed media respond to marketers' demands, not simply to consumer/user demands (as those who equate 'free markets' with consumer sovereignty, or media provision with popular demand assume; see Gitlin 1997; Meehan 2005). Commercial media do not give the people what they want; they give what is profitable to provide. Further, they give what the advertising system will support. This classic critique is relevant for 'free' ad-financed social media whose economic model has affinities with FTA commercial television. The critique needs updating, however, as what is provided is not content so much as services or software for user communication and (co)creation.

Advertising influence and media

To fully understand media we need to understand how media content and services are financed and paid for. A rich tradition of CPE work on media finance and advertising shares with mainstream media economics a concern to examine the resources for media firms, matters of growing importance and complexity given the proliferation of modes of delivery and consumption of digital content. However, CPE analysis goes beyond a narrow concern with profitability or promotional effectiveness, to consider the spectrum of advertising influence. The first question to ask is the level of economic dependence by media on advertising finance. We can ask this question historically to trace the development of commercial mass media, and ask it in relation to media sectors, businesses, types of products and specific media vehicles. In broad outline, revenues from advertising represent 50–60 per cent for magazines, up to 80 per cent for newspapers and 100 per cent for FTA commercial radio and television (Bagdikian 2004: 230; Bettig and Hall 2012).

Media dependence on advertising can be exploited by advertisers to secure favourable conditions such as discounted pricing. However, advertisers can also intervene to influence editorial content, as Chrysler did when it requested that magazine editors notified the car manufacturer of editorial matter adjacent to its adverts that it deemed detrimental to sales (Soley 2002: 210–11). In this instance the American Society of Magazine Editors rallied successfully against a crude demand for censorship, but Soley surveys numerous advertiser efforts to censor media. Bagdikian (2004) documents how tobacco companies used their influence as heavy advertisers to curtail media discussion of the health effects of smoking. Procter and Gamble prohibited programmes 'which could in any way further the concept of business as cold, ruthless, and lacking all sentiment or spiritual motivation' (cited in Herman and McChesney 1997: 7).

Instrumentalist and structuralist explanations

There have been debates between two main alternative explanations of advertiser influence. Instrumentalist explanations focus on the intentional actions and behaviour of actors in seeking to control communications. These may range from efforts to shape specific communications, actions to influence the editorial environment, to efforts to influence the broader orientation of media vehicles and their allocation of resources to tell stories and reach particular audiences. However, other critical scholars argue that the influence of advertising on media is better understood as an impersonal force and offer a structuralist explanation. Curran describes how advertisers in nineteenth century Britain refused to place advertisements in radical newspapers on political grounds. But he argues that the main way in which advertising influenced British media from the early twentieth century was not through deliberate acts of control or political censorship. Advertising operates as an 'impersonal force'; the cumulative decisions of advertisers seeking the most cost-effective vehicles to reach target consumers, creates a source of finance that is unevenly distributed across media.

However, while advancing a structuralist explanation against an instrumentalist one, Curran provides a carefully circumscribed historical analysis. Changing conditions 'made it easier for radical journalism to make a breakthrough in the first half of the twentieth century' (Curran 2011: 5). Advertising agencies became established as intermediaries, evidence-based selection of media vehicles for advertising improved (reducing political bias), and the rising worth of working class consumers helped papers like the *Daily Mirror* and left-wing *Daily Herald*, aimed at those readerships, attract advertising finance. Yet the structure of the press after 1945 was one in which papers with more upscale readers gained greater advertising revenue. The *Daily Herald* had a circulation share of 8 per cent when it ceased publication in 1964 but its advertising share had slumped to 3.5 per cent. Advertising was a largely impersonal force, but a powerful one, delivering market censorship: the distribution of ad finance across newspapers remained very unequal because of the 'advertising bounty' that flowed to papers attracting upscale readers while minority papers with low-income readerships 'were not viable, because they did not attract the same commercial subsidy' (2011: 166).

Advertising subsidy functions as a *de facto* licensing system, determining which ad-dependent media have the resources to survive and thrive. Yet, advertising influence is usually impersonal, first, in that decisions are based on advertising effectiveness (reaching the right prospects in as cost effective a manner as possible) rather than judgements concerning the media vehicle or editorial content as such. Second, the 'licensing' effect arises from the innumerable decisions of individual advertisers. Baker (1994) highlights another dimension: ad-placement decisions can lead to outcomes which are not intended by advertisers, and are detrimental to their interests. Directing advertising income to the media vehicle that can reach the largest number of the target market at low cost may drive competitors out of business, but then advertisers face a monopolist who can raise advertising rates. That occurred, argues Baker, when the distribution of ad finance contributed to monopolisation in US local newspapers from the late nineteenth century. Baker concludes (1994: 103):

> Advertiser influence is so built in to the market context that not only is it often difficult to prove, but advertiser influence frequently occurs without the advertiser's inducing it by any specific act, sometimes even without the advertiser's wanting it.

Oscar Gandy (2000: 48; 1982, 2004) examines the implications of the uneven distribution of commercial subsidy for media serving poorer, ethnic minority audiences in the US, concluding: '[t]o the extent that advertisers place a lower value on gaining access to particular minority audiences, those who would produce content for that segment will be punished by the market ... '.

The structuralist analysis is helpful in highlighting theoretical deficiencies in instrumentalist explanations but historical analyses show that the forms of influence change under different conditions and that advertising influence can take a complex combination of forms. We may continue to ask: under what conditions can marketers or agencies successfully intervene to influence editorial decisions? Yet as marketing decouples from traditional media vehicles we need to frame this more broadly to examine how marketing finance and decisions affect the range and nature of communication services. How do the various influences operate and interact, from more 'impersonal' market signals to the interactions between media, agencies and marketers themselves?

Leiss et al. (1990: 121), drawing on Murdock's (1982) distinction between allocative and operational control, argue that the influence of advertising tends to be of the allocative type, namely shaping the goals and scope of media firms and determining the general ways in which firms deploy resources, rather than directly influencing operational decisions. Other studies have suggested that advertising influence is largely internalised by media management, influencing editorial strategies designed to maximise revenue (Curran 1978, 1986). As Fenton (2007: 13) writes: '[Advertiser] influence commonly functions pre-emptively: the sensibilities of the advertiser are taken into consideration by the media company prior to the screening of contentious material'. TV programming is required to provide a suitably positive selling environment by 'privileging genres that employ the same capitalist realist aesthetic as the advertising that surrounds them' (Murdock 2011: 29; Herman and Chomsky 2008).

Baker (1994: 44) summarises how ad dependence encourages the media to shape and adapt media content:

1 to treat advertisers' products and their broader interests charitably in both news reports and editorials
2 to create a buying mood that will induce readers or viewers to react favourably to advertisements
3 to reduce partisanship and often reduce controversial elements in order to avoid offending advertisers' potential customers and to increase the media's potential reach
4 to favour the middle- to higher-income audiences whose greater purchasing power advertisers value most.

Baker (1994: 45–49) also offers a useful summary of factors that can affect the extent of advertising's influence within a given medium or firm. These include the level and kind of economic dependence on advertising, whether widely distributed amongst many advertisers or concentrated on individual advertisers or organised groups. Another factor is the acceptability of advertising influence on content decisions (and the 'cost' of public disapproval arising from knowledge of influence), which varies according to the media format and type of enterprise. When this 'cost' is internalised by media managers and workers it is related to another key factor, the influence of 'professionalism', which may act to resist advertiser pressure. In addition, 'accepted industry practice' in the sector can in turn influence the behaviour and demands of advertisers. Consumer identification with the advertising and level of actual awareness of separation between advertising and non-advertising content are other, increasingly significant factors. Finally, Baker includes the implications of conglomeration, citing examples of advertisers applying pressure on one part of the conglomerate's business in order to influence another.

The main factors affecting advertising influence on media can be summarised as:

1 levels of dependence on advertising finance and support
2 institutional traditions of specific parts of media and media–advertiser relations
3 behaviour and influence of owners
4 professional norms of media workers and managers
5 formal regulations
6 self-regulation influenced by users (including anticipated consumer responses).

Five and six include the range of interests shaping the practices of firms and regulators, variously stakeholders, policy networks and civil society. A common theme of studies across media is that with increasing commercial pressures comes increasing dependence on advertising and accommodation of advertiser interests. However, this is always a dynamic process since there are various countervailing forces to counter advertiser influence, and advertiser power is mitigated by the unavoidable uncertainty of securing advertising effectiveness in any given promotion (see McAllister 1996).

Institutionalised professional practices can limit advertiser influence. The 'firewall' separating 'Church' and 'State', that is separating editorial from advertiser or corporate interests, are central tropes structuring debate about US journalism (Bagdikian 1997). The firewall concept provides a normative standard for critique while spotlighting profound economic, structural and behavioural changes in journalistic media, especially news journalism. In his extensive participant observation in the 1970s, Gans (1980) noted the strength of US news journalists' resentment of advertiser influence and their partial, institutionalised insulation from such pressure. National news firms could limit advertiser interference by their ability to attract and substitute other advertisers (1980: 257, see also McQuail 1992: 135). All these conditions have been significantly eroded since the 1980s with the firewall protecting the integrity of journalism from corporate interests crumbling; 'That's all gone now. Out the window' the veteran journalist Dan Rather is quoted as saying (McChesney 2013: 178). The results of surveys, interviews with practitioners, commentary and analysis of corporate data indicate how pressures have increased on advertising-dependent media to comply with advertiser demands and offer a host of added benefits (Hardy 2010a). Advertisers have been able to exact more and more 'editorial support' beyond paid advertising (McAllister 1996, 2000). Further, as Bogart (2000: 290) observes, such journalistic professionalism as existed in news journalism was never as firmly established in the entertainment business, or in media sectors like consumer magazines based on close relationships between media and marketers. Herman and McChesney (1997: 140) describe how:

> major TV networks offer their 'stars' to sell commercials and appear at advertiser gatherings; they enter into joint promotional arrangements with advertisers, each pushing the other's offerings; they show 'infomercials' produced entirely by or for advertisers and displaying their products; and they co-produce programs with advertisers and gear others to advertiser requests and needs.

Various studies show increased integration of advertising through plugs in news programmes (Compton 2004; Hardy 2010a; McAllister 2002), entertainment marketing and cross-promotion.

Advertiser pressure to integrate promotional content into 'independent' editorial content is a complex matter for analysis, but three main considerations are pertinent. First, strategies of 'embedded persuasion' (advertising in media content) increase the promotional content of media discourse. Second, such promotional practices influence how media adopt and adapt to them. Third, they influence norms and professional ideology as increased reliance on and accommodation to advertiser interests shapes a more commercial and promotional orientation. At its best, CPE work has brought a long-range historical and analytical perspective and resisted the tendencies to presentism, and autonomisation, in media analysis. Scholars have identified various factors influencing a return and reworking of promotional practices which dominated the early years of radio and television broadcasting in the United States, such as advertiser influence through programme sponsorship, in-programme promotions and product placement and plugola (Newell et al. 2006; Smulyan 1994). Baker (1994: 105) notes, for instance, how programme-length commercials and product placement are 'basically identical' to the paid 'reading notices' which appeared in American newspapers at the turn of the century. Another approach has been to identify the close and enduring relationship between promotional and media content in both news and entertainment media, against either ahistorical idealisations of media performance, or generalised accounts of commercialism.

Media and advertising integration and disaggregation

The characteristic relationship of media and advertising in mid twentieth century media was integration with separation. Advertising was integrated in the sense that it was physically combined with the media product. In newspapers and magazines, adverts appeared alongside editorial; in linear television, spot (or block) advertising appeared in designated breaks within or between programmes. While advertisers controlled their commercial communications, media firms controlled the packaging and distribution of the ad-carrying media. Media and advertising were kept separate on the whole. There have always been opportunities and pressures to integrate but the principles of separation were generally upheld by journalists, and by creative professionals in television, supported by managers, underpinned by self-regulatory codes of conduct in both media and advertising and subject to stronger statutory regulation in some sectors, such as European broadcasting.

Media and advertising integration is by no means a new phenomenon and has a long history across all media forms. Yet, arguably the most profound change in the twenty-first century is that the commercial digital environment has brought increased pressures from marketers, met with increased accommodation by media (McChesney 2013: 155). The emergent forms are *integration without separation*, but this coexists with trends towards *disaggregation* of media and advertising. While these trends are in some senses diametrically opposed, they both reflect a new shift towards marketer power in an era of increased competition for and dependence on advertising finance. One of the most documented forms of media–advertiser integration is product placement and brand integration (Hardy 2010a; Murdock 1992a). Product placement in audiovisual media has a long history but has increased significantly across North America, China and Western European systems after liberalisation, with media and marketing integration extending through computer games (advergames) and social media.

Like integration, disaggregation of media and advertising takes various forms with different consequences. The most challenging feature is that advertising is much less dependent on media vehicles; advertisers can buy access to selected audiences without the need for publishers. Media content still matters, since it attracts consumers that advertisers seek to reach. However, marketers have much greater opportunity to reach consumers without subsidising or accommodating media content providers. The intermediary role of media, creating an audience to sell to advertisers, is being undermined, in part because the production and distribution of physical goods are expensive ways to reach audiences, and in part because of the advantages of new ways to reach target consumers for data gathering, data management and precision targeting. Content is becoming less important than the person being tracked. Adverts can be linked to search and users' activity online so that advertising follows people's profiles rather than being bundled with media content. The affordances of digital communications are driving marketers to demand that they pay only the actual costs of delivering an advert onto a selected platform (Turow 2011). Consequently the traditional subsidy supporting the news, information or entertainment surrounding advertisements is set to diminish, with profound consequences for democratic communication resources, public media and cultural pluralism. At the same time the costs of managing the data that brings together advertising and consumers have created new industries and intermediaries. Paying these is one factor in the reduced income from online advertising for publishers. Publishers receive only around 20 per cent of the amount spent on advertising on their site with the remaining 80 per cent going to ad networks and data handlers (Pariser 2011; McChesney 2013: 156)

Advertising integration and disaggregation trends are obviously contrary tendencies: the embedding of advertising within content, and the disembedding of advertising from content publishing and packaging online. Yet both tendencies spring from the same underlying dynamics and reflect responses to increasing dependence of media on advertising finance. Taking advantage of the competition among web creators and distributors, 'media buyers are eroding the power of web publishers and causing them to play by advertisers' new rules to survive' (Turow 2011: 112).

Marketing professionals identify three main kinds of media: paid, earned and owned. Traditional advertising is 'paid', inserting advertisements into media vehicles or other advertising spaces. Earned media describes public relations activities to generate editorial coverage. The third area, owned, has been transformed by the opportunities for marketers to reach consumers directly via the Internet. Owned media has taken various forms such as contract publishing, that have been aided by but also pre-date digitalisation. But the commercial expansion of the Internet has been a game-changer: the increasing accessibility and reach of owned media increases pressures on media for accommodation in paid and earned media.

Advertising, regulation and democracy

Product placement and invasive advertising have intensified not because of technological capabilities or market forces alone but because the constraining force of societal regulation has been relaxed in favour of corporate actors. The significance of regulation and the struggles between state, market and civil society actors to shape governance are neglected in some culturalist accounts, which treat promotional culture as the outcome of cultural and market evolution. The political economy tradition, by contrast, identifies regulation as a site of struggle between private and public interests and examines how policies that favour market actors over citizens' interests have arisen. No other group in democratic societies commands the same power as marketers to speak. The critical tradition explores the relationship between advertising and systems of domination that restrict capacities for human emancipation and for democratic rule. The relationship between corporate media and advertising narrows the range of information, ideas and imagery in media. Advertisers tend to reinforce politically conservative content and values and tend to be hostile to criticisms of consumerist ideologies and arrangements of which they are major beneficiaries (Herman and McChesney 1997: 6–7). In these ways advertising reinforces the tendencies in corporate media that filter content. Herman and McChesney describe a media/advertiser complex that prefers entertainment over cultivation of the public sphere. 'Advertisers have ideological – and practical – biases that have nothing to do with viewer demand' Lewis (2010: 343).

Renewing the critical tradition

Critical political economy has insisted on examining the economic, political and cultural aspects of media and advertising relationships. Yet, the radical tradition needs to be revised and renewed to take account of changes in media and to offer a suitably rich and compelling analysis and theorisation of media–advertising relationships.

Radical perspectives lost ground in the 1980s subject to revisionist attacks from media and cultural studies. Culturalist approaches emphasised people's immersion in branding and brand culture, and turned away from what were regarded as crude, Marxian domination theories. Critical accounts of advertising have been critiqued as misplaced and displaced: misplaced because they focus on selective visible aspects (advertising texts) to the detriment of analysing production, labour and consumption (Nava 1997); displaced because '[s]ociological critiques of advertising are, in any event, really critiques of market society' says McFall (2011: 93).

The culturalist critique makes valid points but the attack is lopsided. Critical scholarship is not wedded to presumptions of strong ideological effects or manipulation associated with mass media domination paradigms. Instead, it is distinguished by the concern to identify and address problems arising from the manner in which resources, including communication resources, are organised in social life. The radical tradition can be renewed by addressing the ways in which marketer power can be realised and undermined, challenged and contested.

Marketers' 'economic surveillance' combined with social segmentation presents profound challenges for democracy, social inclusion and cultural exchange (Turow 2011). At the same time, the marketing communications industries are adapting to challenging new conditions and volatility across markets. US consumers are spending nearly 30 per cent of their time online with media but while part of that time is spent with ad-supported destinations, such as branded websites, most is spent on communications including email and social media. 'As a result, only eight per cent of total ad spending is going to online media' (Mandese 2010). The challenges for advertising, and the work of creative professionals to achieve advertising effectiveness, must be fully addressed and incorporated into analysis.

CPE attention to advertising as a support mechanism for media remains of central importance but needs updating as 'possibilities for the direct influence of content keep changing' (Leiss et al. 2005: 120) and, as contemporary environments, involve the blurring of pro-am identities, co-creation and networked social communications. Greater attention to media work cultures links to the need for an expanded account of governance, including how formal regulation and informal rules influence practices such as commercial integration in news, entertainment and social media. Where postmodernists have tended to argue that the separation of media and advertising is irretrievable, a revised radical approach can inform a more nuanced analysis of the conditions in which commercial communications and media content combine and influence one another.

So we need a revised mapping of the main factors that tend to strengthen marketers' influence on media and communications services and countervailing forces. Here I draw on Curran's (2002) essay 'Renewing the Radical Tradition' in seeking to identify for media–advertising relationships what that essay considers for media as a whole, in the same effort to offer a conceptual mapping and toolkit for a more open interrogation of influences operating in specific instances. The focus here is on the power of marketers to influence editorial, operational or strategic decisions by communication providers in ways that favour marketing communications messages and interests. In conjunction with each of the factors identified below, we need to consider a *structural* dimension (economic), *sectoral* dimensions (institutional cultures shaping relationships in how communication services are organised) and *behavioural* dimensions (interactions of specific agents, such as particular brand marketers, agencies and media firms). We need to consider specificities of firms, forms and formats, which have different norms and expectations influencing behaviours and which together form the institutional and cultural contexts for media–advertiser relationships.

Factors that tend to enhance advertising influence on media

1 Media dependence on advertising finance

> In general, we can say that the impact of any channel's ad-carrying role on the fashioning of its non-advertising contents is proportional to the extent of its dependence on such revenue.
>
> Wernick (1990: 100)

Dependence on advertising finance is the single most important way in which advertising influences media content. The level of dependence varies according to such factors as the proportion of total revenue made up from advertising, and reliance on particular advertisers or groups of advertisers. The dependence of media on advertising revenue tends to influence media decisions at various levels, from corporate-strategic to operational and editorial.

2 Market conditions and the structural influence of ad finance

The second key factor is the way advertising finance influences how media markets are organised. The structural effect of advertising finance is to grant more resources to media serving wealthy consumers. Much media provision is shaped to appeal to the interests of the affluent because their high disposable incomes make them a prime target for advertisers.

3 Technical capabilities and marketing effectiveness

The third key factor arises from the technical capabilities and resources for marketing effectiveness that affect marketers' demands on media. Digital media capabilities for tracking and targeting consumers provide enhanced opportunities for marketer-controlled content. Marketers' capabilities and opportunities to *disaggregate* advertising from media vehicles (behavioural advertising, owned media, etc.), and to *integrate* advertising with media (product integration, advergames, etc.), both contribute to pressures on media to accommodate marketers in ostensibly media-controlled content.

4 Advertiser–media placement behaviour

Ad influence on non-advertising content (affecting both what is promoted or suppressed) arises also from the instrumental interactions between marketers, marketing agencies, media firms and content makers. Advertising decisions can be ideological, intentional and instrumentalist, so this category includes corporate censorship and other forms of advertising influence arising from the behaviour and interaction of media and marketing actors.

5 Corporate ownership and relationships

Media conglomerates interlock with advertising in a variety of ways. There is corporate cross-ownership of media and advertising businesses, and interlocking at the level of boards and strategic management. Media firms are major advertisers and involved in extensive intra-firm as well as external advertising. Such corporate integration, joint ventures and common corporate interests between marketers, marketing communications agencies and media firms strengthen ad influence.

6 Producer/produser cultures and relationships

Advertising influence is enhanced when marketing goals and promotional cultural values are accepted and normalised by media providers and content creators.

7 User activity – practices and cultures

Various kinds of user interactivity and (co-)creation can promote ad-integration into media content and communications and increase the acceptability of marketers' presence in media.

8 Marketers' influence as media content providers

Marketers engage in communications across their own media channels (owned), advertising (paid) and through public relations (earned). There is increasing convergence and blurring of forms as marketers invest in owned media content (websites; native advertising), commissioned content (paid bloggers, content farms), co-owned media content and public relations activities with media firms.

9 Governance and regulation

Liberalisation of regulations concerning corporate consolidation, media owner-ship, marketing behaviour, advertising placement, advertising content and media content, can all enhance marketers' power and influence.

Countervailing pressures

1 Governance and regulation

Both media and advertising are subject to regulations designed variously to protect and promote values such as consumer welfare, competition, technical operability, quality, or the public interest. The countervailing force of regulation is weakening in areas such as product placement, where the principle of separation of media and advertising is being eroded. Yet, there are also pressures on politicians and regulators from civil society, consumers' and interest groups to restrict advertising.

2 State support and public media

States have a central role in governance and regulation but, as well as powers of *imperium* (the command of law), they can use *dominium* power (employment of the wealth of government). Public service media (PSM) can provide a countervailing force to advertiser influence not only by sustaining non-commercial media, but by shaping media cultures in ways that influence private media too, for instance through movements of professionals and values between sectors, and by influencing consumer expectations, cultural and policy environments.

3 Market conditions

Media–advertiser relationships are shaped by market conditions, including competition and the behaviour of other firms as well as consumer behaviour. Powerful inhibitors on marketers' integration into media content can arise from the actual/anticipated responses of users/consumers, and also from the behaviour and norms of other market actors. Many media markets are 'two-sided' – two groups interact through a media platform or intermediary: advertisers and consumers. Advertisers benefit from reaching more viewers; but too much advertising (or the wrong kinds) may alienate consumers/users. Media face pressures to balance the needs and interests of both parties.

4 Content producers: professional cultures and values

How media engage with advertisers depends not only on economic dependencies but also on institutional arrangements and cultures influencing interactions between actors. As studies such as Gans's (1980) analysis of US journalism show, staff power, professional codes and governance can counter pressures to accommodate advertising. Trade unions can also organise effectively, not only on behalf of workers but in advancing wider social and cultural interests. The Writers Guild of America has organised in opposition to product integration, in part on the grounds of it undermining the artistic integrity of writers. Journalists have organised on behalf of editorial integrity and PR professionals have advanced codes on transparency and disclosure.

5 Civil society action

Consumer and citizens' activism need civil society resources to thrive but have had a distinguished history of interventions (Stole 2006; Mukherjee and Banet-Weiser 2012). Long-standing forms of community action and organised lobbying have been aided by the power of online activism. Civil society activism can counter marketers' power by influencing policy-makers and groups in society.

6 User activity practices and cultures

At the heart of much critical investigation of contemporary digital media is recognition of the influence and potentialities of non-commodified creativity and communication, together with the constraints of corporate and governmental controls. The various cultures and practices that challenge commodification, from piracy to gift exchanges, serve to counter advertising influence, yet they can also be imbricated with advertising too. Independent fan websites may secure income from advertising or media merchandise. Examining how user activity can be a countervailing force, but often complexly implicated with commercial communications, is one of the tasks for critical scholarship.

This mapping is designed to invite more open investigation of advertising influence on non-advertising content and media–advertiser relationships. To examine these factors requires a combination of quantitative measurement and qualitative assessment. The radical tradition highlights key problems arising from media dependence on advertising finance – but to investigate and challenge this persuasively we need to examine the configuration of influences in a more dynamic and open manner; the approach above is designed to contribute to that task.

Conclusion

The critical political economy tradition is guided by critical social theory to identify and address problems. Critical scholarship from the 1970s established studies of advertising finance but tended to provide an aerial view with limited close observation of advertising practices and processes. The rise of sociological and culturalist studies of advertising fills this gap but tends towards an uncritical account of marketing, partly in its effort to distinguish itself from earlier critical discourses. The extension of advertiser power, as well as its limits, cries out for analysis and public debate. What is needed now is critical scholarship that is informed by the theoretical sophistication of new media studies and which includes a close attention to material practices, but which continues to ask and address larger, critical questions about the ways that advertising shapes communication environments.

Notes

1 Smythe answered with a rejoinder to Murdock (Smythe 1978; see also Smythe 1981: 22–51).
2 Previously in 2009, Facebook paid $9.5 million to charities to settle another class action on privacy concerning Beacon, the company's short-lived sharing of users' purchases that caused a storm of protest.

Chapter 7

Globalisation, media transnationalisation and culture

Introduction

Critical political economy is closely associated with a critique of imbalances and inequality in the global flow of media and cultural goods. This cultural imperialism thesis was advanced by prominent CPE scholars in the 1960s and 1970s. It was challenged and lost ground in the 1980s as various critiques coalesced around a cultural globalisation thesis (Tomlinson 1991, 1999). In the conventional version told, crude, neo-Marxist accounts of cultural imposition, American hegemony and 'one-way' cultural flows have given way to an appreciation of multidirectional cultural flows. Yet such framing offers a misleading account of the analysis and contribution of critical scholarship: past and present. Both theory and analysis have developed to try to match the ever more complex patterns and implications of media globalisation. Critical political economy is not characterised by adherence to formulations of cultural imperialism from the 1970s but rather to exploring problems of power in communications that belie more benign accounts of reciprocation and cultural exchange.

Rival perspectives on cultural domination have structured debates on media transnationalisation and so reviewing these serves as a good way into making sense of contemporary analysis. Yet approaching these debates through media and cultural studies literature alone makes it all too easy to disconnect them from their historical and political economic contexts and their relevance to interventions in policy arenas. This chapter seeks to place contemporary debates on globalisation and media in a wider framework, encompassing the geopolitical shifts to neoliberalism and the political challenges to inequalities in media and cultural flows. Rival polarities of cultural imperialism and cultural globalisation still influence debates but, after reassessing their legacy, this chapter goes on to examine divisions (not least amongst radical scholars themselves) between 'strong' globalisation theories and those emphasising the continuing importance and influence of the state and 'national' media systems. The chapter also assesses current developments in the transnational political economy of media.

Modernisation theory

A loosely affiliated group of scholars in North America promoted an account of social and economic transformation in which the advanced capitalist economies would lead the development of market economies in other nations by non-coercive means. This account assigned a key role to communications and to the diffusion of communications technologies, media content and media models derived from the West. For Daniel Lerner (1969, quoted in Schiller 1989: 139)

> The long era of imperialism (subordination) is recently ended: the campaign for international development (equalisation) has just begun.
>
> [...]
>
> Under the new conditions of globalism, [international communication] has largely replaced the coercive means by which colonial territories were seized and held.
>
> [...]
>
> The persuasive transmission of enlightenment is the modern paradigm of international communication.

Modernisation theorists such as Lerner, Ithiel de Sola Pool, Wilbur Schramm, argued that the phase of imperialism was ending with the creation of newly independent nation-states and that communication had a vital role in 'training for self management' and promoting the aspirations of a modernised market economy to both citizens and elites. Capital would have rich new seams of cheaper labour and emergent consumer markets. Transformation would be aided by the benign diffusion of enlightened values. 'Backward' and particularist forms of thought would be replaced by more 'universalistic' values of enterprise and possessive individualism. In reality, the media systems in many developing nations supported authoritarian power rather than popular emancipation and education and on this the US modernisers were ambivalent, paying little attention to how media pluralism could be secured (Curran and Park 2000b).

Cultural imperialism

Radical scholars advanced the concept of cultural imperialism in the 1960s and 1970s. Its major achievement, argues Nordenstreng (2001) was to challenge the then dominant, benign account of Western modernisation; radical scholars argued instead that 'Western culture' was being imposed on newly independent states in the 'third world', eroding cultural autonomy. Their core claim was that the imperialism had not ended with decolonisation; rather colonial powers had found other means to sustain relations of dominance, including the unequal exchange of cultural products, technologies, skills and resources (Said 1993;

Boyd-Barrett 1977). Scholars drew on dependency theory, grounded in neo-Marxist political economy, which argued that core nations maintained peripheral nations in relations of economic and political dependence. Transnational corporations, mostly based in the North, exercised control over developing countries in the South through setting the terms of global trade and exchange, aided by the active support of their respective governments. Dependency theories were developed by Latin American scholars in particular but influenced and joined a broader swathe of subaltern and anti-imperialist work. These analyses also informed the work of CPE scholars in North America (Dallas Smythe, Herbert Schiller, Hamid Mowlana) and Europe (Karle Nordenstreng, Peter Golding).

Leading authors of modern critical economy such as Herbert Schiller and Dallas Smythe were trailblazers for international media analysis. They set out to understand global geopolitical and economic forces and their relationship to communications and cultural exchange. They also made efforts to understand the increasingly complex relations between transnational and national cultural production. However, to reduce their work to the stock features of what is labelled, and critiqued, as the cultural imperialism thesis is misleading. Criticisms can certainly be made of their analysis but they invariably engaged in more sophisticated ways than the standard critique allows with the patterns of an emerging transnational political economy and its cultural implications. Schiller's work, in particular, examined the growth of transnational media corporations in the period after 1945 and the transformation of US national firms into 'huge, integrated, cultural combines', that controlled the means of producing and distributing 'film, TV, publishing, recording, theme parks, and even data banks' (Schiller 1991: 14). Such concerns were supported by studies of global television markets showing that programming flows were dominated by US production. A UNESCO report found that more than half the countries studied imported over 50 per cent of their television, mostly entertainment and most imported from the US (Nordenstreng and Varis 1974; Straubhaar 2002: 194). Calculating an 'index of dependence' based on the proportion of imported television programmes, one UNESCO study in 1972 found that 40 per cent of Latin America television broadcasts came from the US; Guatemala had an index of dependence on US television of 80 per cent.[1] Another focus was the ideological encodings of internationally distributed (mainly Western) media and advertising, and the importation of forms, models and practices derived from Western commercial media and advertising. In *How to Read Donald Duck: Imperialist Ideology in the Disney Comic*, Ariel Dorfman and Armand Mattelart (1975) argued that Disney texts promote Western capitalism, caricature and denigrate 'third world' cultures and consistently carry messages of how such people should aspire to live.

Cultural imperialism (CI) emerged in the context of the wider struggles crystallised in demands for a new world information and communication order, which arose against a background of decolonisation (Mattelart and Mattelart 1998: 137–38; Mosco 1996: 75–76). Pressure to remedy inequality in information and communication flows was an important but always relatively minor aspect of contestation over a new world economic order. These debates occurred in the 1970s when the so-called non-aligned states, including many newly formed nations, could exert pressure at a moment of heightened influence. The two Cold War superpowers, the US and the USSR, vied for their support while capitalist crises that followed in the wake of the OPEC oil price rise in 1973 shifted the bargaining power to resource-rich regions. The United Nations had been established as a for-mally inclusive body with voting equality between member nations. While largely deemed unworkable by US leaders, as the 'executive' powers of the Security Council remained locked in Cold War antagonists, the UN provided a platform and forum for debate. UNESCO began to promote the international circulation of media, the protection of journalists, and promotion of Article 19 of the UN Declaration of Human Rights (1948). By the 1970s the ranks of the UN had swelled as former colonies gained independence and many were unsurprisingly vocal in opposing Western efforts to retain or reimpose arrangements of dependency (Schiller 1996: 99). A UNESCO meeting of experts 1969 concluded:

> At the present time, communication takes place in one direction ... the image given of developing countries is often false, deformed, and what is more serious, this image is the one presented in these countries themselves. The participants in the Montreal meeting believe that the exchange of information and of other cultural products, particularly in developing countries, is in danger of modifying or displacing cultural values and of causing problems for the mutual understanding among nations.
>
> (cited in Mattelart 1994: 180)

Amidst broad-ranging concern about inequality in cultural flows from North to South and from core to periphery a key target was news and news agencies. According to Masmoudi (1979) five Western news agencies were responsible for 80 per cent of the world's news – only a quarter of which was about developing countries. At a UNESCO meeting in Montreal in 1976 the proposal for a New World Information and Communication Order (NWICO) was launched by non-aligned countries and in 1977 UNESCO established an International Commission for the study of communications problems. The Commission, backed by some hundred studies, papers and submissions, was presided over by Sean MacBride, a former Chief of Staff of the Irish Republican Army who went on to become an Irish Government Minister and human rights campaigner. The MacBride Commission report (1980) produced eighty-two recommendations for action set out under the following themes: strengthening independence and self-reliance; social consequences and new tasks; journalistic professional integrity and standards; democratising communication; and fostering international co-operation. It called for guaranteed pluralism, a more just world communication order, support for third world development, limits on the activities of transnational corporations, measures to tackle media concentration, better conditions for journalists, and democratisation of communications, including the abolition of censorship. It called for equal distribution of the electronic spectrum as well as national protection against cross-border satellite communications. The report was fiercely attacked by corporate media in their own news outlets, in publications (Righter 1978), and in lobbying, serving as a foretaste of the mobilisations carried out since by TNMCs such as Rupert Murdoch's News Corporation against politicians threatening their interests in Australia and Britain. The United States left UNESCO in 1984, unhappy at the turn of debate and maintaining its doctrine of 'free flow of information' which for its critics advanced free speech claims while buttressing the existing dominance in US exports and influence. Britain left too in 1985 but the exit of the US, UNESCO's major funder, was a significant blow and the body has not regained the same resources or influence since, even though the US rejoined in 2003 in time to intervene in debates on what became the Convention on the Protection and Promotion of the Diversity of Cultural Expressions (UNESCO 2005).

The MacBride report marked an end point; its conclusions were worthy but woolly and it failed to provide a guide for action in a hostile environment. The report 'failed to galvanize private and public sector participants into action to promote the massive investment ... needed' argue Mansell and Nordenstreng (2007), who draw parallels with the influence of civil society organisations in the World Summit on the Information Society 2003–5. Yet, there were some positive outcomes, notably regional initiatives to support cultural production and the expansion of the Inter Press Service news agency (originally founded in Argentina 1964) across Latin American and Africa.

The new world communication order sought by non-aligned countries of the South did not just fail because of Western neoliberalism. Third Worldism became discredited because of the practice of reactionary states. Contradictions were exposed between the authoritarian, statist demands to control communication inside national borders and pleas to democratise communications and deepen cultural diversity. Calls for a new world order were used as an alibi for failures of domestic action. Internal inequalities were exacerbated between elites welcoming new circuits of modernisation and large sections of society (Iran under the Shah; Kenya under Moi). Internal state attacks on popular culture (such as reggae and Rastafarianism in Jamaica) exposed contradictions, as did the high levels of internal political censorship, state repression and media control. There were ongoing efforts by some states to erect barriers to foreign media influence. The Soviet Union moved to block satellite transmissions. In 1996, the Taliban shut down Afghanistan's only TV station when it took control of Kabul, banning televisions, videocassette recorders and satellite dishes.

Cultural imperialism was invoked to support authoritarian controls in the developing world. 'Defence of Asian values and eastern essentialism against Western imperialism is even now a standard pretext used by conservatives and communists alike to legitimate illiberal controls against their own people' (Curran and Park 2000b: 5). NWICO, argues Miller et al. (2005: 76), offered an inadequate theorisation of capitalism, class relations and postcolonialism; it 'risked cloaking the interests of emergent bourgeoisies seeking to advance their own market power under the sign of national cultural self-determination, national capital over transnational capital' (Miller et al. 2005: 80).

The relationship between radical critics of cultural imperialism and these outcomes is an important but complex one. One key charge is that the CI thesis framed the problem as the erosion of authentic culture whereby 'culture is defined in national terms, within which it is reasonably integrated and homogeneous' (McKay 2004: 71). On the contrary, Dan Schiller, Herbert Schiller's son, argues, persuasively in my view, that the radical critics of cultural imperialism saw culture as in formation; far from assuming an affinity between statist and popular perspectives they saw the struggle for cultural self-determination as part of a struggle for revolutionary social change. In *Communication and Cultural Domination* (1976: 96), Herbert Schiller draws on Frantz Fanon's *The Wretched of the Earth* (1963) and Amilcar Cabral's writings to advocate a cultural revolution, not through nativist traditionalism but communications policy reform: 'National communications policy making is a generic term for the struggle against cultural and social domination in all its forms, old and new, exercised from within or outside the nation'. An appreciation of these tensions is certainly evident too in Herbert Schiller's (1976: 9) statement that:

> The concept of cultural imperialism today best describes the sum of the processes by which a society is brought into the modern world system and how its dominating stratum is attracted, pressured, forced, and sometimes bribed into shaping social institutions to correspond to, or even promote, the values and structures of the dominating centre of the system.

Yet, Dan Schiller also rightly acknowledges that the response to these contradictions was inadequate; faith in the triumph of popular communication was exposed as naïve.

Various critiques are bundled together as the 'cultural imperialism thesis' often to dispatch them more swiftly, but each needs to be assessed on its merits. One such is analysis of the links between the 'military-industrial complex' and the media, developed by Hans Enzenberger, Schiller and others, examining the growth of state-sponsored information and propaganda as part of wider military and covert operations to secure compliant states. As well as producing communications directly, the State–Military complex financed and participated in Hollywood production; President J.F. Kennedy instructed the US Information Agency to use film and television to propagandise, establishing funding for 226 film centres in 106 countries (Miller et al. 2005: 106–7). More contemporary links between Hollywood, Silicon Valley, the US military and government across information management and imagery are explored by Rampton and Stauber (2003). The various forms of US government support for the interests of TNMCs have also been examined, showing how film and other cultural exports were regarded as vital as key economic sectors, for their role in encouraging the consumption of other goods and services, and in contributing to 'soft power' (Nye 2005) promoting strategic and popular support for US-led global capitalism.

What is labelled the 'cultural imperialism thesis', was in reality a short-lived formulation which was criticised 'from within' by critical scholars such as Tunstall (1977) and Mattelart et al. (1984), within a revising tradition of critical political economy. Armand Mattelart argued for recognition of growing complexity in cultural flows (Mattelart et al. 1984: 22):

> One could easily continue to accumulate evidence of the dominant position of American firms. But in so doing we run the risk of enclosing ourselves within a condemnation without perspective.
>
> [...]
>
> For just a few illustrations will ... show that there are nuances to the map of global 'one-way traffic'.

Tunstall (1977: 40) both confirmed and challenged the CI thesis; focusing on TV exports, the 'television imperialism thesis ignores the much earlier pattern of the press and news agencies which quite unambiguously did have an imperial character'.

Cultural globalisation

Three kinds of criticism, in particular, informed what became the 'revisionist orthodoxy' of cultural globalisation theory in the 1990s and beyond (Curran 2002: 171). *Multiple flows*: the notion of predominantly 'one-way' flows from the West to the rest, was challenged by evidence that global flows were always but increasingly 'multidirectional' and so, it was argued, not reducible to a dependency model that conceived influence emanating from 'core' nations to 'peripheral' ones (Sreberny-Mohammadi 1996). *Media audiences*: the second main area of critique focused on the failure to analyse and appreciate audience reception and meaning making. While much can be said about media and cultural flows, the *implications* for those who consume them remained largely obscure. Early studies assumed that the transnationalisation of cultural production led to transnationalisation of reception (Madger 1993). In his nuanced critique, Thompson (1995: 171) argues that Herbert Schiller 'tries to infer, from an analysis of the social organization of the media industries, what the consequences of media messages are likely to be for the individuals who receive them'. Such inferences are speculative and 'disregard the complex, varied and contextually specific ways in which messages are interpreted by individuals and incorporated into their day-to-day lives'. Media consumers are active and creative in selecting and appropriating meanings, argued Liebes and Katz in their reception study of *Dallas*, the global TV export phenomenon of the 1970s (Gripsrud 1995). The affective as well as interpretative relationship of audiences had been neglected (Ang 1991). *Cultural domination*: the third main challenge concerned the notion of *imposition* of culture, usually conceived as Americanisation or Westernisation. By contrast, it was argued that cultural imports, whether products or ideas, are indigenised, hybridised and appropriated in various ways that transform their meaning (Tomlinson 1991). Where cultural imperialism had feared growing cultural homogenisation, it was now argued that more complex processes of differentiation were taking place. Insofar as there *was* a predominant flow of 'cultural discourse' from the West (or North) this should not be regarded as a form of domination but as a multiply directed transition to global modernities.

According to cultural globalisation theories, the global and transnational is eroding the national. Above all, this constitutes a shift from the dominance of national media, such as national broadcasting, to a new media order whereby '[a]udiovisual geographies are thus becoming detached from the symbolic spaces of national culture, and realigned on the basis of the more "universal" principles of international consumer culture' (Morley and Robins 1995: 11). For García Canclini (1995), migration and modernity have broadened cultural territory beyond the traditional nation-state. According to Thompson (1995: 175), 'As symbolic materials circulate on an ever-greater scale, locales become sites where, to an ever-increasing extent, globalized media products are received, interpreted and incorporated into the daily lives of individuals'.

Beyond cultural imperialism and cultural globalisation

Globalisation theory challenged and helped to discredit the cultural imperialism thesis. In place of what were regarded as crude domination theories, cultural globalisation emphasised popular agency, yet downplayed the problems of power, inequality and imposition that gave rise to the original CI thesis. There are ongoing efforts to move beyond the limitations of both paradigms and to integrate cultural theory into critical media scholarship more effectively. We will examine these perspectives below but first it is helpful to identify some key responses from critical political economy and key areas of divisions.

Imbalances in cultural flows

That cultural flows are diverse and multidirectional is uncontested; what is challenged is the claim that significant imbalances no longer remain as problems to tackle. While US cultural hegemony is declining, the US remains the world's leading exporter of audiovisual content. There was a fivefold increase in US film and TV exports between 1992 and 2004, largely serving the massive expansion of private TV channels worldwide. There are contra-flows, 'subaltern' flows such as films from the global South and East. There is increasing global circulation of products from a much wider range of creative hubs such as Mumbai challenging US cultural hegemony, yet no cultural exports match the global reach and influence of US-led Western media, which represent the dominant media flows.

Western TNMCs have regionalised and localised their content, with many Southern media organisations involved in this production and cultural glocalisation. Against tendencies to valorise the rise of non-Western media, Thussu (2007: 11) cautions this 'may reflect a refiguring of hegemony in more complex ways'. A 'global popular' is being created with 'media content and services being tailored to specific cultural consumers not so much because of any particular regard for national cultures but as a commercial imperative' (Thussu 2007: 21). Much of the contra-flow highlighted in accounts of increased cultural diversity is commercial and interlocks into a global corporate system. The diversity of multiple flows advanced within cultural globalisation masks the global extension of a commercial system. This does not produce homogenisation of cultural output; commercial dynamics respond to a diversity of local tastes and interests. However, it does mean that there is sameness arising from the commercial dynamics towards privileging entertainment and other content that does not mount sustained challenges to governing interests and values.

The neglect of economic power

Cultural globalisation theory conceives globalisation as a decentred process. In doing so it '[f]ails to capture the agency of large profit making corporations in affecting, but not completely determining the new cultural world order' (Hesmondhalgh 2007: 238). It reflects what Curran describes as a 'blind spot' in cultural globalisation theory, a reluctance to critically address economic power (Curran 2002: 174). Instead we must begin with an analysis of corporate capitalism.

The critical discourse of cultural imperialism has been challenged for its inadequate account of *cultural processes* (how culture makes us, individually and collectively, and how we make use of culture). Its continuing relevance is in foregrounding questions of inequalities in the distribution of cultural resources and the organisation of cultural markets. It is primarily concerned with *cultural resources*: who has access to the resources to produce, circulate, consume and use cultural forms (Hardy 2008)? Yet, cultural imperialism has always been an 'evocative metaphor' (Sreberny-Mohammadi 1997: 49) rather than a distinct analytical concept and cumulative critiques have prompted efforts to revise and reformulate the problem.

From American cultural imperialism to transnational corporate domination

Throughout the twentieth century, especially after Europe was ravaged by two world wars, American industries grew to become the dominant cultural exporters. The variety of factors explaining American cultural dominance makes the case for a synthesis of strictly political economic and broader cultural explanations. We must account for both the push and pull of American culture (Gitlin 2002; Morley and Robins 1995), for the influences that honed cultural forms and formats valued by audiences worldwide (Tunstall 1977). American popular culture has become the 'central bank of international mythologies, circulating two major dreams: the dream of freedom and the dream of wealth' (Gitlin 2002: 22–23). Key political economic factors have been the size and wealth of the domestic market in the US, allowing products to be sold to other markets at lower prices. In the 1980s the cost of acquiring one hour of *Dallas* would pay for approximately one minute of original Danish drama production (Gitlin 2002: 25). Economic resources also helped to create the formats, production values that cultivated audience tastes and expectations.

Another key factor was the active role of the US state in promoting its cultural industries abroad (Hesmondhalgh 2013: 271–72). Yet the notion of American cultural exports has always been vulnerable on empirical and theoretical grounds. What is 'American' about them? For some critics of domination theories, part of the attraction of US productions is that they are oriented to appeal to a culturally rich and diverse audience at home, qualities that help explain their wider global appeal (Hoskins et al. 2004). Large-scale film and television productions engage international teams of cultural workers so that locating 'Americanness' is problematic. In response, for Schiller (1996), the critical charge is not the export of American culture but 'transnational corporate cultural domination'. An essentialist notion of 'Americanisation' has been replaced by an emphasis on the reach and influence of commercially driven transnational corporations.

Radical accounts such as Herman and McChesney (1997) examine 'a world communication order led by transnational businesses and supported by their respective national states, increasingly linked in continental and global structures' Thussu (2006: 64). This is not an Americanisation thesis; McChesney (2002: 157) writes, 'the notion that media are merely purveyors of US culture is ever less plausible as the media system becomes increasingly concentrated, commercialised and globalised'. Instead, the global system is better understood as 'advancing corporate and commercial interests and values and denigrating or ignoring that which cannot be incorporated into its mission' (McChesney 2002: 157). Globa-lisation here is largely conceived as a process driven 'from above', by the activ-ities of transnational communication conglomerates supported by neoliberal states and supranational institutions such as the WTO and the EC. Herman and McChesney (1997: 9):

> regard the primary effect of the globalization process … to be the implan-tation of the commercial model of communication, its extension to broad-casting and the 'new media,' and its gradual intensification under the force of competition and bottom-line pressures.

The focus is on the nature and influence of corporate transnationalisation and links to commercialisation of culture. Commercialisation of media systems around the world has created new private networks that are primarily interested in markets and advertising revenues. There is cultural critique here but it is not founded on essentialising American culture but on arguing that there are values promoted within a system driven by profits from sales and commercial advertising. Yet such reformulations do not entirely evade problems of cultural definition. For Thompson (1995: 169), Schiller's 'transnational corporate cultural domination' 'still presents too uniform a view of American media culture (albeit a culture which is no longer exclusively at the disposal of American capital) and of its global dominance'.

Measuring exports does not resolve the problems. Transnational co-production, co-ownership, as well as 'translation, franchising, reversioning, and piracy' make the task of distinguishing the originating sources, much less linking these to 'national' cultural characteristics, increasingly difficult (Tunstall 2008: 251). Other analysts highlight the complexity and contradictions within cultural texts. As Mirrlees (2013) shows, *Avatar* can be read as engaging counter-hegemonic discourses as well as hegemonic ones of imperialism and orientalism. *Avatar* is a form of global popular culture whose transnational creative production, mainly across the US and New Zealand, problematises national cultural frames, as do the diverse interpretations of the film including the appropriation of the Na'vi as symbols of the people and groups oppressed by neoliberalism and militarism worldwide. Produced by News Corporation, *Avatar* became the highest grossing film of all time, the top selling cinema release in China and with some 70 per cent of revenue generated outside the United States. Critical political economy rightly highlights the structural imbalances in cultural flows and points to detrimental consequences, but this must be allied to analysis of the influences shaping specific cultural production, circulation and reception, and considerations of the ideological boundaries and polyvalency of texts.

Another set of problems concerning 'transnational corporate domination' concerns the articulation of relationships between capitalist enterprises, states and imperialism. Boyd-Barrett advocates a 'reformulation' of media imperialism, replacing the international, territorially based concept of imperialism with one of 'colonization of communications space', the latter taking greater account of the increasing hybridity of media systems (Boyd-Barrett 1998: 167). McPhail (2006) proposes electronic colonialism. Yet such reformulations are challenged for their conflation of economic, cultural and political power. For Pieterse (2004: 34) the idea of 'corporate imperialism' 'is a step too far and a contradiction in terms, for it implies non-state actors undertaking principally political (not just economic) projects'. This is certainly not to argue that corporations do not support political regimes or 'projects', or that political power is not used instrumentally to further corporate interests. Rather, different kinds of power and agency, while interlocking, still need to be distinguished analytically. Most transnational corporations, Pieterse argues (2004: 34) 'can achieve their objectives without control over sovereignty; economic influence of the type provided by the IMF, World Bank, and WTO regulations suffices, along with lobbying and sponsoring political actors'. This debate raises an important set of issues addressed in theories of imperialism, capitalism and empire. Harvey's concept of 'capitalist imperialism' serves as a rejoinder to Pieterse. Capitalist imperialism refers to a shared system of capital accumulation and power that aims to create worldwide conditions favourable for 'economic power to flow across and through continuous space' (Harvey 2003: 26).

As we have seen, in some Marxist accounts the state is regarded as an agent for capitalism. In crude versions imperialism is undertaken by the state on behalf of capital to meet its expansionist needs and to overcome crises of accumulation. However, most critical theorists advance a more complex account. One entry point is historical analysis. The pursuit of state interests through territorial imperialism and the advancements of capitalist economic interests took multiple forms. For instance, the Dutch East India Company ruled territories in Java with its own apparatus of sovereignty. Winseck and Pike (2008) show that state and private agencies were complexly interlocked in providing the telegraphic cable networks on which imperialism depended. Global media evolved as part of a project of creating a worldwide system of accumulation and modernisation, they argue. Yet, if imperialism contributed to capital's survival and expansion, it also conflicted with capital; 'imperialism created and reinforced rigid boundaries among the various global spaces that blocked the free flow of capital, labor and goods precluding the full realization of the world market' (Hardt and Negri 2000: 305). The second entry point is theoretical elaboration based on analytical distinctions between economic and political processes and actors. As Jessop (2008) argues, there is no determinate relationship between processes of accumulation, institutional orders and forms of consciousness. Capitalist dynamics of the profit-oriented, market-mediated process of accumulation may be supported by different forms of state and supranational governance. Capital accumulation depends upon extra-economic factors and so cannot be regarded as the cause of these.

Capitalist development

To understand fully the problems of global cultural exchange requires an understanding of the development and management of capitalism. A key process has been capital becoming freer of controls exercised by states and state systems. The organisation of economic life around nation-states emerged gradually but was the dominant form by the time of the First World War and the Russian Revolution. In the period from around 1870 to 1914 businesses in advanced economies were subject to increased state oversight. Capital mobility was restricted by imperial networks and trade protectionism, while industrial production tended to be organised territorially under state jurisdiction. Increased public scrutiny with the rise of electoral democracy and public criticisms of 'irresponsible' capitalism also contributed to efforts to make businesses more publicly accountable and regulated (Curran 2002: 175). The period from the 1940s to the 1970s saw further attempts to ameliorate the excesses of capitalism responding to the scarring crises of global depression in the 1930s and the unresolved crises of imperialist expansionism that had led to a second world war.

Western European social democracies sought to secure welfare states, by supporting macroeconomic intervention including state-run industries to provide 'full employment', social and health provision for all. In advanced capitalist economies the period from the 1950s to the early 1970s had been marked by economic growth and rising living standards. Western liberal democracies established welfare systems providing unemployment and other benefits, free or heavily subsidised healthcare and state pensions. Such policies drew on the organised strength of the labour movement and the support of the industrial working class. Europe had fascist and authoritarian states during this period but in democratic systems even mainstream conservative parties, such as the Christian Democrats, supported key tenets of welfare state provision. Demand for labour-saving consumer electronic goods helped to create a 'golden age' for Western capitalism in the 1950s and 1960s, as well as fuel the expansion of East Asian economies.

A global financial regulatory system was established following the Bretton Woods reforms of 1944–46. This organised an international system to manage cross-border capital flows, fix exchange rates (to the dollar standard), gradually reduce protectionism by removing trade tariffs, and make credit available to countries facing economic difficulty. This system of global governance was organised primarily through national governments. The influence of sovereign states was highly unequal, but the system 'enabled the governments of developed economies to give precedence to employment and social welfare over those of global financial interests' (Curran 2002: 176). From the late 1960s this system was strained and gradually undermined. In what Brenner (1998) calls the 'long downturn', the advanced capitalist economies suffered a series of shocks, such as the OPEC oil price rise of 1973, and severe recessions, in 1974–75, 1979–82 and 1991–95. Profit rates fell across all sectors but especially in manufacturing, causing waves of unemployment. Growing competition to US manufacturing output from Germany, Japan and the newly industrialised 'tiger' economies in East Asia, led to a crisis of overproduction in the automobile and other industries.

Capitalist states responded by attacking the labour movement with states and private businesses reducing pay levels for the majority of workers, although wage cuts and increased labour productivity proved insufficient to sustain growth (Harvey 2011). At a domestic level this encouraged a shift away from forms of state intervention that had prevailed since the 1950s. Keynesian policies to maintain growth through state spending failed in recessionary conditions and were repudiated by an increasingly assertive 'new right', who advocated deep cuts in public spending. Within international financial governance, the fixed exchange rate system was abandoned in 1971–73, capital controls were relaxed or abandoned amongst OECD countries in the 1980s and 1990s, financial deregulation increased in the European Union and in other 'free trade' areas. Where the earlier settlement had broadly reflected the strengths of social democracy in curbing market liberals, the latter regained their ascendency with the rise of a neoliberal agenda. During the 1970s multinational corporations expanded their size and operations. Increasingly able to relocate production, operations and finance they gained leverage over governments forced to compete for their patronage under terms that favoured transnational capital at the expense of labour and frequently of national capital too.

In the 1980s and 1990s the financialisation of capitalism increased with the growth in private banking, currency and derivative trading (including by multinational corporations). International transactions were facilitated by new technology, notably satellite and fibre optic cable communications and computing. Market pressures and government liberalisation produced an increasingly unregulated flow of capital between countries on an unprecedented scale. The main features have been a weakening of state-centred economic sovereignty, and the emergence and consolidation of a neoliberal global order formed from the second half of the 1980s. The transformation to a neoliberal governance system was precipitated by the collapse of bureaucratic party-states in the communist East. The welfare states in the capitalist West were weakened. Post-war settlements based on institutionalised compromise between capital and labour shifted to neoliberal economic policies based on liberalisation, deregulation, privatisation, market proxies in the residual public sector, internationalisation and reduced direct taxation – a set of policies intended to alter the balance of forces in favour of capital. The international financial and trading system was reshaped. The implications for media and cultural policy are examined further in the next chapter.

Since the ascendency of neoliberalism in the 1990s and 2000s there have been a series of crises in global capitalism, with a major global recession in 2007–8. As the rise of the so-called BRIC countries (Brazil, Russia, India and China) illustrates, some economies have been relatively insulated from or aided by crises affecting the older advanced economies. China was insulated from the crises afflicting Western capital in the 1970s and grew its economy in the 1990s with China's telecommunications market, the world's largest, developed by national capital and the party-state (D. Schiller 2007: 180, 177–97). US hegemony, including cultural hegemony, has been weakened, although the US remains the world's geopolitical superpower (Tunstall 2008).

The consequence of the global reorganisation of capital has been a significant net loss for democratic governance. The consequence of an adverse reaction from financial markets has disciplined governments into maintaining a raft of policies favoured by private capital interests from privatisation and deregulation, cuts to welfare programmes and tax cuts for corporations and wealthy individuals. Multinational corporations have used diverse means to extract market-friendly policies from huge investment in lobbying to regulatory and industrial arbitrage. The second main consequence has been to strengthen capital and weaken labour.

Globalisation, states and culture

Informing the clash between cultural globalisation enthusiasts and radical political economy's critique of neoliberal ascendancy are differences in conceiving the state.

Where both agree that the powers of the nation-state are being eroded, the cultural globalisation literature associates the nation with 'invented tradition, manipulative ideology, hierarchical control, intolerance, conformism and nationalism' (Curran 2002: 178). Globalisation is thus seen as a largely emancipatory force allowing new identities and solidarities to be forged that enable a new progressive politics to come into being. Global capitalism is viewed as an enabling force for cultural pluralisation.

A central concern in radical analysis is the weakening of democratic controls and oversight as a consequence of power shifting from national electorates and organised labour to global capital. Within CPE there are strong anti-statist, libertarian and anti-nationalist strands, but most share a general conception of the democratic state as a key agency in the realisation of social and economic objectives. More narrowly, the state remains the principal agency in communications policy and central to prospects for greater democratic oversight of media and cultural provision. The internationalisation of communications systems and ownership makes it more, not less, imperative to assess how states use their actual powers of imperium (law and regulation) and dominium (use of resources, subsidies and support mechanisms) over communications and cultural activities.

Morris and Waisbord (2001) argue that it is premature to conclude that the state is withering away and to assume a post-state world. States remain fundamental political units retaining significant law-making powers. Globalisation has challenged but not eliminated states as power centres, as sets of institutions where decisions are made regarding the structure and functioning of media systems. For Mattelart (2002: 609):

> [the nation-state] remains the place where the social contract is defined. It has by no means reached the degree of obsolescence suggested by the crusade in favour of deterritorialization through networks. It takes the nearsightedness of techno-libertarians to support this kind of globalizing populism, which avails itself of the simplistic idea of a somewhat abstract and evil state in opposition to that of an idealized civil society – an area of free exchange between fully sovereign individuals

Rather, a task for organised civil society is 'to ensure that the state is not robbed of its regulatory function' (Mattelart 2002: 609). Cultural (globalisation) theory addresses media processes, and theorising about and beyond ethnocentric frameworks, but has tended to neglect national organisation of communications, to overstate the decline of the nation-state and to ignore the political economic dynamics of 'globalization'.

Media internationalisation

Two radically different perspectives, transnational corporate domination and cultural globalisation, agree that transnational media are eroding national media. The first is critical, neo-Marxist, and highlights imbalances in the global flow of communications output. The second, cultural globalisation, focuses on reception and cultural identity formation and generally regards transnationalisation more favourably (in some cases akin to the modernisation paradigm). Yet, both tend towards a one-way unilinear model of change. Both 'strong globalisation' arguments tend to focus on processes eroding state-based media from above. An alternative perspective argues instead that we need to be more discriminating in assessing the nature and influence of transnational media flows. This might be called 'weak globalisation' but that is misleading since the argument does not revolve around the strength or weakness of global forces but rather on the need to attend to how these are manifested differentially within and across media systems. The objection is not to evidence of 'strong globalisation' but rather to its generalisation and organisation into normative narratives of change. A better term is internationalisation (Hesmondhalgh 2013).

Media internationalisation is pervasive but uneven. Globalisation is transforming 'media fiction and music' (Curran 2002: 179) while production and consumption (as opposed to gathering) of news remains largely organised around the nation-state and locality. The audience for global news channels such as CNN remains small and, with exceptions such as Al Jazeera, has remained predominantly elite. While terrestrial broadcasters' audience share has certainly eroded, this 'has not to any significant extent been caused by the rise of a global news service taking viewers for their national products as part of the growth of a global public sphere' (Sparks 2000a: 84). Cross-border press readership is mostly small and elite (Hafez 2007), with the important exception of minority ethnic and diasporic press readerships. Local media ownership tends to be relatively independent of the global media operators described by Herman and McChesney (Sparks 2000a: 86) and the overwhelming majority of news outlets target national or sub-national audiences. The main categories of multi-region media globalisation are:

- mass market entertainment including audiovisual, audio, computer games, music
- news and information serving business elites (CNN, Wall Street Journal, etc.)
- media serving diasporic communities
- media serving specialist transnational communities of interest
- subaltern media flows especially in news (i.e. Al Jazeera) but also in Third Cinema and other contra-flows.

To analyse these complex flows requires attention to all the factors shaping market supply and demand, which means political economic and cultural elements.

The analysis of television provision and cultural proximity is a good example of the need to integrate the two. Across Western media systems, US premium fiction commands the greatest share of imports, but the maturation of commercial networks in Western Europe 'has dented the appeal of US fiction as audiences demonstrate liking for home-grown programming' (Iosifides et al. 2005: 6). Audiences around the world prefer to watch their own locally made programmes in their own national language (Tunstall 2008). This preference for 'cultural proximity' is an important corrective to 'strong globalisation' theories, although the pattern varies. As Straubhaar (2002: 200) argues 'National cultures vary in their appeal to domestic audiences, although this tends to be a crucial local advantage. National media's ability to compete with foreign imports varies depending on homogeneity and acceptance of local culture'. Cultural proximity also provides another dimension of localisation. Producer behaviour 'follows commercial imperatives but will tend to follow the demands of the domestic market or audience when resources allow' (Straubhaar 2002: 200).

Flows, formats, production and labour

The importance of integrating political economic and cultural analysis is especially evident in tracing contemporary features of media globalisation, notably the cultural and economic dimensions of formats and the internationalisation of cultural labour. In fact, early academic formulations of cultural imperialism were attentive to the diversity of such flows, even if these were conceived within a restricted conception of interstate relations. In his 'generic' concept of media imperialism Boyd-Barrett (1977: 120) identified transnational flows as taking four main forms:

1 the shape of the communication vehicle
2 a set of industrial arrangements
3 a body of values
4 specific media contents.

Dissemination ranged from hardware and content to professional values as well as domination of international news reporting by Western agencies. Later scholars extended analysis of the range of cultural flows, encompassing language, religion, education and travel (Sreberny-Mohammadi 1996), and acknowledging media as only one part of broader cultural interconnectedness (Held et al. 1999). Above all, multidirectionality came to be emphasised, and by the late 1990s at least was confirmed by the growing media influence and 'software' exports of East Asia (Japan, South Korea), Latin America (especially Brazil and Mexico), Australia, India and China (Tunstall 2008).

The transnationalisation of media production has long been a focus for CPE scholars but more recent work has brought renewed attention to labour. The spatial mobility of capital has been enhanced, weakening state power and weakening the power of organised labour. Capital has shifted from regarding developing countries as suppliers of raw materials to treating them as setting the price of labour. Developing countries, regions and 'free trade zones' within states compete to attract capital investment. Shifts in bargaining and power relations between capital and labour have been facilitated by transportation and ICTs. Miller et al. (2005) propose a New International Division of Cultural Labour, adapted from the concept of a New International Division of Labour (NIDL). They examine how Hollywood has reorganised production to take advantage of labour costs and resource efficiencies. Hollywood's proportion of productions shot overseas increased from 7 to 27 per cent in the decade to 2000 (Miller et al. 2005: 137). Production is disaggregated across space, and labour is organised across a world centre (Hollywood), intermediate zones (Western Europe, North America, Australia) with outlying regions of labour subordinate to the centre (the rest of the world).

There is a diminishing need for co-location of aspects of production and post-production. So firms can take advantage of lower studio costs in Eastern Europe and Mexico, high tech but lower costs post-production in India, tax incentives in Europe, and so on. The result has been to depress labour costs and unevenly deskill workers, whilst boosting jobs in lower-wage economies. The development of digital technologies and global transportation are factors, but Miller et al. (2005: 131) highlight corporate efforts to weaken organised labour and boost capital accumulation; 'Hollywood's hegemony is built upon and sustained by the internal suppression of worker rights, the exploitation of a global division of labour and the impact of colonialism on language'. The international division of cultural labour depends on a range of factors determining capital outlay including favourable exchange rates and tax regimes, the weakness of organised labour, specialist skills requirements, through which Hollywood investors seek to minimise costs and maximise revenue in the organisation of film production, manufacturing and services distributed around the globe. This approach engages a 'political and ethical regard for labour and its alienation into a model of citizens and consumers that allows us to question the role of states and markets in extending or stemming global Hollywood' (Miller et al. 2005: 350–51). It also contributes to necessary synthesising of political economic and culturalist studies. By examining the 'global infrastructure of textual exchange', the authors invite examination of the kinds of texts that get produced and circulate, the patterns of (unequal) exchange, and their consequences.

Formats

The importance of integrating political economic and cultural analysis is also illustrated by formats. To understand the growing market in formats we need to examine the capital accumulation logics, the relationships between capitalist (and PSM) firms, the trading and management of intellectual property rights as well as the drives to various forms of localisation, adaption and cultural hybridisation. While the US remains the world's leading exporter of audiovisual programmes, the UK has become the leading exporter of TV formats. In 2004 the UK exported sixty-four formats, France fifty-six, Germany fifty, the US forty-six and the Netherlands forty-six (Ofcom 2006: 118). The format for *Who Wants to be a*

Millionaire? has been sold to at least 106 countries, and the *Pop Idol* format has been shown in countries as diverse as Iceland, Kazakhstan and Lebanon. France earned ECU108 million ($136 million) in 2004 with worldwide sales of its animation series *Totally Spies*, including to Time Warner's Cartoon Network, as well as documentaries and dramas.

Yo Soy Betty, la Fea, a television show developed by a private channel in Colombia RCN in 1999 and later also aired on Telemundo (one of the largest Spanish-language American television networks) was licensed as a format worldwide, including as *Ugly Betty* in the US. It was adapted by Sony for India, where the show became hugely popular, with over twenty worldwide adaptions including in Russia, Germany, Israel and Egypt, blending elements of the Latin American telenovela, the US soap and localised features. The story of Betty, rooted in the Ugly Duckling and other fairytales, had wide cultural appeal and adaptability but also held appeal for businesses as a vehicle for brand promotion. In China, Betty returned to her original work-setting of an advertising agency, rather than magazines as in the US version, providing an ideal vehicle for brand integration. Dove (skin care products) were brand partners for a fifty minute episode in the first series in China in which Betty works on a pitch for the Dove account.[2]

As Arsenault and Castells (2008: 708) observe: 'local and regional players are actively importing and/or re-appropriating foreign products and formats while corporate transnational media organizations are pursuing local partners to deliver customized content to audiences'. Transcultural adaptions are creating hybrid formats – rooted in local markets in which audiences have knowledge and expectations of different genres, visual and narrative styles. With format licensing amongst other transactions we see national firms 'eagerly and actively enter into strategic alliances with TNMCs to serve their local profit interests. Media imperialism, which assumes the coercive domination of one national media industry by another, is not the appropriate way to describe the global-local relationship between TNMCs and NMCs' (Mirrlees 2013: 101).

Conclusions

Cultural imperialism was too crude and vulnerable both to critique and to geo-political and cultural changes. However, the orthodoxy of cultural globalisation that supplanted it failed to address economic power and the detrimental influence of global capital on cultural diversity, labour and democracy. What is needed? Put simply, attention to economics, politics and culture. There is no need to privilege economics or overstate its explanatory value in understanding cultural texts, processes and reading. Yet efforts to explain media internationalisation without adequate regard for economic and political aspects are non-starters and should be challenged just as relentlessly as the caricature of cultural imperialism chased off the stage by neo-modernisation theories. The rejection of 'crude' domination theories gave way to a reluctance or refusal to acknowledge power imbalances in cultural flows that had inspired the original critique. There is much to be done to make up deficiencies but synthesis of political economy and critical cultural analysis demonstrates ways forward.

Notes

1 Access to television schedules worldwide, for instance via www.tvguide.com, offers a useful tool for carrying out similar research today.
2 In the US the first series, shown on ABC in 2006–7, won a Golden Globe award but over four series audiences fell and in 2010 ABC announced it was ceasing production.

Chapter 8

Media convergence and communications regulation

Introduction

This chapter offers an overview of changes in communications regulation and examines national variations and transnational influences in selected policy areas to ask: How is media policy being reshaped in the context of globalisation and internationalisation? Has the national level of media regulation diminished in scope, relevance and influence? The political economy tradition examines how media and communications are organised and in doing so pays particular regard to regulations and governance. Communications policy analysis has always been a core focus for critical political economists, such that the two have sometimes been regarded as almost synonymous. CPE's attention to and analysis of regulation is also in stark contrast to the neglect or limited conceptualisation of regulation across media and cultural studies. This chapter outlines critical issues in communications policy-making, reviews alternative perspectives on policy analysis, and explores connections between radical scholarship and media policy activism.

Why policy matters

Critical concerns with policy are rooted in claims to communication rights derived from democratic theories of communication. The right to communication adheres not only to providers (privileged in liberal press theory) but also to recipients and users. Communications are integral to modern life and to the circulation of ideas and opinions required for democratic participation, and the information and imagery required for human flourishing and freedom. It follows that the outcome of policy decisions affecting how communications resources and services are organised are immensely important. Media policy analysis considers how, why and in whose interests governments, public agencies, and others, act or fail to act, and how others interact with such decision-making and its repercussions. Governments engage in media policy in three main ways: through creating laws (legislation), applying rules directly or through agencies (regulation), or by using grants or subsidies to assist media provision.

If policy matters to CPE because of outcomes, analysts have also been concerned to examine how policy-making processes influence those outcomes. In
liberal democratic systems, policy-making is legitimised by its relative openness
to the widest range of interested parties and their ability to inform decisions and
influence outcomes. For CPE scholars, policy is political action marked by conflict. Policy-making is a process in which different political positions fight for
'material advantages ... and for ideological legitimation' whereby certain ideas
are normalised and others problematised (Freedman 2008: 3).

Defining the terms of debate within media policy has been central to the
contest for power to implement and legitimate change. Recognising this, critical
scholars have given greater attention to discursive power and ordering. They
have also given particular attention to the way power is ordered within policy
networks and their links to broader social formations, sometimes adopting a neo-
Gramscian perspective. Analytically this draws attention to the ways in which the
policy process is ordered, and the structured inequality of access and influence
that tends to be downplayed in liberal-pluralist accounts. Liberal pluralism relies
on claims that media policy-making is open to and influenced by a range of
interests within society none of which are systematically dominant – if not some
other account (such as elite domination) must be invoked. Yet, CPE accounts
have been rightly criticised for adopting limited, mechanistic, instrumentalist or
conspiracy theories, and so more synthesising perspectives are required.

Neoliberalism in communications policies

Neoliberalism (see chapter three) has been the dominant (ideological) force in
media policy since the 1980s in most advanced economies although it has also
been contested, resulting in more mixed, diverse and less predictable policy
outcomes. It has also been rejected in various 'post-neoliberal' systems, such as
the left/populist democracies in South America (Bolivia, Venezuela, Argentina,
Ecuador). For media, neoliberals have espoused the dismantling of public subsidies
and market interventions, such as public service media, and advocated relaxation
of regulations on media ownership and content as barriers to a functioning
market. The guiding principles of neoliberalism are the substitution of market
mechanisms for statist interventions. This has certainly provided ideological
support for processes of marketisation that have shifted media resources and
controls from public to private. Yet a key focus for CPE analysts has been to
challenge the ideological framing of neoliberalism in order to highlight contradictions, anomalies and the highly selective manner in which state intervention is
repudiated. One focus, already examined, concerns selectivity towards market
competition. Since policy influences, and sometimes determines, the conditions
for market entry and exit, this is one source of contradiction when firms
espousing liberalisation of regulation also seek to uphold incumbency rights and
regulatory barriers to competitors. US scholars have challenged the premise that
the state should not be involved in free enterprise by highlighting the extent to

which states are always and already involved. The issue then is not state vs. market – but what kinds of state policy interventions are made and on whose behalf.

Neoliberalism was promoted not merely for domestic governance but to challenge protectionism by foreign states that prevented TNC expansions and efficiencies. Here, CPE scholars highlighted the contradictions between the neoliberal path espoused for others and the massive state support and subsidies that had contributed to successful cultural industries, such as the US film industry. In contrast to free trade rhetoric, in the US, France, Germany, Japan, Korea and China, 'each story of successful industrialisation follows the same path: state subsidy, import taxation, high regulation, welfare protection. Then there was liberalisation, the results of which remain as yet unclear' (Miller et al. 2005: 109).

The starting point for a political economy of communication, argues McChesney (2003: 28) 'is the recognition that all media systems are the direct and indirect result of explicit public policies'. Marketisation, the opening up of space for private enterprise, is not the result of autonomous, 'natural' free markets or the logical outcome of converging technologies, but is constructed by the decisions (or non-decisions) of public authorities. This does not mean that we should substitute one simple model of causality for another; the processes of media change are multicausal and invariably multidirectional. It means that to understand the organisation of communication resources requires understanding the efforts to shape and contest public policy, across supranational, national and sub-national levels. Over the last twenty-five years, the dominant tendency has been the worldwide pursuit of marketisation (chapter three), a term used to describe a shift in governing values that privileges and promotes freedom of action for private businesses and market mechanisms over state regulation and public provision.

Media ownership

Nation-states have adopted anti-monopoly controls to prevent undue concentration in media markets, rules on cross-media ownership (usually across print, radio and television) and rules governing what persons or bodies may own media. From the 1980s national media ownership rules have been relaxed across all advanced economies and most developing countries. By the 1990s it was clear that convergence processes challenged various existing regulatory arrangements and divisions, which would have to be renegotiated. Corporate interests, while by no means unified, formed powerful lobbies advocating relaxation of ownership rules. Governments advanced a variety of arguments led by the claim that digital abundance is overcoming scarcity, so that market mechanisms will ensure diversity of supply without the need for structural intervention (Hardy 2008: 145–52; Doyle 2002a).

Liberalisation has been powerfully advocated but there are also tensions and fault lines. Policy-makers have promoted liberalisation on behalf of increased market competition yet also endorsed corporate consolidation. European Union policy in the 1990s endorsed the case for relaxing ownership rules to enable private firms to grow to generate the resources required to deliver the 'global information infrastructure' required for the information society. This, it was argued, would sustain large firms capable of competing with foreign (principally US) cultural producers. This links to another tension, between market liberalisation and policies to protect 'national champions'. When the UK government removed restrictions on non-EEA ownership in the 2003 Communications Act it favoured market liberal principles over national protection, influenced by arguments that foreign ownership and investments were required to revitalise the creative industries sector. In the UK (Hardy 2012b) and elsewhere there have been policy tensions between the promotion of global competitiveness (corporate growth) and local competitiveness (plurality in services) and, more fundamentally, between market-based and citizen-based models of empowerment and accountability. There are contradictions between projections of self-correcting markets realising digital plenitude and the persistence of problems of media concentration and market control.

There has been a wave of liberalisation. Yet, across a variegated landscape of ownership regulations, two prominent features stand out. First, most states retain at least some rules on media ownership. To explain this we need to consider the importance for states of not relinquishing important levels of control at national (or sub-national) levels, the economic, cultural and political significance of media ownership policy, and the strength of contending forces influencing policy. Media ownership continues to be one of the most sensitive issues in media regulation and a principal means to influence the operations of private media firms in markets. The second prominent feature is a shift from media-specific rules to general competition regulation. The latter has been regarded as more flexible in adapting to rapid changes in media markets, whereas specific rules on cross-ownership have been regarded as rigid, prone to obsolescence and increasingly difficult to enforce. This also represents a broader shift from qualitative judgement to precise economic measurement and legal processes that ensure regulation is more predictable, transparent and consistent for market actors. Within the European Union, competition regulation also developed in the gap created when various efforts to establish and harmonise media ownership rules across the community foundered.

When News Corporation sought total ownership of BSkyB in 2010 it persued and obtained approval on competition grounds from the European Commission, although the Commission (2010) reaffirmed that, under Article 21 of the EU Merger Regulation, the United Kingdom 'remains free to decide whether or not to take appropriate measures to protect its legitimate interest in media plurality'.

As many commentators, including the Commission, acknowledge, the provisions of competition policy address market dominance and cannot grasp the more complex operations of cultural or symbolic power which regulation of media pluralism has traditionally sought to address. The EU lacks rules on media ownership and pluralism following the failure of efforts in the 1990s (Harcourt 2005) and modest initiatives to monitor and examine concentrations since then. In 2012–13 media reform groups, academics and media from nine European member states launched a European citizens' initiative on media pluralism, using the EC petition mechanism to demand action by European institutions to safeguard the right for independent and pluralistic media.

In Western media systems policy-makers have favoured the convergence, consolidation and integration of communication companies. Cross-ownership and integration has become an increasingly accepted norm despite opposition from civil society groups, some political actors and bodies such as the Council of Europe. Processes of digitalisation and technological convergence, while complex and uneven, have undoubtedly influenced the weakening of sectoral regulation and of command and control measures (such as entry control) which have underpinned broadcasting regulation. Technological change, it is argued, has undermined the rationale (scarcity, market failure), desirability and capacity of sectoral regulation, in particular content regulation. The locus of communications policy is shifting from traditional to convergent media and to the broader areas of information and digital communications policy. This involves a host of critical issues for researchers amongst which are data protection, privacy, Internet content controls and censorship, Big Data and the implications of copyright, digital rights management and other intellectual property rules.

Internationalisation of communications policy

The internationalisation of communications policy in its modern form may be traced to the co-ordination of global telegraphy networks established by the colonial powers and the US in the nineteenth century. Yet from the early years of radio, policy actors and debate focused on mass communications, organised mainly within national boundaries. Regulatory power was distributed among governments and parliaments, regulatory agencies and the judiciary, with varying levels of influence and accommodation for businesses, political parties and organised civil society groups. Through the twentieth century, cultural regulation of broadcasting was a matter of national sovereignty, even though the allocation of radio spectrum was and remains a matter requiring international co-operation to minimise interference and 'spill over' effects. From the 1970s, however, internationalisation of telephony (beyond international connectivity of mainly monopoly national services) and broadcasting was accompanied by a shift towards transnational policy regimes.[1] Key trends include:

- shifts from national to transnational regulatory authority
- erosion of distinctions between different media through convergence, conglomeration and new media developments
- strengthening of private media industry rights, especially in intellectual property rights (IPRs), with global rules imposed on national-level regimes

- media ownership increasingly private, multimedia and transnational, with firms market oriented and subject to 'light touch' regulation and oversight
- shifts from 'command and control' regulation towards industry self-regulation and co-regulation
- shifts from public to supranational and private governance.

Under the influence of neoliberalism, governance as well as production of culture is shifting to non-state institutions, notably global corporations and private foundations, as states cut back on investment (Yúdice 2003). The latest phase of communications policy has involved an enhanced role for international institutions in media governance, creating a 'complex ecology of inter-dependent structures' (Raboy 2002: 6). Global institutions include various United Nations bodies (UNESCO, ITU) and more recently established, commercially focused bodies such as the WTO and WIPO. There are multilateral exclusive 'clubs' such as the Organisation for Economic Co-operation and Development (OECD) and the Group of Eight (G8)[2] and G20 groupings of powerful nation-states. The European Union and Council of Europe form 'regional multistate groupings', as does the North American Free Trade Agreement (NAFTA) between the US, Canada and Mexico. An important difference, however, is that the European Union is a politically integrated institution of global governance, with the European Parliament providing a level of democratic deliberation absent in the WTO and weaker in NAFTA (Chakravartty and Sarikakis 2006: 87).

The WTO, along with the World Bank and International Monetary Fund, has been one of the principal instruments of neoliberal policy. The WTO is charged with administering a multilateral trading system that involves 159 countries (March 2013). It was established in 1995 as the successor to the General Agreement on Tariffs and Trade (GATT), which was created in 1947 with a mandate to reduce tariffs, trade barriers and preferences between member countries (initially 23, representing around 80 per cent of world trade). The WTO differs from GATT in being a permanent institution with greater powers to ensure compliance with WTO agreements, which are binding on all members, and in handling trade disputes.

The place of media within the WTO regime is a matter of some complexity and ongoing dispute (Hardy 2008). WTO trade issues now include trade in services, trade in ideas (intellectual property rights) and liberalisation of telecommunications. Among the WTO-administered agreements, the TRIPS Agreement (Trade-Related Intellectual Property Rights) and, to a lesser extent, the ITA (Information Technology Agreement) have implications for the audiovisual sector. However, there have been strenuous efforts by some member countries, and the EU trade delegation, to keep their audiovisual trading out of the WTO rules. By contrast, WTO agreements covering books and magazines already prevent member governments from introducing measures that would tend to favour national products over imports, on the grounds that such measures distort competition.

These disputes have been characterised by tensions between the values of trade versus culture (Harvey 2002). An example is the bilateral free trade agreement reached between the United States and South Korea in 2007. South Korea has actively supported its film industry including through screen quotas in force since 1967. The quotas contributed to the rapid increase in the film market which created conditions for successful regional exports, part of the so-called Korean wave. Under pressure from the US government, lobbied by the Motion Picture Association of America (MPAA) and Hollywood, South Korea reduced the screen quota by half, from 146 days to 73 days in 2006 in the lead-up to signing the free trade agreement in 2007. Korean films regularly outsell Hollywood movies but cultural protectionism was a casualty of broader trade negotiations. Taiwan dropped its film import restrictions in 2001 when it joined the WTO, and a decade on foreign movies took 97 per cent of box office revenues (Jaffe 2011). China has faced increasing pressure via the WTO to end its twenty-foreign-films-a-year quota, and open its cinemas to foreign films. The twenty foreign titles previously allowed each year would compete with more than five hundred domestic movies. Even so, they accounted for around 45 per cent of Chinese box office revenues. In 2010, *Avatar* grossed £125 million, totally dwarfing the £65 million made by China's highest-grossing domestic film ever, *Let the Bullets Fly* (Jaffe 2011). In February 2012 China announced it would permit fourteen premium format films (IMAX, 3D) to be exempt from the twenty-film import quota.

One of the most significant challenges to the powerful, trade-based approach of the WTO has been the effort to support cultural diversity through UNESCO, a strategy pursued by countries such as Canada and France, recognising that this offered potentially more durable protection than that provided by 'cultural exception' exemptions within the WTO. The UNESCO Convention on the Protection and Promotion of the Diversity of Cultural Expressions (UNESCO 2005) states that 'cultural activities, goods and services have both an economic and a cultural nature, because they convey identities, values and meanings, and must therefore not be treated as solely having commercial value'. By July 2013 when El Salvador ratified, there were 130 state parties to the Convention, as well as the European Union, but it lacked the influence of such agreements as the Kyoto Protocol, which 150 countries ratified. The United States voted against the Convention, together with Israel, when 148 countries originally supported it; Australia, Honduras, Liberia and Nicaragua abstained. The Convention does not formally impinge on states' agreements under other treaties, including WTO agreements, so its impact on trade rules remains unclear, but it marked an important symbolic victory for an updated model of *l'exception culturelle*, the concept France introduced into GATT negotiations in 1993.[3]

Nation-states and policy

The reconfigurations of state power have been more varied and complex than is captured by the language of *erosion* of state power, or *transfer* of power from states to supranational governance. Nation-states remain lead players in the design and implementation of media policy and in the application of structural, behavioural and content rules, technical standards and interoperability, production incentives and subsidies, tax and financial rules (Straubhaar 2002: 187; Goldsmith and Wu 2006). Yet supranational governance increasingly shapes all these policy areas.

EU states are subject to European Union Directives across television, telecoms and computing, rules on competition and restrictions on 'state aid' and subsidies for enterprises including public service media. States are differentially involved in and affected by supranational bodies from issue to issue, but they are increasingly constrained by supranational agreements on market openness, competition and trade. Yet states can be key agents here, depending on the flows of influence, not merely acted upon 'from above'. Individual states may succeed in influencing 'supranational' regulation. States may also manage domestic opposition by presenting supranational decisions that they have actively pursued as being imposed upon them, as Thatcher (2000) examines in the case of European telecommunications regulation.

Policy convergence is a predicted consequence of convergence in media systems as the forces of the global market 'tend to displace the national political forces that once shaped the media' (Hallin and Mancini 2004: 276). Shared processes of internationalisation, digitalisation, convergence and market expansion influence the adoption of similar policy solutions. Supranational governance also imposes greater uniformity. Powerful lobbying by transnational corporations and industry bodies shapes policy convergence. Civil society coalitions and networks have some influence too, for instance at the World Summit on the Information Society (Chakravartty and Sarikakis 2006), but represent a considerably weaker force and one that has very often been eclipsed as policy-making shifted from societal to pro-market values. Societal regulation at international level has been limited (Ó Siochrú et al. 2002).

Analysing policy

Amongst the many approaches to explaining policy and regulation are those that can be identified as institutional, socio-economic, ideational and public choice (also referred to as rational choice) (John 2003; Baldwin and Cave 1999). CPE analysis has had an affinity with Marxist socio-economic accounts, yet, as in other areas, is characterised by a more complex interaction with other theories. This involves a shift from determinism and functionalism to radical pluralist analysis. It acknowledges that neither the state nor policy process is monolithic but involves a diverse range of policy agents and interests. It is radical in its focus on power relations and asymmetries within the policy process and their connection to societal orderings of political and economic power. However, in doing so it draws upon mainstream policy analysis and other approaches such as new institutionalism, pursuing various efforts at synthesis. There is no space to do justice to all these alternative perspectives but the following summary seeks to trace their influence on CPE approaches.

Marxist approaches

Marxism regards the prime function of the capitalist state as assisting the process of capital accumulation. This then led to debates on the relationship between politics and economics and the relative autonomy of states. In 'orthodox' Marxism the capitalist state is the superstructural form that corresponds to the capitalist mode of production (the base) and so the state, and policy, serve to reflect the class interests of the bourgeoisie and seek to sustain the capitalist economic system. So-called Marxism–Leninism attacked the Second International proponents of 'reformism', who argued for the peaceful transition to socialism through the electoral success of socialist parties and reform of the state from within. Lenin advocated the overthrow of the state and its replacement by workers' councils. The failure of the Soviet system and other communist states to sustain democratic involvement prompted efforts to rethink revolutionary change and democratic rule (Hardt 1992). From the mid 1960s, with the consolidation of welfare state systems in some Western liberal democracies and the apparent quelling and incorporation of class-based opposition to capitalism, Western Marxists showed renewed interest in explaining the forms and functions of the capitalist state (Jessop 2008: 55). A second revival occurred from the late 1970s, including efforts to examine the role of the state in sustaining relations of power based on gender, race, sexuality and expanding the articulation of politics, particularly through renewed attention to culture and identity. Feminists examined the patriarchal ordering of the state, and rejected conventional demarcations of public and private to trace social reproduction throughout, from education and employment to the division of labour and sexual politics. This late 1970s revival involved more theoretical currents and was more institutional in approach. It also involved multifaceted critiques of the teleological role ascribed to the (male) proletarian worker in revolutionary change to examine how power relations were lived out across multiple forms of oppression and how radical politics involving new social movements might be advanced (Laclau and Mouffe 1985).

In the earlier phase (from the 1960s) Marxist state theory advanced in two main ways. Instrumentalist accounts such as Miliband (1973, 1977) stressed the power of the capitalist class forged through close linkages between political elites and economic leaders. The main alternative account was structural and functionalist, proposing that the state produces policy in the interest of capitalism by virtue of its role, rather than from the power of the capitalist class and its supporting networks. In early phases, state policy is concentrated on establishing a regulatory framework to support capital accumulation, in mature systems state action encompasses the resources needed for growth and social reproduction, including education. Debates on integrating agency and structure have continued since, but both main variants of Marxist state theory were regarded as restricted and rigid as Marxism lost wider academic influence in the 1980s. In policy analysis, Marxists tended towards 'interest' theories in which policies reflected the interests of the dominant class. However, such accounts were criticised for their crude determinism, and failure to adequately explain the variation and complexity of public policy. Explanations derived from capitalist class dominance or the 'logic of capital' failed to engage adequately with the variety of groups usually involved in the policy process and the multiplicity of social and political objectives expressed, and had difficulty, in moving from abstract to concrete analysis, in explaining how specific policies were required by the functional needs of capitalist societies (John 2003: 97–98; Mosco 2009).

In response, radical scholars tended to depart from classic Marxist formulations and totalising accounts, sharing a criticism of social determinist readings that 'read off' politics and policies from an account of the most powerful forces at work in the economy and society (Hill 1997). The so-called regulationist school sought to reintegrate the economic and political, focusing on the role of public authorities in regulating 'regimes of accumulation' (Aglietta 1979; Jessop 1995; Sum and Jessop 2013). A 'regime of accumulation' refers to the economic, social and political framework that allows capitalism to extract a surplus and stave off a crisis of instability. State structures and policies reflect and regulate the techno-logical basis of capitalist accumulation. Policy change is driven by the effect of shifts in production techniques on capital accumulation strategies, the rate of profit, the state and regulatory arrangements. As a regime of accumulation, 'Fordism', comprising mass-production techniques in large factories, required a well-developed state bureaucracy to create conditions for mass markets, manage demand (through Keynesian economic management), and sustain and reproduce a healthy, trained workforce through welfare state provision. Post-Fordism arose from responses to the crisis of capital accumulation from the late 1960s to early 1970s. With falling rates of profitability in more competitive markets, firms sought to become more efficient and flexible in operations, and developed products for niche markets in seeking out higher rates of profitability. With the shift from mass production, the regulatory framework that had supported Fordism lost its legitimacy and salience. The state came to reflect post-Fordist characteristics and developed a new regulatory framework to assist new forms of capital accumulation. Examples include moves toward more flexible local government, with services contracted out to non-state providers. This new capi-talist logic was served by the deregulation of state controls over the economy, job protection and social welfare. The regulationist account provided an analysis of policy shifts from welfarism, corporatism and state management of nationalised industries, to privatisation 'deregulation' and promotion of labour market 'flexibility' (Jessop 1995).

Shifts from Fordism to post-Fordism have become staples of media and cultural analysis, particularly in exploring shifts in cultural production and consumption, for instance in fashion and advertising, as well as in work practices. However, regulationist accounts are critiqued for their technological determinism in seeing technological change as the generator for the production of public policy. The stagist nature of such accounts is also problematic in downplaying the significance and implications of the coexistence of features from different regimes of accumulation. Such problems are compounded when the analysis shifts to global capitalisms, and the varieties of state–capitalist formations.

Public choice theory

Public choice is a form of 'positive' political economy as it both celebrates and founds its theory of human action on principles of possessive individualism, rational self-interest and acquisitiveness. Analytically, public choice analysis focuses on explanations for rational decision-making. According to this public choice (or rational choice) theory 'preferences and bargaining of actors explain decisions and outcomes' (John 2003: 15). Drawing its methods and inspiration from neoclassical economics, rational choice tests hypotheses about human behaviour based on the premise that individuals make choices based on self-serving preferences. In doing so it 'replaces the institutional language of political structure and power with the economic language of markets, utilities, and preferences' (Mosco 1996: 264). For advocates such as John (2003: 18), rational choice theory provides the basis for an integrated explanatory account, linking individual action to the changing structures individuals face – which include the constraints of institutions, influence of group membership, socio-economic structures and preferences of other individuals. However, proponents offer a reductive account of motivation as anchored in rational self-interest (although altruistic behaviour can be modelled too). People seek to maximise their personal utility rather than serve collective goods. Accordingly, 'policy entrepreneurs' act to advance their careers if their policy ideas are successful. Rational choice is also unable to explain adequately the basis on which preferences are formed, why decision makers select a particular course of action, or why a policy may be desirable over and above the interests of the actors involved. Public choice, though, has had a significant influence on policy-making activity, influencing analysis of how markets can operate more effectively and how regulation and other 'opportunity costs' influence market actors' decision-making.

Institutional and other approaches

Institutional approaches examine the ways in which political organisations, such as parliaments and legal systems, structure policy decisions. So-called new institutionalism developed from the 1980s with renewed academic interest in the role of institutions, the state in particular, in politics. This approach sees institutions as sites in which norm and conventions of behaviour are reproduced, but addresses critiques of institutional approaches being overly static and structuralist by seeking to assess the role of institutions alongside other influences on political action.

New institutionalists have adopted and broadened the economic concept of path dependency, to examine how the institutional and other arrangements established by policy action can constrain, without entirely determining, subsequent policy debate and action (Starr 2004; Galperin 2004). Another approach, actor–network theory (ANT), provides conceptual resources for a radical pluralist analysis of the interaction of diverse sets of actors in efforts to shape and influence policy. ANT is closer to Foucaultian approaches to power than Marxist ones. It proposes a 'flat ontology' (Latour 2005) that rejects a pre-ordering of power in contrast to Marxian and CPE efforts to understand how power structures and the economic influence conditions for exercising agency.

CPE has looked to revisions in social theory to break out of the problems of structure and agency. Mosco, drawing on the work of Anthony Giddens, proposes structuration as offering a more dynamic and integrated approach. In Mosco's formulation 'social action takes place within the constraints and the opportunities provided by the structures within which action happens' (2009: 16). Going further, Jessop (2008: 41) proposes a 'strategic-relational' account that dialectically relativises both analytical categories:

> social structure can be studied in 'strategic-relational' terms as involving structurally inscribed strategic selectivity; and action can likewise be analysed in terms of its performance by agents with strategically calculating structural orientation. The former term signifies that structural constraints always operate selectively; they are not absolute and unconditional but are always temporally, spatially, agency- and strategy-specific. The latter term implies that agents are reflexive, capable of reformulating within limits of their own identities and interests, and able to engage in strategic calculation about their current situation.

Structure here is conceived in relational rather than reified terms, 'structural constraints comprise those elements in a situation that cannot be altered by agent(s) in a given time period and will vary according to the strategic location of agents in the overall matrix of the formation' (Jessop 2008: 44). This hardly reduces the challenges for analysis in identifying what is structural within particular practices but it does provide grounds for more productive engagement. For media political economy analysis it invites attention to what serve as structural constraints in a given situation. The interweaving of critical political economy, sociology and critical cultural theory has produced synthesising 'radical pluralist' accounts that are more open and less deterministic, while sharing a focus on the nature and effects of power imbalances in communication resources. CPE approaches have moved towards more dynamic accounts of structuration but accounting for political and economic structures remains a defining feature, distinguishing CPE from varieties of voluntarist actor theories, whether liberal or postmodernist.

For CPE scholars communications policy must be situated in the broader context of the regulation of the economy and connected policy areas, notably information, trade and culture. There have been valuable efforts to counter the compartmentalisation of a media-centric policy perspective. Leys (2001) examines marketisation in Britain by researching and comparing impacts in broadcasting and in the health service. Lunt and Livingstone (2012) explore the performance of regulators and public engagement across media and financial services. However, there is scope for greater engagement with theories of policy and policy analysis so as to match the ambition of the regulationist school, while moving beyond its restrictive explanatory framework.

In radical analysis there has been a shift from totalising frameworks derived from Marxism towards greater use and interaction with political science theories that emphasise 'politics matters', policy actors and networks, together with new institutionalism, and renewed attention to discourse. Another emphasis, drawing on ideational approaches, has been to stress the importance of struggles to set discursive agendas and to frame policy problems. Here Hancher and Moran's (1989: 271–99) conception of regulatory space offers a useful synthesis, examining the discursive and non-discursive space in which regulatory issues are identified, framed and enunciated. Likewise, Sum and Jessop (2013) emphasise discursive struggles in processes of legitimation for regimes of accumulation and regulation. There have been overarching shifts to neoliberal policy values, as many analysts have examined. However, policy and regulation tends to be more complex, contingent, contradictory and contested than stagist. Engaging with this complexity involves attention to the discursive and ideational aspects of policy. In democracies, governments and regulators have pressures and motivations to address a range of values which may be conflicted or undermined by policies. Media attracts special concerns regarding the quality of democracy, culture, communication and the public good that influences discursive struggles. The policy environment and organisation of 'regulatory space' is therefore of critical interest and importance. Another key qualification is recognition of the varied, often conflicting interests of media businesses.

Policy actors and interests

Policies affect media sectors, and firms within those sectors, in different ways. These may be regarded by some as superficial differences and antagonisms that can serve to mask the underlying 'pro-business' orientation of policies and the displacement, or exclusion, of values and concerns other than those of private business interests. However, the manner in which policies impact on different sectors and firms has become increasingly significant as convergence, digitisation and regulation confer differential advantages on firms and business models. Firms also seek to use regulation, and associated legal action, as a tool for competitive advantage.

In addressing these issues, media policy analysts, including radicals, have tended to move beyond the framework of interest group analysis and regulatory capture. In its left inflection the latter tends to focus on the 'capture' of regulators in the service of big business. For right-wing public choice advocates, it refers to regulators' affiliation to incumbents and tendencies to defend current regulatory arrangements against market innovation. The promotion of deregulation from regulators was a factor in contradicting predictions of statist conservatism. The assumption that state bureaucrats would seek to enhance their power and status by increasing the size of their budgets was at odds with evidence of active engagement in deregulation, for instance in the FCC and Ofcom.

The significant political roles played by actors with key economic interests in 'deregulation' policies have been examined in accounts of UK and European policy (Humphreys 1996; Freedman 2008). Companies have supported formidable trade associations such as the National Broadcasters Association and Motion Picture Association of America, or sometimes short-lived tactical alliances for lobbying. There are usually tensions between competing interests that render such combinations dynamic, if not unstable. Yet there has been significantly increased investment by corporations in trade associations. One coalition, the International Communications Round Table (ICRT), represents twenty-five leading media, computer and communications companies, including Time Warner, Walt Disney, News Corporation, Reed Elsevier, Sony Entertainment, Bertelsmann, Philips, Siemens and Microsoft. This grouping urged revision of the 1997 Television Directive, opposing EU quotas as no longer viable or justifiable in a global, technologically converging environment. There has continued to be extensive lobbying of Brussels by national and transnational industry interests (Sarikakis 2004; Harcourt 2005), joined by Facebook and other digital giants such as Google, who spent $5 million lobbying Congress in the first quarter of 2012 alone (McChesney 2013: 144). Such corporate interests are far from unopposed by media reform lobbies (discussed below), yet the disparity in resources tends to be enormous. The US corporate interests seeking copyright extension and enforcement outspent public domain and fair use advocates by an estimated 1,300-to-1 ratio on lobbying and public relations (McChesney 2013: 92).

Media reform

There have been two principal alternatives for those who came to a radical and critical view of mass media: establish alternative communications or advocate and agitate to change the organisation of the media, through policy change. These paths have been richly interlocked in radical media history, as well as prompting sometimes bitter debates over where and how political energy should be invested. More constructively, radicals have advanced the right to communication as a central demand. This includes freedom of expression but seeks to balance the libertarian and free-market emphasis on the property rights of providers, with the rights of everyone to enjoy access to communications. This articulates obligations for democratic states to ensure the conditions for communication rights to be realised. In turn, this supports state intervention to tackle and counter market failure and provide the resources and arrangements for media pluralism and diversity to be strengthened.

We now have a growing literature on media policy activism (Hackett and Carroll 2006). My own involvement has been with the Campaign for Press and Broadcasting Freedom, a UK media reform organisation established by media trade unionists, whose work has of necessity become more internationalist and networked since its foundation in the late 1970s. Media reform agendas engage with the specificity and complexity of local policy-making but there have been many efforts to co-ordinate global responses and articulate common demands. One such effort has been the coalition, Voices 21, described as 'a global movement for People's voices in Media and Communication for the twenty-first century'. This association of media activists and academics set out a reform agenda under various themes (Voices 21 2002: 261–73) including:

1 access and accessibility: 'Participation in social communication presupposes access: to big media, to community media, to computer networks, to information sources and to other tools'
2 right to communicate: 'Around the world, new and old forms of state and commercial censorship are rampant, they threaten not only the independence of conventional mass media, but also the right to communicate through new channels like the Internet. Universal access to media means little in the absence of adequate public space where information, opinions and ideas can be freely exchanged and debated.'
3 diversity of expression
4 security and privacy
5 cultural environment: global media foster a 'culture of violence, discrimination, exclusion and consumerism'.

Media reform agendas generally seek to establish some degree of citizen control over the controllers of communication as well as asserting rights in communication space. For CPE there is a vital and close link between the academy, radical media practice and policy activism (chapter nine). There are also often tensions too, between and amongst NGOs, activists, community media, labour groups and academics. These include tactical tensions between 'insider' strategies to win credibility and support within policy networks and strategies to build popular support for more far-reaching reforms which are marginalised or dismissed by elites. McChesney (2013) reflects on the failures of the Obama administration, the corporate capture of politicians and regulators as well as the difficulties faced by the media reform movement he co-founded, *Free Press*, to sustain widespread popular support. At a time of crisis, and opportunity, when debates in the decade ahead may settle the contours of communication control for the century, reform cannot succeed while governments are doing the bidding of capital. While there have been important victories, like stalling Stop Online Privacy Action (SOPA), the coalition of people power needed to win the big Internet policy fights has not yet been assembled and remains an immense challenge.

Conclusion

Neoliberalism has become a dominant force in supranational and national communications policy. Corporations have also increased their influence to unprecedented levels. The corporate grip on policy in the US poses risks that communications arrangements for the next century will be decided with minimal democratic involvement. Yet analysis needs to have regard for dynamic openness to understand variations across different media systems and the complex configurations of power shaping specific policy issues when viewed in more granular detail. Attention to openness and contestation is required for media reform politics as well as analysis. Reform requires us to identify and build on openings and possibilities for change. Ó Siochrú et al. (2002) outline two main alternatives for global media governance. The first is a dominant trade and liberalisation paradigm in which a logic of commercialisation pervades the media and communication sphere. The second, 'multilateral cooperation reborn', privileges democratic, cultural and societal governance based on peoples' communication rights. The dominance of the first appears even more entrenched today, but as the authors argue, the outcome is still not settled.

Notes

1 Hardy (2008) provides a summary of changes in international communications regulations. See also accounts of media policy paradigm shifts (Hoffman-Riem 1996; Van Cuilenburg and McQuail 2000) and the internationalisation of media policy (Ó Siocrú et al. 2002).
2 In March 2014 the G7 nations agreed to suspend the G8 until Russia changed its policy towards Ukraine.
3 In July 2013 the cultural exception re-emerged as key sticking point in the negotiations between the European Union and the US on what will be the world's largest free trade agreement.

Part III

Interventions and change

Chapter 9

Media power, challenges and alternatives

Introduction

How should we understand and assess the alternatives and challenges to 'big media' in an era of increasing digital communications? Are distinctions between radical, alternative and community media pertinent? How do they relate to media personalisation and new forms of exchange as digital tools for creativity and communication become more widely diffused? How should claims of a power shift from producers to producer–consumers be assessed? What is the contribution of political economy in assessing the challenges and implications of alternative media? During the twentieth century, the radical tradition called for greater media diversity and argued that this required structural reforms in media systems and the break-up of corporate giants in oligopolistic markets. This chapter returns to consideration of the degree to which these arguments remain compelling, and addresses the extent to which they are challenged by the way media markets, and social movements, have developed.

Conceptualising media power

For Thompson (1995: 16) symbolic power 'stems from the activity of producing, transmitting and receiving meaningful symbolic forms'. This includes power over how people and things are represented. Media power is defined by Couldry (2002: 4) as 'the concentration in media institutions of the symbolic power of "constructing reality" (both factual representations and credible fictions)'. We can justify focusing on various aspects of media power – for instance how resources for symbolic meaning are organised and concentrated in media organisations – the focus of political economy. But meaning is the complex outcome of social interaction. If symbolic power is the power of media to construct reality then a full account of symbolic power must include reception and audiences, what people think and do. Symbolic power is one of four main types of power and can be understood best in relation to the others: economic, political and coercive (Thompson 1995). These are analytically distinct but combine in complex ways. Investigating connections between symbolic power and the other types of power may be regarded as one of the central tasks in media political economy.

Coercive and symbolic power are frequently combined. When NATO bombers started to attack Serb forces in 1999, the then President of Yugoslavia, Slobodan Milosevic, removed the head of Belgrade's independent radio station B92. Later, masked police took over Studio B, Serbia's main opposition-controlled TV station (as well as two Belgrade radio stations). When Milosevic was deposed in 2000 demonstrators set fire to the state TV station, an act common across modern and ancient regime change.

In 2008 Vladimir Putin's anointed successor Medvedev was voted president with just over 70 per cent of the vote. Medvedev had refused to take part in debates between candidates and officially did not campaign, but as deputy prime minister he received what *The Times* (Halpin 2008) called 'blanket Soviet-style coverage on state television as he tours the country inspecting factories, hospitals and ice rinks'. When Putin was elected president in 2004, international monitors reported that the elections were flawed because of an 'overwhelming' bias towards Putin in the media (as well as election count irregularities). The media gave 'an overwhelming advantage to the incumbent' and fiercely attacked Putin's main opponent (Sergei Glazyev). According to *The Guardian* newspaper, by 2003 Putin had 'emasculated' NTV, the only national TV station; 'such is the level of control that no political chat show can be broadcast live'. The federal government maintained strong control over the nationally distributed state and private channels.

In addition to instrumental, structural and symbolic forms of power, Braman (2009: 25) adds informational, as 'power that shapes human behaviour by manipulating the informational bases of instrumental, structural, and symbolic power'. Her focus is on strategies of state power, where informational power alters how other powers are exercised. An example is states using private sector entities as regulatory agencies, for instance requiring ISPs to help states monitor Internet use, or as the revelations of whistle-blower Edward Snowden exposed in 2013, weakening commercial encryption systems subject to state approval. The informational state involves network relationships with other states and with non-state actors of whom TNCs are pre-eminent. Nation-states vie to provide favourable conditions for corporate activities and these relationships encompass and connect the global political economy with states' information policies and activities, including their generally supportive (if also complexly policed and negotiated) relations with media providers. Castells (2009: 50) too emphasises communicative action as the key to power, such that while fundamental sources of power have not changed 'the terrain where power relationships operate has changed'.

The definitional or *discursive* power of the media is identified by Street (2011) as one of three main forms of media power, the others being access and resource power. Discursive power operates through the way the media privilege particular discourses and construct particular forms of reality. This has been developed in research on agenda-setting (McCombs 2004) and framing (Entman 2007) as well as content (Glasgow Media Group, see Eldridge 1993; Berry and Theobald 2006: 109–24) and critical discourse analysis (Fairclough 1995). *Access* power concerns whose voices, identities and interests get heard in the public media. This includes addressing how particular interests or identities are articulated or excluded in the media and how media institutions and systems are structured in relation to access to communication. The third type of power is *resource* power, which refers to the ways in which those who own and control the media can affect the actions of state authorities.

In another useful formulation, Street distinguishes between two dimensions of media power. The first is power *over* the media (what gets shown and reported), the power of social actors to influence the discursive power of the media. The second dimension is the power *of* the media to shape meanings and effect change (what gets changed by the media). As Curran and Couldry (2003: 3) emphasise, accounts that focus exclusively on power over the media can treat the media as merely 'the door through which the contestants for power pass en route for battle'. Instead, they suggest the media are better understood as a processing plant, that converts inputs rather than merely carrying them (like a waterfall carries water). The media do not just mediate what lies outside them, they generate. If we overemphasise the impact of external power on the media we risk losing sight of what happens inside the so-called 'black box', how media process and create meanings, and crucially too what difference they make in the world. The media cannot be viewed merely as a watchdog against other forms of power, they need to be scrutinised as central generators of power in contemporary societies.

My own preferred metaphoric concept for the media is that of apparatus. The term apparatus is used in a variety of ways in media studies from production to ideology critique (Althusser's Ideological State Apparatuses). An apparatus means both the technical resources required for particular activities or purposes, and the complex structure of an organisation or system. An apparatus may be used and occupied, but it is also actively shaped and constructed. Crucially, an apparatus has affordances (qualities which enable and may also prompt the performance of certain actions) but all the possible uses cannot be simply read off from structure alone. Apparatuses are constraining frames but also enabling of multiple uses and unpredictability. If this serves as a general term, there are clearly also variations in the design, complexity and variability of uses, access rights and control over apparatuses that CPE explores. Apparatus-as-object is vulnerable to Foucault's important critique that both Marxism and liberalism regard power as a possession that is exercised repressively from a centralised source. Yet accounts of the diffusion of media power, some influenced by Foucault, can end up dissolving power altogether. To pursue the metaphor of apparatus, there are indeed apparatuses of communication, institutionalised orderings of power, but power arises from relationships with apparatuses, it does not merely inhere in apparatuses themselves. Power is produced through interactions (instrumental and structural) across various levels or domains of activity in markets where communications are produced, bought, sold and exchanged. It is produced within and across levels of ownership and management of communication services; media–external relationships; access and reception; user activities; social and cultural practices.

The aspects of media power outlined above – discursive, access and resources – are central concerns for CPE analysis but also relatively uncontested across media and cultural studies. Mainstream scholarship does not share the same evaluation of problems but there are few challenges to the theoretical validity of these concepts. By contrast, considerable criticism is directed at CPE's understanding of reception and meaning-making. Pursuing the nature of communication power as 'framing of the mind', Castells (2009: 155, 416) argues 'Power is primarily exercised in the construction of meaning in the human mind through processes of communication enacted in global/local multimedia networks ... '. If media power is rightly regarded not as inhering in production or texts but as a process involving the construction of meanings and their influence, then we need an account of psycho-cognitive reception and psycho-social action. CPE does not investigate these in any adequate manner. In so far as critical scholars do infer media effects and influence (which they do) they are open to this critique, but a CPE approach that acknowledges explanatory limits carefully can insist on the value of its analysis of media power. Instead two other key challenges, introduced already in chapter two, are considered further here. These are that CPE offers a theoretically impoverished domination model, and one that does not adequately address shifts in communication power in twenty-first century media.

Critical political economy and media problems: beyond mass media

We have examined political economy as any approach concerned with the political and economic organisation of media, while focusing on a critical tradition that aims to identify and address problems in the media. This tradition is diverse in orientation and examines the full variety of political and media systems but, while never uniform, its critical normative perspective clusters around concerns about democratic life in its broadest sense, efforts to distribute power more equitably in the world and to make communications democratic and sustainable. Taking off in the 1960s, the tradition dealt largely with problems of mass media. This included production and engagement with alternative media (considered below) but CPE analysis focused on problems in dominant mass communications, in particular:

- ownership and (capitalist) control of media
- the framing of media issues and discourses (and links between media organisation, media access and media discourses)
- a presumption of influence in the information, ideas and imagery conveyed by mass media.

A central set of questions are therefore: to what extent do these problems persist given profound transformations of media? Which problems persist? How has change in media systems served to reduce, ameliorate or render redundant 'old' problems? What new problems arise? Any answers to such questions need to acknowledge partiality in both positive and negative senses. In its positive sense partiality, having a particular preference, refers to emotions of fondness and judgements of value. In its negative sense partiality refers to bias and suggests a distorted or at least limited perspective. I think both meanings are pertinent and that advancing any positive partiality benefits from recognising positionality and the limitations of perspective in addressing the problems of media. Second, we need to ask these questions of specific practices in specific contexts. That does not mean that analysis must remain micro in focus at all, but that the local and specific context of problems is always relevant. Third, it must be an ongoing, collective task to map, understand and assess problems in the media. To be salient critical media analysis must engage with changes affecting communication systems, relevant developments in theory and analysis, as well as diverse political and social priorities, all reflexive of more international and comparative perspectives.

In chapter two I reviewed the division between liberal and radical perspectives used to structure formative university courses in media in the 1970s. In Western media studies a version of the liberal paradigm remains dominant, even though advocates are more likely to self-identify as postmodernist, in viewing mediated communications as increasingly pluralistic and open (Deuze 2006). The majority tradition does not see major problems in commercial media cultures surrounding access, and voice, and so is generally not concerned with remedies (including institutional reform). The foundation is a positive assessment of the capabilities of capitalism to generate and circulate information, including radical ideas. For McNair (2006: 41) capitalism 'has evolved into providing the most open and receptive space for dissenting voices of any form of society in human history'. He acknowledges there are still dominant forces of state and market influencing media but offers an optimistic conclusion. In contemporary cultural capitalism, commercial viability and political radicalism coexist; 'The market provides a highly efficient mechanism for the circulation of dissenting, progressive ideas in commodity form' (McNair 2006: 88). The distribution of films by Michael Moore (*Capitalism a Love Story*; *Fahrenheit 9/11*) and Morgan Spurlock (*Super Size Me*; *The Greatest Movie Ever Sold*) are amongst the supporting examples. McNair celebrates the capacity of the market to bring about self-corrective reform. The competitive logic of cultural capitalism placed *Fahrenheit 9/11* at the heart of the mainstream media marketplace, it was the highest-grossing documentary film release, generating more than $222 million worldwide on a production budget of $6 million, although McNair does acknowledge the difficulties Moore had in securing a distribution deal after Disney's Miramax withdrew. The market is an aid not a barrier to the circulation of diverse viewpoints. Market competition also spurs critical journalism: 'In the global news market ... critical, revelatory journalism is not a luxury ... but a marketing necessity, as is the visible demonstration of reliability, objectivity, independence and diversity' (2006: 97). McNair (2006: 94) concludes:

> When ... it is recognised that capitalism is here to stay, and that the critical task is to reform and humanise rather than replace it, the capacity of the media to channel dissidence and diversity becomes a valuable political tool in the progressive project.

To summarise an opposing, radical perspective, Robert Entman and Clay Steinman (2008: 12) argue:

> We see the dialectic of resistance and hegemonic power as largely unaffected by ICT at the start of the new millennium, in part because of the wide availability of these communication resources, and in part because the structures of inequality ... remain largely in place.
>
> Fiscal and physical necessities continue to exert their traditional constraints on political consciousness-raising and activism ... The limits of time and energy, the need to work ever more hours to support households and still spend quality time with children, friends, parents, and relatives – especially for women who work the double-shift of full-time work and most household care – puts a premium on relaxing rather than agitating for solutions to global warming, heterosexism, inequality, militarism, and racism.
>
> Meanwhile, powerful institutionalized interests fund full-time advocates and communication campaigns; entrenched interests do not have to rely on voluntarism. This imbalance gives the lie to celebratory democratic theory. The very forces that make life so hard for so many people have legions of spokespeople whose jobs depend on promoting corporate and to a lesser extent bureaucratic interests in a disciplined way to dominate public policy discussions.

Here, the emphasis is on the structured imbalance of communication resources between those serving power holders and those of civil society interests. Close to Habermas's pessimistic account of refeudalisation of the public sphere, the focus is on public relations serving corporate and elite interests to shape awareness and discussion of public policy. These alternative perspectives do not address the same ground and it is possible to combine them. The reach of well-crafted filmic essays such as *Capitalism: A Love Story* becomes even more important to lift spirits, provide collective points of reference for debate, nurture counter-hegemonic values and analysis, blend politics and entertainment. What they do highlight are different assessments of the suitability of capitalism to serve democracy. Capitalist markets do circulate diverse content. The radical paradigm does not seek to deny or minimise the presence of such diversity, including radical content. It fully shares the celebration. The corollary, though, is that CPE insists on highlighting problems in the organisation of communications that connect to problems for democracy, communication empowerment and cultural exchange. How far do these problems persist? One set of answers is derived from the continuing relevance of mass media and the attendant problems that the CPE tradition has outlined since the 1970s: concentration, control, commercialisation. However, it is argued that CPE is stuck gazing backwards at problems that are being resolved in the reconfigured environments of new media.

New media: participation and empowerment

The context of broad claims and counterclaims for the Internet was examined in chapter five. Here I want to pursue claims for digital empowerment and their consequences for media power. To clear some ground, there is little disagreement that we are in the midst of a digital revolution that has already had profound impacts, including the diffusion of new forms of communication power to users. In the mass media era of the mid twentieth century, communication power was concentrated in the hands of providers and most people lacked ready access to channels of mass communications. Today, a rapidly increasing number of people worldwide have individual access to communication resources that allow them to publish to mass audiences, to access billions of gigabytes of information and to exchange and share all kinds of data. The 'people formerly known as the audience' (Rosen 2006) can now participate, can create and co-create as well as consume. For Castells (2009: 57) this diffusion of communication power means that 'social actors and individual citizens around the world are using the new capacity of communication networking to advance their projects, to defend their interests, and to assert their values'. Meikle and Young (2011: 10) concur, 'The convergent media environment is making possible an enormous redistribution of a certain kind of power – the power to speak, to write, to argue, to define, to persuade – symbolic power ... For many people, the media are no longer just what they watch, listen to or read – the media are now what people *do*'.

CPE responses

Many of the claims of Internet celebrants are directly countered by sceptics who argue that there is rising disinformation and disempowerment rather than advancement. However, there are a number of important arguments advanced by CPE scholars against aligning with either. First the celebrants include many like Benkler (2006) who offer a compelling and progressive vision of non-commodified communication that radicals share. The key disagreement is not the vision but the capability of realising it, given the dominance of capital. Second, the choice between celebrant and sceptic accounts cannot be easily or satisfactorily decided. It is better, argue Curran et al. (2012), to examine specific contexts in their complexity than adopt simple explanatory narratives. McChesney (2013) argues that both celebrants' and sceptics' accounts lack what a political economy approach can provide, analysis of how corporate capitalism has shaped and continues to shape how the Internet develops.

Other CPE scholars have addressed the specific claims for participation and co-creation. Celebrant accounts of digital capitalism often adopt terms associated with political democracy and apply these to communication activities in general but also to specific claims that user-generated content platforms facilitate a participatory culture and economy (Tapscott and Williams 2006). Fuchs (2011) advocates returning terms such as participation to their roots in theories of 'strong' participatory democratic so that participation claims are assessed in regard to such criteria as control over decision-making, ownership and democratic empowerment, Fuchs critiques the shallow and restricted conception of participation on offer and the way this misrepresents the dominance of corporate ownership and commercial provision.

> Statistics such as the ownership structures of web 2.0 companies, the most viewed videos on YouTube, the most popular Facebook groups, the most popular topics on Google and Twitter, the Twitter users with the highest number of followers show that the corporate web 2.0 is not a democratic space of equal participants, but a space, in which large companies, celebrities and entertainment dominate. They achieve a much higher number of followers, readers, viewers, listeners, re-tweets, likes, etc. than the everyday users.
>
> (Fuchs 2012: 728)

Fuchs concludes that Web 2.0 and such like are ideological categories that serve the interests of capital and ignore the power structures that shape the Internet.

The smooth harmonising of commercial and consumer interests underpinning a benign vision of the market require the expansion of such critique. However, as Fuchs (2011: 324) also emphasises, a dialectic analysis of media and society will 'try to identify the positive and negative potentials and effects ... and how they come to contradict each other'. Highlighting contradiction as a key tool for contemporary Marxist analysis, Fuchs (2011: 325) proposes four main themes; how and to what extent:

1 media play a role in capital accumulation and commodification
2 they advance ideologies or are surrounded by ideologies about their own (positive and negative) effects
3 they advance one-dimensional instrumental and/or complex critical modes of thinking and practices
4 there are potentials that media act as alternative media in social struggles that want to bring about a better world that benefits all and not only certain groups or individuals.

Accordingly, researchers should examine how these are present in concrete situations and systems, and how they interact and contradict each other.

The task for CPE, in my view, is not to cement an orthodox reading but to continue to pose and investigate critical questions of power. One requirement concerns research design and agendas. A strength of the CPE tradition is the capacity for making empirically testable propositions, within a theoretically reflexive critical realism that rejects naïve positivism. As Fuchs demonstrates, we can pursue sets of claims through empirical research into market provision and social usage. In this way, critical Internet studies can generate more empirically rich, situated analysis, serving not least as forms of ideology critique. A second key requirement is to attend to the complexity of power dynamics and modalities of power. The 'free' distribution of public cultural goods, and gift relations based on the reciprocal exchange and pooling of services, are both cultivated and vie with the dominant modality of commercial transactions. CPE analysis insists that we must understand the workings and influence of economic power on both Internet provision and on policy-making in order to assess how the social uses and capabilities celebrated by writers like Benkler may be realised and restricted.

Contesting media power

There have been four main types of activity through which media power has been contested: integration, alternative media, media reform and protest. The first, which I call integration, refers to efforts to gain access to or influence symbolic meanings in public media. The second, alternative media, refers to media production and communications that challenge, at least implicitly, central concentrations of media resources. The third, media reform, refers to action to democratise media systems by means of changes in policy and governance. The fourth category, protest, differs in that it can be directed at a variety of actors or structures affecting communications and may not seek or value remedies from policy reform. Common to each are efforts to alter the conditions in which media resources are organised. This description fits present conditions but it also reflects the logic of mass media arrangements, characterised by sharper divisions between mainstream and alternative than exist today. Approached more dynamically, the mapping can be used to explore how these activities are connected and combined.

Integration

At its broadest, integration reflects the tensions between creativity and autonomy of cultural workers and efforts of managers to discipline and organise them on behalf of commercial or other purposes. As the literature on cultural work examines, there are problems for capital in organising creativity to both cultivate and capture value.

More narrowly, there are moments of social action to contest media power by attempting to reshape media production. This is one reason why the binarism mainstream/alternative media is problematic, because there can also be fluid movement and merging across these spheres. Social movements in the 1960s and

1970s challenged dominant power and social arrangements including media provision and representation. Social movements provided the impetus and support for alternative media production but also agitation to gain access to media apparatuses. This pressure for change also blends with drives to incorporate at least some of the new currents from within the mainstream.

In the UK one important and well-documented moment of integration was the opening up of Channel Four television in 1982 (Curran and Seaton 2010). Channel Four was the last terrestrial television service created with a full public service remit. It developed from an establishment policy process, the Annan Committee, that was nevertheless open to influences from the left, such as socialist intellectuals and activists in the Free Communication Group, and from new social movements, feminists, LGBT, Black and ethnic minority activists. Lord Annan's committee challenged the 'cosy duopoly' of mainstream provision and advocated a more radical remit for Channel Four to cater for tastes and interests not otherwise served by the BBC and ITV. The committee rejected calls for workers' representation on governing bodies, but adopted calls for an 'open broadcasting authority', a publisher model in which the broadcaster would commission programmes from independent providers. The Annan Committee reported to a Labour government, but when Channel Four began broadcasting Britain was being reshaped by the New Right government of Margaret Thatcher. The publisher model of entrepreneurial independent producers appealed to the right, against that of strongly unionised in-house production, and Channel Four survived while providing a programme mix that included some powerful challenges to Conservatism on issues ranging from the conflict in Ireland to gay sexuality and multiculturalism. Channel Four is also an example of institutional communication space being opened up. In a ground-breaking deal, the trade union (ACTT) together with film and arts funding bodies agreed arrangements supporting commissioned programmes from community-based non-profit workshops. The experiment was short-lived and not without tensions but it provided access slots for groups like Amber Films and Sheffield Film Co-op that tackled social action issues in new ways from below. One landmark film was *Handsworth Songs*, by Sankofa, directed by John Akomfrah. Made following urban riots in 1985, it combines newsreel and archive footage to explore the historical, social and political background to the racial unrest in Britain at the time.

Another example from a very different media ecology is Spike Lee's powerful, Emmy award winning film *When The Levees Broke* (2006), examining the poverty of responses especially by the federal government to devastation caused by Hurricane Katrina in New Orleans. Here a distinguished Black independent filmmaker produced work financed ($2m) by a premium subscription channel, HBO, and subsequently shown worldwide. This example, in contrast to Channel Four, may fit McNair's celebratory account of capitalism's capacity to invest in dissent if this fits into the logic of capital accumulation overall. Yet, such overtly critical filmmaking remains exceptional in the media cultures of commercial television. In the case of HBO, a niche market service could cultivate and respond to audience interests not catered for by ad-financed or thoroughly commercialised channels. In the case of Channel Four, greater openness came from a public service system responding in part to the growing cultural power of new social movements. Channel Four, a public trust organisation, initially cross-subsidised by ITV's advertising revenue, subsequently became more exposed to commercial pressures, contributing to a programming shift that was less experimental and less open to hitherto excluded voices. The conditions that enable dissident voices to use public media apparatuses to reach large audiences remain restricted and in an era of supposed digital plenitude these examples are reminders too of the protracted social and institutional struggles that carve out the space that courageous creative workers seize.

Alternative media

The second key form of contesting media power arises from within the broad and fluid category of alternative media. Critical political economy has a strong affinity with forms of 'radical' and 'alternative' media whose practices pursue similar purposes. Radical media can challenge and contest dominant media power, can advance and realise different kinds of communication than those available across 'mainstream' media. Yet, the relationship between CPE and alternative media has often been more fraught and complex than these obvious affinities would suggest. Despite its commitment to expanding communications freedom and diversity, the CPE tradition has been erratic in its engagement with alternative or radical media, sometimes dismissing it as marginal to the task of democratising 'mass' public media (Couldry 2006: 182–83).

Within the broad and fluid category of 'alternative' media, 'radical' media have helped constitute counterpublics beyond the dominant public sphere (Fenton and Downey 2003; Milioni 2009). North American examples include websites such as CounterPunch.org, radio shows such as *Democracy Now!*, culture jammers like Adbusters (Atkinson 2008) as well as social-justice-oriented Independent Media Centres (IMC). Non-commercial community media have been heralded as a counterforce against corporate media, notably in systems such as the US where the latter dominate (McChesney and Nichols 2002), and increasingly embraced by media activist movements aiming to democratise public communication (Hackett and Carroll 2006). More broadly, community or 'citizen's media' (Rodriguez 2001) are valued as media serving, often empowering, minority social or ethnic groups and interests in geographic or geocultural communities (Buckley et al. 2008). 'Alternative' media, then, covers a range of practices resistant to simple categorisation or even common attributes but generally comprising 'small, alternative, nonmainstream, radical, grassroots or community media ... that is often based on citizen participation' (Fenton and Downey 2003: 185; Coyer et al. 2007).

Recognising that alternative media can be viewed via their products or their processes, Atton (2002) suggests that it is the tendency away from professionalised, capitalised and institutionalised media that identifies 'alternative'. Atton favours the term alternative over that of radical media for the former's embrace of a wider range of media types, and freedom from revolutionary connotations, which may or may not be present in the various media. Rodriguez (2001: 20) rejects the term 'alternative' as likely to 'entrap us in binary thinking: mainstream media and their alternative', and limit the 'potential of these media to their ability to resist the alienating power of mainstream media'. Her preferred term is citizens' media, which implies

> first that a collectivity is enacting its citizenship by actively intervening and transforming the established mediascape; second, that these media are contesting social codes, legitimized identities, and institutionalized social relations; and third, that these communication practices are empowering the community involved, to the point where these transformations and changes are possible.
>
> (Rodriguez 2001: 268)

Bailey et al. (2008) identify four approaches to alternative media: as media that serve specific communities and facilitate participation; as 'alternative' to mainstream (in organisation and content); as part of civil society; and their preferred rhizomatic approach focusing on the fluidity of the boundaries that structure the other approaches, whereby relationships between alternative media and with mainstream media are recognised as sometimes transient and elusive, but also complex and overlapping. Culture-jamming activists use a mixture of street, old and new media, mainstream and alternative media to circulate their jams. The part-professional, part-citizen journalist *OhmyNews*, in South Korea, for instance, demonstrates 'a hybrid structure of publication organization, combining elements of traditional commercial organizations with those typically regarded as alternative' (Kim and Hamilton 2006: 544). Such approaches can help shift from definitional debates, to theoretically informed yet grounded analyses of different media practices in their political, social and geocultural contexts. They can also bridge divisions between media-centric analysis, political science, and civil society/social movement research, by examining relationships between social movement media and social change (Downing 2008; De Jong et al. 2005; Cammaerts and Carpentier 2007). Other analysts have favoured radical media as a term associated with the history of revolutionary, communist, socialist and anarchist media. 'Radical' media have a rich history (Pajnik and Downing 2009), including the Levellers pamphlets of the English Civil War, the smuggled publications that helped to foment revolution in eighteenth century France, and onwards. CPE has an affinity with radical media and delineating the extent of radical media activity today is critical to debates on the Internet.

Alternative media, argue Bailey et al. (2008: 153) range from

> some totally independent of market or government, some dependent on the state for their resources, others drawing on advertising to finance their

operations; some re-producing hegemony, others clearly counter-hegemonic; some reactionary, some reformist, some revolutionary, and others less obviously political.

Contrary to the voluntarist notion of independence deployed by Bailey et al., alternative media do not operate entirely outside forces of state and market. Many internal and external factors shape the performance and social influence of alternative media but CPE gives particular attention to issues of financing and resources. Most alternative media involve small-scale production, taking advantage of cost-benefits from technology for production and/or distribution (such as 'desk-top publishing' and video technology in the 1980s). Sources of income have included sales (music fanzines for instance) but also subsidies and support. There is media produced directly by organisations and subsidised from income generated elsewhere or included in costs of membership or services. There is media funded wholly or partly by third-parties: grant-funding bodies, civil society organisations, trade unions, political parties, states.

A key issue for contemporary debates is the relationship between technological resources and financing: does digitalisation lessen problems of a lack of financial resources, and problems of patronage and control by funders? Second, much alternative media production has relied heavily on 'free labour', individuals giving their labour and time. Such altruism is rightly celebrated at the heart of Benkler and others' visions for non-commodified Internet exchange. However, that connects to the emergence of more critical readings of free labour as exploitation and the limits imposed by capital and states on co-operation (Fuchs 2011). This links to a third key area for analysis: the distribution of resources for alternative media. Entman and Steinman (2008) highlight the pressures that draw working people away from contesting dominant power interests. Increasing marketisation and the global recession has meant, in much of the West, a weakening of the labour movement and socialist parties, shrinking state and non-state funding for civil society organisations. In general, the traditional funding resources for alternative media have declined. This increases the importance of assessing how the affordances of digitalisation affect the capacity to generate alternative media.

Internet and radical media

One of the most researched exemplars of radical media in recent years has been Indymedia. This also serves to highlight some of the strengths and limitations of radical media. Indymedia (www.indymedia.org) activist network grew out of a collective that produced live information during the 'Battle of Seattle' against the WTO meeting held there in 1999. By 2004 Indymedia had 142 affiliated sites in 54 countries, in 2013 it had around 150 (not all active). Indymedia has been a celebrated experiment in democratic media as well as 'globalisation from below', encouraging and empowering people to 'be the media', providing a focus for events, issues and explanations largely ignored by corporate media, and in doing so foregrounding struggles over media power (Curran and Couldry 2003). Committed to decentralised structures, combined with collective decision-making, Indymedia built an 'open publishing' model in efforts to create open source, automated systems for posting, archiving, editing and syndicating networked information.

Indymedia has been heralded as illustrating a new and continuing challenge to the infrastructure of global media power, taking advantage of the affordances of the Internet to create a global means of self-representation, and changing the scale on which social conflicts are played out. The Internet 'opens up public space beyond the nation-state and, thereby, to some extent, bypasses, or rather escapes, state and market colonization' (Bailey et al. 2008: 153). As a mobilising resource for activists, the Internet offers an audience-building capacity greater than most resource-poor groups and social movements groups have hitherto assembled. Also highlighted is the capacity to overcome the narrow reach and limited distribution that has been a feature of much radical, resource-poor media; the Internet makes it easier to distribute beyond activist circles, and for Internet users to access and encounter radical communications.

Discussions on the potentialities of the Internet for alternative media follow the contours of larger debates on the Internet (chapter five). What is more distinctive though are concerns about what kinds of power relations are challenged in terms of content, form, who speaks and who is heard. Indymedia has served to highlight limitations within alternative media, including the (hidden) subsidies of time, money and computing resources that enable speakers to participate. Such resources are unequally distributed according to gender in that women's 'free' time in households with children tends to be considerably less than men's. Occupation, wealth and location are other critical factors in differential access to computing resources, stable electricity, connectivity. This does not diminish the value of critical communication, nor the resource-building capacity that even poor Internet capabilities can bring to communities and individuals worldwide, but it does suggest that alternative media do not escape the effects of global orderings of wealth and social power, even if they mobilise to contest them. A key limitation remains the 'enormously unrepresentative social base' (Bennett 2003) for Internet activism.

A study of openDemocracy, a web-based magazine of politics and culture produced with the avowed aim of ensuring that 'marginalised views and voices are heard' from around the world, found that most contributors came from elite backgrounds: in 2006–8, 78 per cent of authors (mostly unpaid) were academics, journalists or professional writers; 72 per cent were men and 71 per cent came from Europe and the Americas with only 5 per cent from Africa (Curran and Witschge 2009). Important claims can be made for openDemocracy's efforts to foster international dialogue but discussions of new media democratisation must take account of the unrepresentative and skewed social base of online participation, the relatively marginal space of political engagement online, and the distance between realised exchanges and the grassroots communication of world citizenry. The publics emerging in cyberspace do establish some conditions for a transnational public sphere, but they are not themselves fully democratic (Hackett and Carroll 2006: 49). A related concern has been with the quality of communications exchange in counterpublic spheres. In a study of Indymedia Athens, Milioni (2009: 427) offers a qualified endorsement of exchanges that nevertheless challenge normative ideals of public sphere deliberation; even though debates 'are often swarming with aggression and fail to reach consensus, participants debate argumentatively about the issues under consideration and define, autonomously and intersubjectively, the rules and terms of their own discussion'.

The adoption of the Internet by civil society organisations over the last two decades has brought about an expansion in scale and scope, made both alternative media and civil society networks more visible, and accessible, and encouraged a flourishing of investigation that has helped move research from the margins towards the mainstream. Even so, significant gaps remain in understanding 'the norms, processes and discourses that are developed [in alternative media], the activists who sustain them, the publics who use them, the reach of their products within the general public, and the reception and interpretation of their content' (Milioni 2009: 413).

Citizen journalism

The deficiencies of adopting a simple opposition of mass and alternative media are amply revealed by the practices labelled as 'citizen journalism'. These range from images captured by the public and offered (or sold) to mainstream media, to online comments on professional published work, to blogs and web publishing, through to unpaid or underpaid journalism. Citizen journalism has emerged as the loose, indistinct term for diverse forms of participation and production ranging from ordinary people (often witnesses to news 'events') supplying material to mainstream media, to contributors to competitor news services such as the *Huffington Post*, to those engaged in radical and oppositional media (Allan and Thorsen 2009). The category of blogger, in particular, is extremely fluid covering the whole range (Bailey et al. 2008: 151, Hindman 2009).

News production has been dominated at a national level by corporate or state institutions and globally by Western news corporations from the nineteenth to the late twentieth century, but today a growing range and variety of non-Western news formations produce subaltern contra-flows (Thussu 2006, 2007). New technologies have aided the expansion of news and cultural flows within geo-cultural and diasporic communities. The main resource-rich providers tend to be commercial firms or state-sponsored providers (Russia Today, CCTV-9, France 24, Al Jazeera), but there are alternative providers, usually resource-poor, financed by various sources, which may include state subsidies, advertising, subscription and 'free' labour. There is no space to do adequate justice to these exciting, emergent activities. The reshaping of media through participation, citizen journalism, user-generated content and 'mass self-communication' (Castells 2009) is likely to be a central focus for future research. Yet, like the Internet in the early 1990s, the topic of citizen journalism is suffused with investments and claims, from solving the crisis of journalism to achieving democratic renewal and deepening political participation. Such important hopes, however, need to be assessed soberly and concretely across different media and political systems, against both empirical evidence and analysis of contending forces. Citizen journalism promises a more diverse array of viewpoints than either prevailing forms of market censorship or state censorship permit, 'yet the idea that citizen media is *more* representative, or open to "everyone's voices" [Gillmor 2004: xiii] … is as mythological as the idea that traditional journalism could ever have been objective' (Tilley and Cokley 2008: 109).

The Internet *has* been a proven tool to challenge 'existing political hierarchy's monopoly on powerful communications media' (Rheingold 1993: 13), yet researchers need to grasp the contradictions and variables that continue to delay such universalist utopian predictions. As one study (Kluver and Banerjee 2005: 40) concludes:

> Although the Internet does indeed increase the potential for mobilization and organization for certain wired segments of society, in much of Asia this means that politics becomes less democratic, as the greater bulk of national populations remain without access to political information and mobilizational capability, and without democratic power.

New media facilitate reactionary as well as 'progressive' counterpublics; the Internet contributes simultaneously to new forms of social solidarity and fragmentation, to shallowing as well as deepening participation, to fostering networked inclusion and new exclusions, to contesting *and* sustaining social power and inequalities. The best CPE work is alert to such contradictions, to openings and possibilities, as well as constraints and restrictions (Raphael 2001). This is then an expanding research agenda that engages CPE's concerns throughout. CPE's distinctive contribution lies in its attention to resources, the resources for sustaining forms of public communication, and the social, cultural and economic resources that shape production and participation in communications (including the class and gendered organisation of time, cultural competencies, and such factors as feedback and the forms of legitimisation that sustain 'voluntary' work and activist participation). CPE can also overcome the much-criticised binarism of 'mainstream' and 'alternative' through its broader concern with the shifting relationships and interconnections between mainstream and alternative media, professional and 'citizen' journalism.

The irresolvable debate between optimists and pessimists would matter less were it not linked to implications for public policy. For a powerful range of interests from liberal academic commentators to transnational corporations, the market can be trusted to realise digital plenitude and create an equitable environment for cultural and democratic exchange. There is undeniably increased digital communication but claims for media pluralism need to be carefully qualified and assessed in regard to the continuing dominance of 'vertical' media content provision and consumption, contractions in public service media and the scarcity and resource limitations of alternatives. While source diversity has undoubtedly increased, understanding which sources are actually used by audiences (exposure diversity) has grown in importance (Napoli 2011; Karppinen 2009). The myth of digital abundance is problematic because it is mobilised to suggest that market mechanisms can secure by themselves what have been formerly recognised as goals for public policy – balancing private and public interests in communications; fostering and safeguarding media pluralism and diversity. For citizens' media to flourish requires financial and regulatory support through public policies.

Media reform and protest

Democratic media activism takes four main forms. Integration involves reforming the media internally. Alternative media means creating new and parallel media activities. Protest involves criticism, action and awareness raising about media problems. Media reform involves efforts to change the conditions in which media operate. As with other categories discussed above the division between protest and media reform is blurred and many media reform strategies and tactics involve both. Media reform is characterised by efforts to ensure communication resources are used for social purposes and shaped by democratic involvement. Protests against media power may not share confidence in or support for such solutions by virtue of critiques of statism (libertarianism, culturalism), majoritarianism, or orderings of mainstream cultural values (some activism on sexuality, race, gender and disability).These are fruitful and important areas of debate within the creation of progressive coalitions. On the whole the CPE tradition has advocated media reform as the logical outcome of a critique both of dominant media and the marginalisation and structured insufficiency of radical media to provide a satisfactory alternative. Writing in a US context, McChesney and Nichols argue (2002: 123):

> It is the result of relentless lobbying from big business interests that have won explicit government policies and subsidies permitting [corporate media] to scrap public interest obligations and increase commercialization and conglomeration. It is untenable to accept such massive subsidies for the wealthy, and to content ourselves with the 'freedom' to forge alternatives that only occupy the margins.

Media reform agendas were outlined in chapter eight. In the context of the discussion here critical issues include which modes of contesting media power are more feasible, desirable and capable of mobilising the necessary support to make gains. That must be debated and answered within and across media systems.

Conclusion

Are there media power problems and if so how should they be addressed? The aim of this book is to promote those questions being answered by readers across myriad media systems and situations. There are, though, some general points that arise from the discussions above.

I Mass media and old problems persist

Mass and electronic media remain the most important means by which people across the world form views on reality beyond their individual experience. So it matters profoundly how key problems facing the world are addressed in public media from ecological destruction to military imperialism. 'Old' problems persist, from media concentration to marketisation and the subordination of public to private interests. We have encountered critiques that marketisation and the expansion and power of corporate media damages the public sphere, cuts down space for debate and involves a number of structural biases that tend to make it conservative in orientation. This makes corporate media an unreliable basis for a properly inclusive, open, diverse and democratic media. If that is so, then action is required to put it right.

2 New media have new problems

Digital media environments involve new controls (instrumental and structural) over production, circulation and exchange arising from private ownership, state surveillance, marketers' advertising and other forms of monetisation. Access to communication resources and to benefits of communication are unequally distributed generating digital divides and democratic deficits. Big Data, something of a buzzword in 2013, nevertheless highlights how the collection and use of digital communications data connects state, corporate and commercial interests. Data from social media, video streaming and personal communications is subject to management and exploitation by commercial providers and varying degrees of state surveillance. Such manifestations of ongoing convergence need an analytically convergent CPE to address issues of control, privacy, security, environmental damage, labour and social use.

3 Old and new media are interconnected, and so too are problems

The Internet has certainly aided the circulation of voices and expanded publishing, yet the financing of newsgathering remains a problem across old and new media. Research has shown that bloggers and citizen journalists rely heavily on journalists for information (Mitchelstein and Boczkowski 2009). An analysis of postings on Indymedia and Slashdot found that 'not only do few weblog writers engage in any independent news reporting, most weblog writers cover the same topics as mainstream news media and, perhaps more significantly, rely on them for information on those topics' (Haas 2005: 393). The web provides a means of expression well adapted to collective forms of organisation (Bennett 2003); it enables mass distribution of movements' own media, with some costs transferred to users. However the Internet does not overcome the challenges of content creation and production costs, or the costs of attracting audiences and sustaining participation (Owens and Palmer 2003).

Analysing how power works in and through media is a vital task for researchers. To do so requires insights from political, economic and cultural approaches, but it also requires connections to wider struggles for media democracy. Critical political economy of communications marks out a dynamic tradition that draws on past work, asks vital questions about media today and will continue to revisit and reinvigorate answers. But its validity and value ultimately resides in contributing to making a difference to people's lives by advancing communication arrangements for societies that draw from each according to their abilities and support each according to their needs.

By exploring connections between how communication resources are organised and how societies are organised, CPE provides the foundations for an inclusive, integrative study of media and communications. Critical political economy provides base nutrients for the revitalisation of media and communication studies for the twenty-first century. Analysing how the production of media takes place under the influence of political and economic forces remains a necessary foundation for enquiry. CPE promotes asking big questions about the relationship between media, capitalism and democracy. CPE's concern to examine the transformation of media also necessitates the long-range historical perspective and cross-disciplinary engagements that the field of media studies requires. Critical political economy is principally concerned with 'problems', and disposed to address these because inequalities in resources affect all aspects of life, including culture and communications. Going forward, it is challenged to help explain in compelling ways how these problems coexist with the pleasures and gains of communication, to persuade a new generation worldwide to join in efforts to tackle and change, as well as investigate, the problems of the media.

Bibliography

Note: some book subtitles have been omitted for reasons of space.

Adam Smith Institute (1984) *Omega Report: Communications Policy*, London: Adam Smith Institute.

Adorno, T. and Horkheimer, M. (1997) [1944] 'The culture industry: enlightenment as mass deception' in T. Adorno and M. Horkheimer, *Dialectic of Enlightenment* (trans. J. Cummings), London: Verso.

Aglietta, M. (1979) *A Theory of Capitalist Regulation*, New York: Verso.

Albarran, A. (2004) 'Media Economics' in J. Downing et al. (eds) *The Sage Handbook of Media Studies*, London: Sage.

Albarran, A. and Chan-Olmsted, S. (1998) *Global Media Economics*, Ames: Iowa State University Press.

Alexa (2013) 'Top News sites'. Available at http://www.alexa.com/topsites/category/Top/News (accessed 27 November 2013).

Alexander, A., Owens, J., Carveth, R., Hollifield, C. and Greco, A. (2004) *Media Economics: Theory and Practice*, Mahwah, NJ: Lawrence Erlbaum Associates.

Alexander, J. (2011) *Performative Revolution in Egypt*, London: Bloomsbury Academic.

Allan, S. and Thorsen, E. (2009) *Citizen Journalism: Global Perspectives*, New York: Peter Lang.

Althusser, L. (1984) *Essays on Ideology*, London: Verso.

Amin, S. (1976) *Accumulation on a World Scale*, New York: Monthly Review Press.

Andersen, R. (2000) 'Introduction' in R. Andersen and L. Strate, *Critical Studies in Media Commercialism*, Oxford: OUP.

Anderson, C. (2004) 'The Long Tail'. Available at http://www.wired.com/wired/archive/12.10/tail.html (accessed 23 November 2013).

——(2009) *The Longer Long Tail*, London: Random House.

Andrejevic, M. (2012) 'Exploitation in the Data Mine', in C. Fuchs, K. Boersma, A. Albrechtslund and M. Sandoval (eds) *Internet and Surveillance*, New York: Routledge.

Ang, I. (1991) *Desperately Seeking the Audience*, London: Routledge.

Arsenault, A. (2012) 'The Structure and Dynamics of Communications Business Networks in an Era of Convergence: Mapping the Global Networks of the Information Business' in D. Winseck and D. Y. Jin (eds) *The Political Economies of Media*, London: Bloomsbury.

Arsenault, A. and Castells, M. (2008) 'The Structure and Dynamics of Global Multi-Media Business Networks', *International Journal of Communication*, 2: 707–48.

Atkinson, J. D. (2008) 'Towards a Model of Interactivity in Alternative Media: A Multi-level Analysis of Audiences and Producers in a New Social Movement Network', *Mass Communication and Society*, 11: 227–47.

Atton, C. (2002) *Alternative Media*, London: Sage.

Babe, R. E. (2009) *Cultural Studies and Political Economy: Towards a New Integration*, Lanham, MD: Lexington Books.

Bagdikian, B. (1997) *The Media Monopoly*, Boston: Beacon Press.

——(2004) *The New Media Monopoly*, Boston: Beacon Press.

Bailey, O. G., Cammaerts, B. and Carpentier, N. (2008) *Understanding Alternative Media*, Maidenhead, Berkshire: Open University Press.

Baker, C. E. (1989) *Human Liberty and Freedom of Speech*, New York: OUP.

——(1994) *Advertising and a Democratic Press*, Princeton: Princeton University Press.

——(2002) *Media, Markets, and Democracy*, Cambridge: Cambridge University Press.

——(2007) *Media Concentration and Democracy*, Cambridge: Cambridge University Press.

Baldasty, G. J. (1992) *The Commercialization of News in the Nineteenth Century*, Winsconsin: University of Winsconsin Press.

Baldwin, R. and Cave, M. (1999) *Understanding Regulation*, Oxford: OUP.

Balnaves, M., Donald, S. H. and Shoesmith, B. (2009) *Media Theories and Approaches*, Basingstoke: Palgrave.

Barbrook, R. and Cameron, A. (1995) 'The Californian Ideology'. Available at http://w7.ens-lyon.fr/amrieu/IMG/pdf/Californian_ideology_Mute_95-3.pdf (accessed 23 November 2013).

Barendt, E. (2005) *Freedom of Speech*, 2nd edition, Oxford: OUP.

Barker, H. (2000) *Newspapers, Politics and English Society, 1695–1855*, Harlow: Longman.

Barlow, D. and Mills, B. (2012) *Reading Media Theory*, Harlow: Pearson.

Beckett, C. (2008) *SuperMedia*, Chichester: Wiley-Blackwell.

Benkler, Y. (2006) *The Wealth of Networks*, New Haven, CT: Yale University Press.

Bennett, W. (2003) 'New Media Power: the Internet and Global Activism' in J. Curran and N. Coundry (eds) *Contesting Media Power*, Lanham, MD: Rowman and Littlefield.

——(2011) *News: The Politics of Illusion*, 9th edition, New York: Pearson.

Benson, R. and Neveu, E. (eds) (2004) *Bourdieu and the Journalistic Field*, Cambridge: Polity.

Berle, A. and Means, G. [1932] (1968) *The Modern Corporation and Private Property*, New York: Harcourt, Brace & World.

Berry, D. and Theobald, J. (eds) (2006) *Radical Mass Media Criticism*, Montreal: Black Rose Books.

Bettig, R. and Hall, J. (2012) *Big Media, Big Money*, 2nd edition, Lanham, Maryland: Rowman and Littlefield.

Biltereyst, D. and Meers, P. (2011) 'The Political Economy of Audiences' in J. Wasco, G. Murdock and H. Sousa (eds) *The Handbook of Political Economy of Communications*, Oxford: Blackwell.

Boczkowski, P. (2004) *Digitizing the News*, Cambridge MA: MIT Press.

Bogart, L. (2000) *Commercial Culture*, New Brunswick: Transaction Publishers.

Bolaño, C., Mastrini, G. and Sierra, F. (eds) (2012) *Political Economy, Communication and Knowledge: A Latin American Perspective*, New York: Hampton.

Born, G. (2000) 'Inside television: television studies and the sociology of culture', *Screen* 41(4): 404–24.

——(2004) *Uncertain Vision*, London: Secker & Warburg.

Boyd-Barrett, O. (1977) 'Media Imperialism' in J. Curran, M. Gurevitch and J. Woolacott (eds) *Mass Communication and Society*, London: Arnold.

——(1998) 'Media Imperialism Reformulated' in D. K. Thussu (ed.) *Electronic Empires*, London: Arnold.

Braman, S. (2009) *Change of State*, Cambridge, MA: MIT Press.

Brants, K. and De Bens, E. (2000) 'The Status of TV Broadcasting in Europe' in J. Wieten, G. Murdock and P. Dahlgren (eds) *Television Across Europe*, London: Sage.

Brenner, R. (1998) 'Uneven development and the Long Downturn: the advanced capitalist economies from boom to stagnation, 1950–1998', *New Left Review*, 11(6): 5–43.

BtoB Media Business (2013) 'Media M&A activity in 2012 doubled'. Available at http://www.btobonline.com/article/20130102/MEDIABUSINESS10/301029996/media-m-a-activity-in-2012-doubled.

Buckley, S., Duer, K., Mendel, T. and Ó Siochrú, S. (2008) *Broadcasting, Voice, and Accountability*, Ann Arbor, MI: University of Michigan Press.

Calabrese, A. (2004) 'Toward a Political Economy of Culture' in A. Calabrese and C. Sparks (eds) *Toward a Political Economy of Culture*, Lanham, Maryland: Rowman and Littlefield.

Calhoun, C. (ed.) (1992) *Habermas and the Public Sphere*, Cambridge, MA: MIT Press.

Cammaerts, B. and Carpentier, N. (2007) *Reclaiming the Media*, Bristol: Intellect Books.

Campante, F. R. and Chor, D. (2011) 'Why was the Arab world poised for revolution? Schooling, economic opportunities and the Arab spring', *Journal of Economic Perspectives*, 26(2): 167–88.

Caraway, B. (2011) 'Audience Labor in the New Media Environment. A Marxian Revisiting of the Audience Commodity', *Media, Culture & Society*, 33(5): 693–708.

Cardiff, D. and Scannell, P. (1991) *A Social History of British Broadcasting. Vol 1, 1922–1939 Serving the Nation*, Oxford: Blackwell.

Cardoso, F. H. and Faletto, E. (1979) *Dependency and Development in Latin America*, Berkeley, CA: University of California Press.

Cassidy, J. (2002) *Dot.Con*, London: Penguin.

Castells, M. (1996) *The Information Age, Vol 1: the Rise of the Network Society*, Oxford: Blackwell.

——(2009) *Communication Power*, Oxford: OUP.

Cellan-Jones, R. (2012) 'Facebook Q&A: The Network Justifies the Cost of Its "Like" Adverts', 13 July. Available at http://www.bbc.co.uk/news/technology-18816674 (accessed 13 July 2012).

Chakravartty, P. and Sarikakis, K. (2006) *Media Policy and Globalization*, New York: Palgrave.

Chakravartty, P. and Zhao, Y. (eds) (2008) *Global Communications: Towards a Transcultural Political Economy*, Lanham, Maryland: Rowman and Littlefield.

Chan-Olmsted, S. and Chang, B-H. (2003) 'Diversification Strategy of Global Media Conglomerates: Examining Its Patterns and Determinants', *Journal of Media Economics*, 16(4), 213–33.

Chomsky, N. (1989) *Necessary Illusions*, London: Pluto.

Christians, C., Glasser, T., McQuail, D., Nordenstreng, K. and White, R. (2009) *Normative Theories of the Media*, Urbana, IL: University of Illinois Press.

Clarke, J., Hall, S., Jefferson, T. and Roberts, B. (1976) 'Subcultures, cultures and class' in S. Hall and T. Jefferson (eds) *Resistance Through Rituals*, London: Hutchinson.

Compaine, B. (2001) 'The Myths of Encroaching Media Ownership'. Available at http://www.opendemocracy.net/media-globalmediaownership/article_87.jsp (accessed 8 November 2013).

Compaine, B. and Gomery, D. (2000) *Who Owns the Media?*, Mahwah, NJ: Lawrence Erlbaum.

Compton, J. (2004) *The Integrated News Spectacle*, New York: Peter Lang.

Conboy, M. (2004) *Journalism: A Critical History*, London: Sage.

Cooper, M. (2011) 'The Future of Journalism: Addressing Pervasive Market Failure with Public Policy' in R. McChesney and V. Pickard (eds) *Will the Last Reporter Please Turn Out the Lights*, New York: The New Press.

Cottle, S. (2003a) 'Media Organisation and Production: Mapping the Field' in S. Cottle (ed.) *Media Organization and Production*, London: Sage.

——(ed.) (2003b) *News, Public Relations and Power*, London: Sage.

Couldry, N. (2000) *Inside Culture*, London: Sage.

——(2002) *The Place of Media Power*, London: Routledge.

——(2006) 'Transvaluing Media Studies: Or, Beyond the Myth of the Mediated Centre' in J. Curran and D. Morley (eds) *Media and Cultural Theory*, London: Routledge.

Council of Europe (CoE) (2004) *Transnational Media Concentrations in Europe*, Strasbourg: CoE.

Coyer, K., Dowmunt, T. and Fountain, A. (2007) *The Alternative Media Handbook*, New York: Routledge.

Cronin, A. (2003) *Advertising Myths*, London: Routledge.

Croteau, D. and Hoynes, W. (2006) *The Business of Media*, 2nd edition, Thousand Oaks, CA: Pine Forge Press.

Curran, J. (1978) 'Advertising and the Press' in J. Curran (ed.) *The British Press: A Manifesto*, London: MacMillan.

——(1986) 'The Impact of Advertising on the British Mass Media' in R. Collins, J. Curran, N. Garnham, P. Scannell and C. Sparks (eds) *Media, Culture and Society: A Critical Reader*, London: Sage.

——(1996) 'Mass Media and Democracy Revisited' in J. Curran and M. Gurevitch (eds) *Mass Media and Society*, 2nd edition, London: Arnold.

——(2000) 'Press Reformism 1918–98: A Study of Failure' in H. Tumber (ed.) *Media Power, Professionals and Policies*, London: Routledge.

——(2001) 'Media Regulation in the Era of Market Liberalism' in G. Philo and D. Miller (eds) *Market Killing*, Harlow: Longman.

——(2002) *Media and Power*, London: Routledge.

——(2004) 'The Rise of the Westminster School' in A. Calabrese and C. Sparks (eds) *Toward a Political Economy of Culture*, Lanham, MD: Rowman and Littlefield.

——(2006) 'Media and Cultural Theory in the Age of Market Liberalism' in J. Curran and D. Morley (eds) *Media and Cultural Theory*, London: Routledge.

——(2010a) 'Entertaining Democracy' in Curran, J. (ed.) *Media and Society*, 5th edition, London: Bloomsbury.

——(2011) *Media and Democracy*, London: Routledge.

——(2012) 'Reinterpreting the Internet' in J. Curran, N. Fenton and D. Freedman (2012) *Misunderstanding the Internet*, London: Routledge.

Curran, J. and Couldry, N. (eds) (2003) *Contesting Media Power: Alternative Media in a Networked World*, Lanham, MD: Rowman and Littlefield.

Curran, J. and Gurevitch, M. (1977) 'The Audience', *Mass Communication and Society, Block 3*, Milton Keynes: Open University.

Curran, J. and Park, M-J. (eds) (2000a) *De-Westernising Media Studies*, London: Routledge.

——(2000b) 'Beyond Globalization Theory' in *De-Westernizing Media Studies*, London: Routledge.

Curran, J. and Seaton, J. (2010) *Power without Responsibility*, 7th edition, London: Routledge.

Curran, J. and Witschge, T. (2009) 'Liberal Dreams and the Internet: A Case Study' in N. Fenton (ed.) *New Media, Old News*, London: Sage.

Curran, J., Gaber, I. and Petley, J. (2005) *Culture Wars*, Edinburgh: Edinburgh University Press.

Curran, J., Iyengar, S., Lund, A. and Salovaara-Moring, I. (2009) 'Media System, Public Knowledge and Democracy: A Comparative Study', *European Journal of Communication*, 24(1): 5–26.

Curran, J., Fenton, N. and Freedman, D. (2012) *Misunderstanding the Internet*, London: Routledge.

Cushion, S. (2012) *The Democratic Value of News*, Basingstoke: Palgrave Macmillan.

Dahlgren, P. (1995) *Television and the Public Sphere*, London: Routledge.

Davies, N. (2008) *Flat-Earth News*, London: Chatto and Windus.

Davis, A. (2013) *Promotional Cultures*, Cambridge: Polity.

Dawisha, A. (2013) *The Second Arab Awakening*, New York: Norton.

Dayan, D. and Katz, E. (1992) *Media Events*, Cambridge, Mass.: Harvard University Press.

DCMS/BERR (2009) *Digital Britain*, London: DCMS/BERR.

Deacon, D. (2003) 'Holism, Communion and Conversion: Integrating Media Consumption and Production Research', *Media, Culture and Society*, 25: 209–31.

Deadline Hollywood (2013) 'Netflix TV Episodes Cost between $3.8m-$4.5m' (10 March). Available at http://www.deadline.com/2013/03/netflix-tv-episodes-cost-3-8m-4-5m-caa/ (accessed 20 March 2013).

De Bens, E. (ed.) (2007) *Media Between Culture and Commerce*, Bristol: Intellect.

De Certeau, M. (1974) *The Practice of Everyday Life*, Berkeley: University of California Press.

De Jong, W., Shaw, M. and Stammers, N. (2005) *Global Activism, Global Media*, London: Pluto.

Demers, D. and Merskin, D. (2000) 'Corporate News Structure and the Managerial Revolution', *The Journal of Media Economics*, 12(2): 103–21.

Dempsey, J. (2008) 'ABC Family under Harry Potter's spell'. Available at http://variety.com/2008/film/news/abc-family-under-harry-potter-s-spell-1117992921/ (accessed 30 September 2008).

Deuze, M. (2006) 'Ethnic Media, Community Media and Participatory Culture', *Journalism*, 7(3): 262–80.

——(2007) *Media Work*, Cambridge: Polity.

——(2009) 'Media Industries, Work and Life', *European Journal of Communication*, 24(4): 467–80.

——(ed.) (2011) *Managing Media Work*, London: Sage.

Dorfman, A. and Mattelart, A. (1975) *How to Read Donald Duck*, New York: International General Editions.

Dover, B. (2008) *Rupert's Adventures in China*, Edinburgh: Mainstream Publishing.

Dovey, J. (ed.) (1996) 'The Revelation of Unguessed Worlds' in J. Dovey (ed.) *Fractal Dreams*, London: Pluto.

Downie, L. and Schudson, M. (2011) 'The Reconstruction of American Journalism' in R. McChesney and V. Pickard (eds) *Will the Last Reporter Please Turn Out the Lights*, New York: The New Press.

Downing, J. (2008) 'Social Movement Theories and Alternative Media: An Evaluation and Critique', *Communication, Culture & Critique*, 1: 40–50.

Doyle, G. (2002a) *Media Ownership*, London: Sage.

——(2002b) *Understanding Media Economics*, London: Sage.

Dubai School of Government (2011) *Civil Movements: The Impact of Facebook and Twitter*, Arab Social Media Report, 2. Available at http://www.dsg.ac/portals/0/ASMR2.pdf (accessed 25 June 2011).

Du Gay, P. (ed.) (1997) *Production of Culture/Cultures of Production*, London: Sage

Dunleavy, P. and O'Leary, B. (1987) *Theories of the State*, Basingstoke: Macmillan.

Eagleton, T. (2003) *Figures of Dissent*, London: Verso.

——(2007) *Ideology*, 2nd edition, London: Verso.

——(2011) *Why Marx Was Right*, New Haven: Yale University Press.

Economist, The (2012) 'Non-news is good news' (9 June). Available at http://www.economist.com/node/21556635 (accessed 30 June 2012).

Edwards, D. and Cromwell, D. (2006) *Guardians of Power*, London: Pluto.

Eldridge, J. (1993) 'News, truth and power' in J. Eldridge (ed.) *Getting the Message: News, Truth and Power*, London: Routledge.

Entman, R. (2007) 'Framing Bias: Media in the Distribution of Power', *Journal of Communication*, 57: 163–73.

Entman, R. and Steinman, C. (2008) 'Tear Down the Walls: Re-envisioning Communication Theory and Research', *Conference Papers – National Communication Association*, 1–32.

European Audiovisual Observatory (2009) *Trends in European Television, Yearbook 2008*, Brussels: European Audiovisual Observatory.

European Commission [EC] (2010) *Mergers: Commission Clears News Corp.'s Proposed Acquisition of BSkyB under EU Merger Rules*. IP/10/1767. Brussels: EC.

——(2013) *High Level Group on Media Freedom and Pluralism*, Brussels: EC.

FAIR (2009) 'Media Blackout on Single-Payer Healthcare'. Available at http://www.fair.org/index.php?page=3733 (accessed 28 July 2009).

Fairclough, N. (1995) *Critical discourse analysis*, New York: Longman.

Faraone, R. (2011) 'Economy, Ideology and Advertising' in J. Wasco, G. Murdock and H. Sousa (eds) *The Handbook of Political Economy of Communications*, Oxford: Blackwell Publishing.

Feintuck, M. and Varney, M. (2006) *Media Regulation, Public Interest and the Law*, 2nd edition, Edinburgh: Edinburgh University Press.

Fenton, N. (2007) 'Bridging the Mythical Divide: Political Economy and Cultural Studies Approaches to the Analysis of Media' in E. Devereux (ed.) *Media Studies: Key Issues and Debates*, London: Sage.

——(ed.) (2009) *New Media, Old News*, London: Sage.

——(ed.) (2010) *New Media, Old News*, London: Sage.

Fenton, N. and Downey, J. (2003) 'New media, counter publicity and the public sphere', *New Media & Society*, 5(2): 185–202.

Ferguson, M. and Golding, P. (eds) (1997) *Cultural Studies in Question*, London: Sage.

Figueiras, R. and Ribeiro, N. (2013) 'New Global Flows of Capital in Media Industries after the 2008 Financial Crisis: The Angola-Portugal Relationship', *The International Journal of Press/Politics*, 18(4): 508–24.

Fiske, J. (1990) *Introduction to Communication Studies*, 2nd edition, London: Routledge.

Fitzgerald, S. (2011) *Corporations and Cultural Industries*, Lanham, MD: Lexington Books.

Flew, T. (2007) *Understanding Global Media*, Basingstoke, Hampshire: Palgrave.

——(2011) 'New Media Policies' in M. Deuze (ed.) *Managing Media Work*, London: Sage.

Fortunati, L. (2005) 'Mediatization of the Net and Internetization of the Mass Media', *Gazette*, 67(1): 27–44.

Foster, J. and McChesney, R. (2012) 'The Endless Crisis', *Monthly Review*. Available at http://monthlyreview.org/2012/05/01/the-endless-crisis (accessed 23 November 2013).

Freedman, D. (2006) 'Internet Transformations: "Old" Media Resilience in the "New Media" Revolution' in J. Curran and D. Morley (eds) *Media and Cultural Theory*, London: Routledge.

——(2008) *The Politics of Media Policy*, Cambridge: Polity.

——(2009) '"Smooth Operator?": The Propaganda Model and Moments of Crisis', *Westminster Papers in Communication and Culture*, 6(2): 59–72.

——(2012) 'Web.2.0' in Curran et al. *Misunderstanding the Internet*, London: Routledge.

Fuchs, C. (2008) *Internet and Society*, Abingdon: Routledge.

——(2009) 'Some Reflections on Manuel Castells' Book "Communication Power"', *tripleC*, 7(1): 94–108.

——(2011) *Foundations of Critical Media and Information Studies*, London: Routledge.

——(2012) 'Dallas Smythe Today – The Audience Commodity, the Digital Labour Debate, Marxist Political Economy and Critical Theory', *tripleC*, 10(2): 692–740.

Galperin, H. (2004) *New Television, Old Politics*, Cambridge: Cambridge University Press.

Gandy, O. (1982) *Beyond Agenda Setting*, Norwood, NJ: Ablex.

——(2000) 'Race, Ethnicity and the Segmentation of Media Markets' in J. Curran and M. Gurevitch (eds) *Mass Media and Society*, 3rd edition, London: Arnold.

——(2004) 'Audiences on Demand' in A. Calabrese and C. Sparks (eds) *Toward a Political Economy of Culture*, Lanham, MD: Rowman and Littlefield.

Gans, H. (1980) *Deciding What's News*, London: Constable.

García Canclini, N. (1995) *Hybrid Cultures*, Minneapolis, MN: University of Minnesota Press.

Garnham, N. (1979) 'Contribution to a Political Economy of Mass Communication', *Media, Culture and Society*, 1: 123–46. Reprinted in N. Garnham, *Capitalism and Communication*, London: Sage.

——(1990) *Capitalism and Communications*, London: Sage.

——(1992) 'The Media and the Public Sphere' in C. Calhoun (ed.) *Habermas and the Public Sphere*, Cambridge Massachusetts: MIT Press.

——(2000) *Emancipation, the Media and Modernity*, Oxford: OUP.

——(2011) 'The Political Economy of Communication Revisited' in J. Wasco, G. Murdock and H. Sousa (eds) (2011) *The Handbook of Political Economy of Communications*, Oxford: Blackwell.

Gilder, G. (1994) *Life After Television*, 2nd edition, London: W.W. Norton.

Gillmor, D. (2004) *We the Media*, Sebastopol: O'Reilly Media.

Ginsborg, P. (2004) *Silvio Berlusconi*, London: Verso.

Gitlin, T. (1997) 'The Anti-political Populism of Cultural Studies' in M. Ferguson and P. Golding (eds) *Cultural Studies in Question*, London: Sage.

——(2002) 'The Unification of the World under the Signs of Mickey Mouse and Bruce Willis: The Supply and Demand Sides of American Popular Culture' in J. Chan and B. McIntyre (eds) *In Search of Boundaries*, Westpost, CT: Ablex.

Golding, P. and Murdock, G. (1979) 'Ideology and the Mass Media: The Question of Determination' in M. Barrett, P. Corrigan, A. Kuhn and J. Woolf (eds) *Ideology and Cultural Production*, New York: St Martin's Press, 198–224.

——(1997) *The Political Economy of the Media*, 2 vols., Cheltenham: Elgar.

——(2000) 'Culture, Communications and Political Economy' in J. Curran and M. Gurevitch (eds) *Mass Media and Society*, London: Hodder Arnold.

Goldsmith, J. and Wu, T. (2006) *Who Controls the Internet?*, London: OUP.

Goldsmiths Media Group (2000) 'Central Issues' in J. Curran (ed.) *Media Organisations in Society*, London: Arnold.

Graham, A. et al. (1999) *Public Purposes in Broadcasting*, Luton: University of Luton Press.

Greenslade, R. (2003) 'Their Master's Voice', *The Guardian* (17 February).

Gripsrud, J. (1995) *The Dynasty Years*, London: Routledge.

Guardian, The (2011) 'The world's top 10 newspaper websites', (19 April). Available at http://www.theguardian.com/media/table/2011/apr/19/worlds-top-10-newspaper-websites (accessed 20 April 2011).

——(2013) 'The Guardian'. Available at http://www.theguardian.com/media/2013/sep/02/the-guardian (accessed 2 September 2013).

Haas, T. (2005) 'From "Public Journalism" to the "Public's Journalism"? Rhetoric and Reality in the Discourse on Weblogs', *Journalism Studies* 6(3): 387–96.

Habermas, J. (1989) [1962] *The Structural Transformation of the Public Sphere* (trans. T. Burger), Cambridge: Polity Press.

Hackett, R. and Carroll, W. (2006) *Remaking Media*, London: Routledge.

Hafez, K. (2007) *The Myth of Media Globalization* (trans. A. Skinner), Cambridge: Polity.

Hall, S. (1980) 'Race, Articulation and Societies Structured in Dominance', *Sociological Theories: Race and Colonialism*, Paris: UNESCO.

Hall, S., Critcher, C., Jefferson, T., Clarke, J. and Roberts, B. (1978) *Policing the Crisis*, London: Macmillan.

Hallin, D. (1994) *We Keep America On Top Of The World*, London: Routledge.

——(2000) 'Commercialism and Professionalism in the American News Media' in J. Curran and M. Gurevitch (eds) *Mass Media and Society*, London: Arnold.

Hallin, D. and Mancini, P. (2004) *Comparing Media Systems*, Cambridge: Cambridge University Press.

Halloran, J., Elliot, P. and Murdock, G. (1970) *Demonstrations and Communication*, London: Penguin.

Halpin, T. (2008) 'Q&A Russia's Presidential Election', *Times Online* (29 February).

Hampton, M. (2004) *Visions of the Press in Britain, 1850–1950*, Urbana, IL: University of Illinois Press.

Hamzawy, A. (2009) 'Rising Social Distress: The Case of Morocco, Egypt, and Jordan', *International Economic Bulletin*, Carnegie Endowment for International Peace. Available at http://www.carnegieendowment.org/ieb/?fa=view&id=23290 (accessed 15 June 2011).

Hancher, L. and Moran, M. (eds) (1989) *Capitalism, Culture and Economic Regulation*, Oxford: Clarendon.

Hannerz, U. (2004) *Foreign News: Exploring the World of Foreign Correspondents*, Chicago: University of Chicago Press.

Harcourt, A. (2005) *The European Union and the Regulation of Media Markets*, Manchester: Manchester University Press.

Hardt, H. (1992) *Critical Communication Studies*, London: Routledge.

Hardt, M. and Negri, A. (2000) *Empire*, Cambridge, MA: Harvard University Press.

Hardy, J. (2004) '"Safe in Their Hands?": New Labour and Public Service Broadcasting', *Soundings*, 27: 100–114.

——(2008) *Western Media Systems*, London: Routledge.

——(2010a) *Cross-Media Promotion*, New York: Peter Lang.

——(2010b) 'The Contribution of Critical Political Economy' in J. Curran (ed.) *Media and Society*, 5th edition, London: Bloomsbury.

——(2011) 'Mapping Commercial Intertextuality: HBO's *True Blood*', *Convergence*, 17(1): 7–17.

——(2012a) 'Comparing Media Systems' in F. Esser and T. Hanitzsch (eds) *Handbook of Comparative Communication Research*, New York: Routledge.

——(2012b) 'Television Policy 2000–2010', *Journal of British Cinema and Television*, 9(4): 521–47.

——(2013a) 'Cross-Media Promotion and Media Synergy: Practices, Problems and Policy Responses' in M. P. McAllister and E. West (eds) *The Routledge Companion to Advertising and Promotional Culture*, New York: Routledge.

——(2013b) 'The Changing Relationship between Media and Marketing' in H. Powell (ed.) *Promotional Culture and Convergence*, London: Routledge.

Harvey, D. (2002) 'Policy' in A. Briggs and P. Cobey (eds) *The Media: An Introduction*, 2nd edition, Harlow, Essex: Longman.

——(2003) *The New Imperialism*, Oxford: OUP.

——(2011) *The Enigma of Capital*, London: Profile.

Held, D., McGrew, A., Goldblatt, D. and Perraton, J. (1999) *Global Transformations*, Cambridge: Polity Press.

Herman, E. (1986) 'Gatekeeper versus Propaganda Models: A Critical American Perspective' in P. Golding, G. Murdock and P. Schlesinger (eds) *Communicating Politics*, New York: Holmes and Meier, pp. 171–95.

——(1999) 'The Propaganda Model Revisited' in *The Myth of the Liberal Media*, New York: Peter Lang.

Herman, E. and Chomsky, N. (1988) *Manufacturing Consent: The Political Economy of the Mass Media*, London: Vintage.

——(2008) *Manufacturing Consent*, 2nd edition, London: Bodley Head.

Herman, E. and McChesney, R. (1997) *The Global Media*, London: Cassell.

Hesmondhalgh, D. (2006) 'Media Organisations and Media Texts: Production, Autonomy and Power' in D. Hesmonhalgh (ed.) *Media Production*, Maidenhead and Milton Keynes: Open University Press.

——(2007) *The Cultural Industries*, 2nd edition, London: Sage.

——(2010) 'Media industry studies, media production studies' in J. Curran (ed.) *Media and Society*, London: Bloomsbury.

——(2013) *The Cultural Industries*, 3rd edition, London: Sage.

Hill, K. (2012) 'Facebook Will Pay $10 Million to Make Its "Sponsored Stories" Problem Go Away', *Forbes* (18 June). Available at http://www.forbes.com/sites/kashmirhill/2012/06/18/facebook-will-pay-10-million-to-make-its-sponsored-stories-problem-go-away (accessed 30 June 2012).

Hill, M. (1997) *The Policy Process in the Modern State*, Harlow: Pearson.

Hills, M. (2002) *Fan Cultures*, London: Routledge.

Hindman, M. (2009) *The Myth of Digital Democracy*, Princeton: Princeton University Press.

Hoffmann-Riem, W. (1996) *Regulating Media*, New York: Guilford Press.

Hoggart, R. (1957) *The Uses of Literacy*, London: Chatto and Windus.

Hoskins, C., McFadyen, S. and Finn, A. (2004) *Media Economics*, Thousand Oaks, CA: Sage.

House of Lords Select Committee on Communications (2007) 'Minutes of the Visit to New York and Washington DC', November 16–21.

——(2008) *The Ownership of the News Volume I: Report*. Available at http://www.publications.parliament.uk/pa/ld200708/ldselect/ldcomuni/122/122i.pdf (accessed 1 July 2008).

Hughes, S. (2006) *Newsroom in Conflict*, Pittsburgh: University of Pittsburgh Press.

Humphreys, P. (1996) *Mass Media and Media Policy in Western Europe*, Manchester: Manchester University Press.

Innis, H. (1950) *Empire and Communications*, Oxford: Clarendon.

——(1951) *The Bias of Communication*, Toronto: University of Toronto Press.

International Federation of Journalists (2012) 'IFJ Renews Call to UN and Governments to Halt Slaughter of Journalists after 121 Killings in Bloody 2012'. Available at http://www.ifj.org/en/articles/ifj-renews-call-to-un-and-governments-to-halt-slaughter-of-journalists-after-121-killings-in-bloody-2012) (accessed 20 January 2013).

Internet Advertising Bureau (2009) *A Guide to Online Behavioural Advertising*. Available at http://www.iabuk.net/sites/default/files/publication-download/OnlineBehaviouralAdvertising Handbook_5455.pdf (accessed 25 January 2010).

Internet World Stats (2011) 'Usage and Population Statistics: China', Miniwatts Marketing Group. Available at http://www.internetworldstats.com/asia/cn.htm (accessed 3 August 2011).

——(2013) 'Internet Users in the World'. Available at http://www.internetworldstats.com/stats.htm (27 November 2013).

Iosifides, P. (1997) 'Methods of Measuring Media Concentration', *Media Culture and Society*, 19(4): 643–63.

Iosifides, P., Steemers, J. and Wheeler, M. (2005) *European Television Industries*, London: BFI.

ITU (2013) ITC Facts and Figures. Available at http://www.itu.int/en/ITU-D/Statistics/Documents/facts/ICTFactsFigures2013.pdf (accessed 17 July 2013).

Iyengar, S. et al. (forthcoming) 'The Prevalence and Correlates of Out-Party Animosity: Cross-National Evidence on Affective Polarisation', article submitted to a journal.

Jaffe, G. (2011) 'Will the great film quota wall of China come down?', *The Guardian*, 24 March. Available at http://www.theguardian.com/business/2011/mar/24/china-film-quota (accessed 21 April 2014).

Jarvis, J. (2009) *What Would Google Do?*, London: Harper Collins.

Jay, M. (1996) *The Dialectical imagination*, Berkeley: University of California Press.

Jenkins, H. (1992) *Textual Poachers*, London: Routledge.

——(2006) *Convergence Culture*, New York: New York University Press.

Jessop, B. (1995) 'The Regulation Approach, Governance and Post-Fordism', *Economy and Society*, 24(3): 307–33.

——(2008) *State Power*, Cambridge: Polity.

Jhally, S. (1990) [1987] *The Codes of Advertising*, London: Routledge.

Jin, D. (2012) 'Deconvergence and Deconsolidation in the Global Media Industries: The Rise and Fall of (Some) Media Conglomerates', in D. Winseck and D. Y. Jin (eds) *The Political Economies of Media*, London: Bloomsbury.

John, P. (2003) *Analysing Public Policy*, London: Continuum.

Joshi, S. (2011) 'Reflections on the Arab Revolutions: Order, Democracy and Western Policy', *Rusi Journal*, 156(2): 60–66.

Karppinen, K. (2009) 'Rethinking Media Pluralism and Communicative Abundance', *Observatorio Journal*, 11: 151–69.

Keane, J. (1991) *The Media and Democracy*, Cambridge: Polity.

——(1998) *Civil Society*, Cambridge: Polity.

Kellner, D. (2009) 'Media Industries, Political Economy and Media/Cultural Studies: An Articulation' in J. Holt and A. Perren (eds) *Media Industries: History, Theory, and Method*, Chichester: Wiley-Blackwell.

Kim, E.-G. and Hamilton, J. (2006) 'Capitulation to Capital? *OhmyNews* as Alternative Media', *Media, Culture & Society*, 28(4): 541–60.

Klaehn, J. (2009) 'The Propaganda Model: Theoretical and Methodological Considerations', *Westminster Papers in Communication and Culture*, 6(2): 43–58.

——(ed.) (2010) *The Political Economy of Media and Power*, New York: Peter Lang.

Klein, N. (2000) *No Logo*, London: Flamingo.

Klite, P., Bardwell, R. and Salzman, J. (1997) 'Local TV News: Getting Away With Murder', *Press/Politics*, 2(2): 102–12.

Kluver, R. and Banerjee, I. (2005) 'Political Culture, Regulation and Democratization: The Internet in Nine Asian Nations', *Information, Communication & Society*, 8(1): 30–46.

Koboldt, C., Hogg, S. and Robinson, B. (1999) 'The Implications of Funding for Broadcasting Output' in A. Graham et al. *Public Purposes in Broadcasting*, Luton: University of Luton Press.

Koss, S. (1981/1984) *The Rise and Fall of the Political Press in Britain*, 2 vols., London: Hamish Hamilton.

Kuhn, R. (1995) *The Media in France*, London: Routledge.

——(2007) *Politics and the Media in Britain*, Basingstoke: Palgrave.

Küng, L., Picard, R. and Towse, R. (eds) (2008) *The Internet and the Mass Media*, London: Sage.

Kunz, W. (2007) *Culture Conglomerates*, Lanham, MD: Rowman and Littlefield.

Laclau, E. and Mouffe, C. (1985) *Hegemony and Socialist Strategy*, London: Verso.

Lai, C. (2007) *Media in Hong Kong*, Abingdon: Routledge.

Latour, B. (2005) *Reassembling the Social*, New York: OUP.

Lazarsfeld, P. (1941) 'Remarks on administrative and critical communications research', *Studies in Philosophy and Social Science*, 9: 2–16.

Leadbeater, C. (2009) *We-Think*, London: Profile Books.

Lee, C-C. (2000) 'State, Capital and Media: The Case of Taiwan' in J. Curran and M-Y. Park (eds) *De-Westernizing Media Studies*, London: Routledge.

Lee, C-C., He, Z. and Huang, Y. (2007) 'Party-Market Corporatism, Clientelism, and Media in Shanghai', *Harvard International Journal of Press/Politics*, 12(3): 21–42.

Lee, R. E. (2003) *Life and Times of Cultural Studies*, Durham, NC: Duke University Press.

Leiss, W., Jhally, S. and Kline, S. (1990) *Social Communication in Advertising*, 2nd edition, London: Routledge.

Leiss, W., Jhally, S., Kline, S. and Botterill, J. (2005) *Social Communication in Advertising*, 3rd edition, London: Routledge.

Leuven, K. U. et al. (2009) *Independent Study on Indicators for Media Pluralism in the Member States – Toward a Risk-Based Approach: Final Report, Prepared for the European Commission Directorate-General Information Society and Media*, Leuven, July, Strasbourg: European Commission.

Lewis, J. (2010) 'The Myth of Commercialism: Why a Market Approach to Broadcasting Does not Work' in J. Klaehn (ed.) *The Political Economy of Media and Power*, New York: Peter Lang.

Lewis, J. and Brookes, R. (2003) 'Reporting the war on British Television' in D. Miller (ed.) *Tell Me Lies*, London: Pluto.

Leys, C. (2001) *Market-Driven Politics*, London: Verso.

Lister, M., Dovey, J., Giddings, S., Grant, I. and Kelly, K. (2009) *New Media: A Critical Introduction*, London: Routledge.

Livingstone, S. (2010) 'Interactive, Engaging but Unequal: Critical Conclusions from Internet Studies' in J. Curran (ed.) *Media and Society*, London: Bloomsbury.

Lull, J. (1995) *Media, Communication, Culture*, Cambridge: Polity.

Lunt, P. and Livingstone, S. (2012) *Media Regulation*, London: Sage.

MacBride Report (1980) *Many Voices, One World*, Paris: UNESCO.

MacKinnon, R. (2012) *Consent of the Networked*, New York: Basic Books.

Madger, T. (1993) *Canada's Hollywood*, Toronto: University of Toronto Press.

Mandese, J. (2010) 'Point of View: Commerce is King', *Admap* (February).

Manning, P. (2001) *News and News Sources*, London: Sage.

Mansell, R. (2004) 'Political Economy, Power and New Media', *New Media and Society*, 6(1): 96–105.

Mansell, R. and Nordenstreng, K. (2007) 'Great Media and Communication Debates: WSIS and MacBride Report', *Information Technologies and International Development*, 3(4): 15–36.

Marx, K. (1980) [1859] 'A Contribution to the Critique of Political Economy' in *Marx/Engels Selected Works*, Moscow: Progress Publishers.

——(1983) [1867] *Capital: A Critique of Political Economy, Volume 1*, London: Lawrence and Wishart.

Marx, K. and Engels, F. (2013) [1848] *The Communist Manifesto*. Available at http://www.marxists.org/archive/marx/works/1848/communist-manifesto/ch01.htm.

Masmoudi, M. (1979) 'The New World Information Order', *Journal of Communication*, 29(2): 172–79.

Mastrini, G. and Becerra, M. (2012) 'Media Ownership, Oligarchies and Globalization: Media Concentration in South America' in D. Winseck and D. Y. Jin (eds) *The Political Economies of Media*, London: Bloomsbury.

Matos, C. (2008) *Journalism and Political Democracy in Brazil*, Lanham, MD: Lexington.

Mattelart, A. (1989) *Advertising International*, London: Routledge.

——(1994) *Mapping World Communication*, Minnesota: University of Minnesota Press.

——(2002) 'An Archaeology of the Global Era: Constructing a Belief', *Media, Culture & Society*, 25(5): 591–612.

Mattelart, A. and Siegelaub, S. (eds) (1979) *Communication and Class Struggle, Volume 1: Capitalism, Imperialism*, New York: International General.

——(eds) (1983) *Communication and Class Struggle, Volume 2: Liberation, Socialism*, New York: International General.

Mattelart, A., Delcourt, X. and Mattelart, M. (1984) *International Image Markets* (trans. D. Buxton), London: Comedia.

Mattelart, M. and Mattelart, A. (1998) *Theories of Communication*, London: Sage.

Maxwell, R. (2003) *Herbert Schiller*, Lanham: Rowman and Littlefield.

——(2009) 'My Media Studies', *Television and New Media*, 10(1): 100–102.

McAllister, M. (1996) *The Commercialization of American Culture*, Thousand Oaks, CA: Sage.

——(2000) 'From Flick to Flack: The Increased Emphasis on Marketing by Media Entertainment Corporations' in R. Andersen and L. Strate (eds) *Critical Studies in Media Commercialism*, Oxford: OUP.

——(2002) 'Television News Plugola and the Last Episode of Seinfeld', *Journal of Communication*, 52(2): 383–401.

McChesney, R. (1998) 'The Political Economy of Global Communication' in R. McChesney, E. Meiksins-Wood and J. Bellamy-Foster (eds) *Capitalism and the Information Age*, New York: Monthly Review Press.

——(1999) *Rich Media, Poor Democracy*, Urbana: University of Illinois Press.

——(2000) 'The Titanic Sails On – Why the Internet Won't Sink the Media Giants', *EXTRA!, Journal of FAIR* (March–April).

——(2001) 'Global Media, Neoliberalism, and Imperialism', *Monthly Review*, 52(10). Available at http://monthlyreview.org/2001/03/01/global-media-neoliberalism-and-imperialism (accessed 20 November 2013).

——(2002) 'The Global Restructuring of Media Ownership' in M. Raboy (ed.) *Global Media Policy in the New Millennium*, Luton: University of Luton Press.

——(2003) 'Corporate Media, Global Capitalism' in S. Cottle (ed.) *Media Organization and Production*, London: Sage.

——(2004a) 'The Sad State of Political Economy in U.S. Media Studies' in A. Calabrese and C. Sparks (eds) *Toward a Political Economy of Culture*, Lanham, Maryland: Rowman and Littlefield.

——(2004b) *The Problem of the Media*, New York: Monthly Review Press.

——(2007) *Communication Revolution*, New York: The New Press.

——(2008) *The Political Economy of Media*, New York: Monthly Review Press.

——(2013) *Digital Disconnect*, New York: The New Press.

McChesney, R. and Nichols, J. (2002) *Our Media, Not Theirs*, New York: Seven Stories.

McChesney, R. and Nichols, J. (2010) *The Death and Life of American Journalism*, Philadelphia: Nation Books.

McChesney, R. and Scott, B. (2004) *Our Unfree Press*, New York: The New Press.

McCombs, M. (2004) *Setting the Agenda*, Cambridge: Polity.

McFall, L. (2004) *Advertising: A Cultural Economy*, London: Sage.

——(2011) 'Advertising: Structure, Agency and Agencement?' in M. Deuze (ed.) *Managing Media Work*, London: Sage.

McGuigan, J. (1992) *Cultural Populism*, London: Routledge.

——(1996) *Culture and the Public Sphere*, London: Routledge.

——(1998) 'What Price the Public Sphere?' in D. K. Thussu (ed.) *Electronic Empires*, London: Arnold.

McGuigan, L. (2012) 'The Commodity Product of Interactive Commercial Television, or, Is Dallas Smythe's Thesis More Germane Than Ever?', *Journal of Communication Inquiry*, 36(4): 288–304.

McKay, H. (2004) 'The Globalisation of Culture' in D. Held (ed.) *A Globalizing World?*, 2nd edition, London: Routledge.

McNair, B. (1998) *The Sociology of Journalism*, London: Arnold.

——(2006) *Cultural Chaos*, London: Routledge.

McPhail, T. (2006) *Global Communication*, 2nd edition, London: Blackwell.

McQuail, D. (1992) *Media Performance*, London: Sage.

——(2010) *McQuail's Mass Communication Theory*, 6th edition, London: Sage.

McStay, A. (2011) 'Profiling Phorm: An Autopoietic Approach to the Audience-as-Commodity', *Surveillance & Society*, 8(3): 310–22.

Meehan, E. (1993) 'Commodity Audience, Actual Audience: The Blindspot Debate' in J. Wasco, V. Mosco and M. Pendakur (eds) *Illuminating the Blindspots: Essays Honouring Dallas W. Smythe*, Norwood, NJ: Ablex.

——(1999) 'Commodity, Culture, Common Sense: Media Research and Paradigm Dialogue', *Journal of Media Economics*, 12(2): 149–63.

——(2002) 'Gendering the Commodity Audience: Critical Media Research, Feminism and Political Economy' in E. Meehan, and E. Riordan (eds) *Sex and Money*, Minneapolis: University of Minnesota Press.

——(2005) *Why TV is Not Our Fault*, Lanham, MD: Rowman and Littlefield.

Meehan, E. and Riordan, E. (eds) (2002) *Sex and Money*, Minneapolis: University of Minnesota Press.

Meikle, G. and Young, S., (2011) *Media Convergence*, London: Palgrave.

Melody, W. (1992) 'Dallas Smythe: A Lifetime at the Frontier of Communications', *Canadian Journal of Communication*, 17(4).

Meyrowitz, J. (2008) 'Power, Pleasure, Patterns: Intersecting Narratives of Media Influence', *Journal of Communication*, 58(4): 641–63.

Miège, B. (1989) *The Capitalization of Cultural Production*, New York: International General.

Miliband, R. (1973) *The State in Capitalist Society*, London: Quartet.

——(1977) *Marxism and Politics*, Oxford: OUP.

Milioni, D. (2009) 'Probing the Online Counterpublic Sphere: The Case of Indymedia Athens', *Media, Culture & Society*, 31(3): 409–31.

Miller, R. (2008) *International Political Economy*, London: Routledge.

Miller, T., Govil, N., McMurria, J., Maxwell, R. and Wang, T. (2005) *Global Hollywood 2*, London: BFI.

Mirrlees, T. (2013) *Global Entertaiment Media*, London: Routledge.

Mitchelstein, E. and Boczkowski, P. (2009) 'News Production: Between Tradition and Change: A Review of Recent Research on Online Alternative Media', *Journalism*, 10(5): 562–86.

Mizruchi, M. (2004) 'Berle and Means Revisited: The Governance and Politics of Large U.S. Corporations', *Theory and Society*, 33: 519–617.

Morley, D. and Robins, K. (1995) *Spaces of Identity*, London: Routledge.

Morris, N. and Waisbord, S. (eds) (2001) *Media and Globalization*, Lanham, MD: Rowman and Littlefield.

Mosco, V. (1996) *The Political Economy of Communication*, London: Sage.

——(2005) *The Digital Sublime*, Cambridge MA: The MIT Press.

——(2009) *The Political Economy of Communication*, 2nd edition, London: Sage.

——(2011) 'The Political Economy of Labour' in J. Wasco, G. Murdock and H. Sousa (eds) *The Handbook of Political Economy of Communications*, Oxford: Blackwell.

Mosco, V. and McKercher, C. (2008) *The Laboring of Communication*, Lanham, MD: Lexington Books.

Motavalli, J. (2002) *Bamboozled at the Revolution*, New York: Penguin.

Mukherjee, R. and Banet-Weiser, S. (eds) (2012) *Commodity Activism*, New York: New York University Press.

Mullen, A. (2013) 'Selling Politics – the Political Economy of Political Advertising', in C. Wharton (ed.) *Advertising as Culture*, Bristol: Intellect.

Murdoch, R. (1989) *Freedom in Broadcasting*, London: News International.

——(2006) Speech to the Worshipful Company of Stationers and Newspaper Makers, London, 13 March.

Murdock, G. (1978) 'Blindspots about Western Marxism. A Reply to Dallas Smythe', *Canadian Journal of Political and Social Theory*, 2 (Spring–Summer): 109–19.

——(1982) 'Large Corporations and the Control of the Communications Industries', in M. Gurevitch et al. (eds) *Culture, Society and the Media*, London: Routledge.

——(1992a) 'Embedded Persuasions: The Fall and Rise of Integrated Advertising' in D. Strinati and S. Wagg (eds) *Come on Down? Popular Media Culture in Post-war Britain*, London: Routledge.

——(1992b) 'Citizens, Consumers, and Public Culture' in I. Skovmand and K. Schroder (eds) *Media Cultures*, London: Routledge.

——(2003) 'Back to Work' in A. Beck (ed.) *Cultural Work*, London: Routledge.

——(2004) 'Past the Posts: Rethinking Change, Retrieving Critique', *European Journal of Communication*, 19(1): 19–38.

——(2011) 'Political Economies as Moral Economies: Commodities, Gifts and Public Goods' in J. Wasco, G. Murdock and H. Sousa (eds) *The Handbook of Political Economy of Communications*, Oxford: Blackwell.

Murdock, G. and Golding, P. (1974) 'For a Political Economy of Mass Media' in R. Miliband and J. Saville (eds) *The Socialist Register 1973*, London: Merlin.

——(1977) 'Capitalism, Communication and Class Relations' in Curran, J. et al. (eds) *Mass Communication and Society*, London: Arnold/Open University.

——(1999) 'Common Markets: Corporate Ambitions and Communication Trends in the UK and Europe', *The Journal of Media Economics*, 12(2): 117–32.

——(2005) 'Culture, Communications and Political Economy' in J. Curran and M. Gurevitch (eds) *Mass Media and Society*, London: Hodder Arnold.

Murdock, G. and Wasko, J. (eds) (2007) *Media in the Age of Marketization*, Cresskill, NJ: Hampton Press.

Napoli, P. (2011) 'Exposure Diversity Reconsidered', *Journal of Information Policy*, 1: 246–59.

Nava, M. (1997) 'Framing Advertising: Cultural Analysis and the Incrimination of Visual Texts' in M. Nava, A. Blake, I. MacRury and B. Richards (eds) *Buy this Book*, London: Routledge.

Negroponte, N. (1995) *Being Digital*, London: Hodder and Stoughton.

Negus, K. (1997) 'The Production of Culture' in P. Du Gay (ed.) *Production of Culture/Cultures of Production*, London: Sage.

Neil, A. (1997) *Full Disclosure*, 2nd edition, London: Pan Books.

Newell, J., Salmon, C. and Chang, S. (2006) 'The Hidden History of Product Placement', *Journal of Broadcasting & Electronic Media*, 50(4): 575–94.

Nielsen (2007) 'Harry Potter Charms the Entertainment Industry' *PR Newswire US* (10 July).

——(2012) *Social Media Report*. Available at http://www.nielsen.com/us/en/newswire/2012/social-media-report-2012-social-media-comes-of-age.html (accessed 30 March 2012).

Nixon, S. (2011) 'From Full-Service Agency to 3-D Marketing Consultants: "Creativity" and Organizational Change in Advertising' in M. Deuze (ed.) *Managing Media Work*, London: Sage.

Noam, E. (2009) *Media Ownership and Concentration in America*, New York: OUP.

Nordenstreng, K. (1968) 'Communication Research in the United States: A Critical Perspective', *Gazette*, 14(3): 207–16.

——(2001) 'Epilogue' in N. Morris and S. Waisbord (eds) *Media and Globalization*, Lanham, MD: Rowman and Littlefield.

—— (ed.) (1979) *National Sovereignty and International Communication*, Norwood, N.J.: Ablex.

—— (ed) (1993) *Beyond National Sovereignty: International Communication in the 1990s*, Norwood, N.J.: Ablex.

Nordenstreng, K. and Varis, T. (1974) *Television Traffic – A One-way Street*, Paris: UNESCO.

Norris, P. (2001) *Digital Divide*, Cambridge: Cambridge University Press.

Nye, J. (2005) *Soft Power*, New York: Public Affairs.

OECD (2008) *Growing Unequal?: Income Distribution and Poverty in OECD Countries*, Paris: OECD.

Ofcom (2006) *The Communications Market 2006*, London: Ofcom.

——(2007) *New News, Future News*, London: Ofcom.

——(2010) *Report on Public Interest Test on the Proposed Acquisition of British Sky Broadcasting Group plc by News Corporation*, London: Ofcom.

——(2011) *Communications Market Report* [UK], London: Ofcom.

——(2012) *Media Plurality and News*. Available at http://stakeholders.ofcom.org.uk/binaries/consultations/measuring-plurality/statement/Annex7.pdf (accessed 23 November 2013).

——(2013) *News Consumption in the UK*, London: Ofcom.

Office of Fair Trading (2009) 'Review of the local and regional media merger regime'. Available at http://www.oft.gov.uk/shared_oft/mergers_ea02/oft1091.pdf (accessed 20 July 2012).

O'Malley, T. (1997) 'Labour and the 1947–49 Royal Commission on the Press' in M. Bromley and T. O'Malley (eds) *A Journalism Reader*, London: Routledge.

O'Reilly, T. and Battelle, J. (2009) 'Web Squared: Web 2.0 Five Years On'. Available at http://www.web2summit.com/web2009/public/schedule/detail/10194 (accessed 20 March 2010).

Ó Siochrú, S., Girard, B. and Mahan, A. (2002) *Global Media Governance*, Lanham, MD: Rowman and Littlefield.

O'Sullivan, T., Hartley, J., Saunders, J., Montgomery, M. and Fiske, J. (1994) *Key Concepts in Communication and Cultural Studies*, 2nd edition, London: Routledge.

Ottaway, M. and Hamzawy, A. (2011) 'Protest Movements and Political Change in the Arab World', Carnegie Endowment for International Peace, Policy Outlook. Available at http://carnegieendowment.org/files/OttawayHamzawy_Outlook_Jan11_ProtestMovements.pdf (accessed 20 June 2011).

Owens, L. and Palmer, L. (2003) 'Making the News: Anarchist Counter-Public Relations on the World Wide Web', *Critical Studies in Media Communication*, 20(4): 335–61.

Pajnik, M. and Downing, J. (2009) *Alternative Media and the Politics of Resistance*, Ljubljana: Peace Institute.

Pariser, E. (2011) *The Filter Bubble*, New York: Penguin.

Paterson, C. (2006) 'News Agency Dominance in International News on the Internet', Centre for International Communications Research, Papers in International and Global Communication, 01/06.

Peck, J. (2006) 'Why We Shouldn't be Bored with the Political Economy versus Cultural Studies Debate', *Cultural Critique*, 64 – Fall.

Peters, J. (2002) 'The Subtlety of Horkheimer and Adorno: Reading "The Culture Industry"' in E. Katz et al. (ed.) *Canonic Texts in Media Research*, Cambridge: Polity.

Petley, J. (2009) 'What Fourth Estate?' in M. Bailey (ed.) *Narrating Media History*, London: Routledge.

Pew Research Centre Project for Excellence in Journalism (2009) *State of the News Media 2009*. Available at http://stateofthemedia.org/2009/overview/ (accessed 23 February 2014).

——(2010a) *State of the News Media*. Available at http://stateofthemedia.org/2010/online-summary-essay/nielsen-analysis/ (accessed 20 June 2010).

——(2010b) 'The Study of the News Ecosystem of One American City'. Available at http://www.journalism.org/2010/01/11/how-news-happens/ (accessed 23 November 2013).

——(2011) *State of the News Media 2011*. Available at http://stateofthemedia.org/overview-2011/ (accessed 30 March 2011).

——(2012) *State of the News Media 2012*. Available at http://stateofthemedia.org/2012 (accessed 20 June 2012).

——(2013) *State of the News Media 2013*. Available at http://stateofthemedia.org/2013 (accessed 10 April 2013).

Philo, G. and Miller, D. (2001) *Market Killing*, Harlow: Longman.

Picard, R. (1989) *Media Economics*, Newburg Park, California: Sage.

Pieterse, J. (2004) *Globalization or Empire*, New York: Routledge.

Pietilä, V. (2005) *On the Highway of Mass Communication Studies*, Cresskill, NJ: Hampton Press.

Piore, M. and Sabel, C. (1984) *The Second Industrial Divide*, New York: Basic Books.

Poster, M. (1997) 'Cyberdemocracy: the Internet and the Public Sphere' in D. Holmes (ed.) *Virtual Politics*, London: Sage.

Press Gazette (2013) 'UK National Newspaper Sales' (8 February). Available at http://www.pressgazette.co.uk/uk-national-newspaper-sales-relatively-strong-performances-sun-and-mirror (accessed 23 November 2013).

Proffitt, J., Yune Tchoi, D. and McAllister, M. (2007) 'Plugging Back into the Matrix: The Intertextual Flow of Corporate Media Commodities', *Journal of Communication Inquiry*, 31(3): 239–54.

Purcell, K. (2010) 'Teens and the Internet: The Future of Digital Diversity', Pew Research Centre. Available at http://www.pewinternet.org/files/old-media/Files/Presentations/2010/Mar/FredRogersSlidespdf.pdf (accessed 23 February 2014).

Putnam, R. (2001) *Bowling Alone*, New York: Simon & Schuster.

Raboy, M. (2002) 'Media Policy in the New Communications Environment' in M. Raboy (ed.) *Global Media Policy in the New Millennium*, Luton: University of Luton Press.

Rampton, S. and Stauber, J. (2003) *Weapons of Mass Distraction*, California: Tarcher.

Raphael, C. (2001) 'The Web' in R. Maxwell (ed.) *Culture Works*, Minneapolis: University of Minnesota Press.

Redden, J. and Witschge, T. (2010) 'A New News Order? Online News Content Examined' in N. Fenton (ed.) *New Media, Old News*, London: Sage, 171–87.

Rheingold, H. (1993) *The Virtual Community*, London: Secker and Warburg.

Righter, R. (1978) *Whose News? Politics, the Press and the Third World*, London: Times Books.

Riordan, E. (2002) 'Intersections and New Directions: On Feminism and Political Economy' in E. Meehan and E. Riordan (eds) *Sex and Money*, Minneapolis: University of Minnesota Press.

Rodriguez, C. (2001) *Fissures in the Mediascape*, Cresskill, NJ: Hampton Press.

Rosen, J. (2006) 'The People Formerly Known as the Audience'. Available at http://archive.pressthink.org/2006/06/27/ppl_frmr.html (accessed 30 November 2013).

Sackrey, C., Schneider, G. and Knoedler, J. (2010) *Introduction to Political Economy*, 6th edition, Boston MA: Economic Affairs Bureau.

Said, E. (1993) *Culture and Imperialism*, London: Chatto and Windus.

Sakr, N. (2001) *Satellite Realms*, London: I.B. Tauris.

Sammut, C. (2007) *Media and Maltese Society*, Lanham, MD: Lexington.

Sarikakis, K. (2004) *Powers in Media Policy*, New York: Peter Lang.

Schatz, T. (1997) 'The Return of the Hollywood Studio System' in E. Barnouw et al. *Conglomerates and the Media*, NY: The New Press.

Schiller, D. (1996) *Theorizing Communication*, New York: OUP.

——(2000) *Digital Capitalism*, Cambridge, MA: MIT Press.

——(2006) 'Digital Capitalism: A Status Report on the Corporate Commonwealth of Information' in A.Valdivia (ed.) *A Companion to Media Studies*, Oxford: Blackwell.

——(2007) *How to Think about Information*, Urbana: University of Illinois Press.

Schiller, H. (1976) *Communication and Cultural Domination*, White Plains, NY: International Arts and Sciences Press.

——(1989) *Culture, Inc.*, New York: OUP.

——(1991) 'Not Yet the Post-imperial Era', *Critical Studies in Mass Communication*, 8(1): 13–28.

——(2000) *Living in the Number One Country*, New York: Seven Stories Press.

Schlesinger, P. (1990) 'Rethinking the Sociology of Journalism; Source Strategies and the Limits of Media – Centrism' in M. Ferguson (ed.) *Public Communication*, London: Sage.

Schlesinger, P. and Tumber, H. (1994) *Reporting Crime*, Oxford: Clarendon.

Schudson, M. (1995) *The Power of News*, Cambridge, Mass.: Harvard University Press.

——(1996) 'The Sociology of News Production Revisited' in J. Curran and M. Gurevitch (eds) *Mass Media and Society*, 2nd edition, London: Arnold.

——(2000) 'The Sociology of News Production Revisited (Again)' in J. Curran and M. Gurevitch (eds) *Mass Media and Society*, 3rd edition, London: Hodder Arnold.

——(2005) 'Four Approaches to the Sociology of News' in J. Curran and M. Gurevitch (eds) *Mass Media and Society*, 4th edition, London: Hodder Arnold.

——(2010) 'Four Approaches to the Sociology of News Revisited' in J. Curran, *Media and Society*, 5th edition, London: Bloomsbury.

Schumpeter, J. (1942) *Capitalism, Socialism and Democracy*, New York: Harper.

Sen, A. (2001) *Development as Freedom*, Oxford: OUP.

Seymour, E. and Barnett, S. (2006) *Factual International Programming on UK Public Service TV, 2005*, London: International Broadcasting Trust.

Shields, M. (2010) 'Murdoch's iBlunders', *Adweek*, 51(45): 15.

Siebert, F., Peterson, T. and Schramm, W. (1963) [1956] *Four Theories of the Press*, Campaign, IL: Univ. of Illinois Press.

Sinclair, J. (2011) 'Branding and Culture' in J. Wasco, G. Murdock and H. Sousa (eds) (2011) *The Handbook of Political Economy of Communications*, Oxford: Blackwell Publishing.

Sinclair, U. (2003 [1920]) *The Brass Check*, Urbana: University of Illinois Press.

Smith, A. (1776) *An Inquiry into the Nature and Causes of the Wealth of Nations*. Available at http://www.econlib.org/library/Smith/smWN.html (accessed 29 October 2013).

Smulyan, S. (1994) *Selling Radio*, Washington, DC: Smithsonian Institution Press.

Smythe, D. (1977) 'Communications: Blindspot of Western Marxism', *Canadian Journal of Political and Social Theory*, 1(3): 1–27.

——(1978) 'Rejoinder to Graham Murdock', *Canadian Journal of Political and Social Theory*, 2 (Spring-Summer): 120–27.

——(1981) *Dependency Road*, Norwood, NJ: Ablex.

Soley, L. (2002) *Censorship Inc.*, New York: Monthly Review Press.

Source Watch (2013) 'Propaganda Model'. Available at http://www.sourcewatch.org/index.php?title=Propaganda_Model (accessed 20 November 2013).

Sparks, C. (1998) *Communism, Capitalism and the Mass Media*, London: Sage.

——(2000a) 'The Global, the Local and the Public Sphere' in G. Wang, J. Servaes and A. Goonasekera (eds) *The New Communications Landscape*, London: Routledge.

——(2000b) 'Media Theory After the Fall of European Communism: Why Old Models from East and West Won't Do Any More' in J. Curran & M.-J. Park (eds) *De-Westernising Media Studies*, London: Routledge.

——(2004) 'The Impact of the Internet on the Existing Media' in A. Calabrese and C. Sparks (eds) *Toward a Political Economy of Culture*, Lanham, MD: Rowman and Littlefield.

——(2008) 'Media Systems in Transition: Poland, Russia, China', *Chinese Journal of Communication*, 1(1) (April 2008): 7–24.

Sreberny-Mohammadi, A. (1996) 'The Global and the Local in International Communication' in J. Curran and M. Gurevitch (eds) *Mass Media and Society*, London: Arnold.

——(1997) 'The Many Cultural Faces of Imperialism' in P. Golding and P. Harris (eds) *Beyond Cultural Imperialism*, London: Sage.

Starr, P. (2004) *The Creation of the Media*, New York: Basic Books.

Stein, L. (2008) *Speech Rights in America*, Urbana: University of Illinois Press.

Stole, I. (2006) *Advertising on Trial*, Urbana: University of Illinois Press.

Straubhaar, J. (2002) '(Re)asserting National Television and National Identity Against the Global, Regional and Local Levels of World Television' in J. M. Chan and B. T. McIntyre (eds) *In Search of Boundaries*, Westpost, CT: Ablex.

Street, J. (2011) *Mass Media, Politics and Democracy*, 2nd edition, London: Palgrave.

Sum, N-L. and Jessop, B. (2013) *Towards a Cultural Political Economy*, London: Edward Elgar.

Sussman, G. (ed.) (2011) *The Propaganda Society*, New York: Peter Lang.

Sylvian, O. (2008) 'Contingency and the "Networked Information Economy": A Critique of "The Wealth of Networks"', *International Journal of Technology, Knowledge, and Society*, 4(3): 203–10.

Tapscott, D. and Williams, A. (2006) *Wikinomics*, London: Penguin.

Terranova, T. (2000) 'Free Labour: Producing Culture for the Digital Economy', *Social Text*, 18(2): 33–58.

Thatcher, M. (2000) *The Politics of Telecommunications*, Oxford: OUP

Thomas, P. and Nain, Z. (eds) (2004) *Who Owns the Media?*, London: Zed Books.

Thompson, E. (1978) *The Poverty of Theory*, London: Merlin.

Thompson, J. B. (1990) *Ideology and Modern Culture*, London: Polity.

——(1995) *The Media and Modernity*, Cambridge: Polity.

Thussu, D. (2006) *International Communication*, London: Hodder Arnold.

——(ed.) (2007) *Media on the Move*, London: Routledge.

——(ed.) (2009) *Internationalizing Media Studies*, London: Routledge.

Tilley, E. and Cokley, J. (2008) 'Deconstructing the Discourse of Citizen Journalism: Who Says What and Why it Matters', *Pacific Journalism Review*, 14(1): 94–114.

Tomlinson, J. (1991) *Cultural Imperialism*, London: Pinter.

Tomlinson, J. (1999) *Globalization and Culture*, Cambridge: Polity.

Tunstall, J. (1977) *The Media Are American*, London: Constable.

——(1996) *Newspaper Power*, Oxford: OUP.

——(2008) *The Media Were American*, New York: OUP.

Tunstall, J. and Machin, D. (1999) *The Anglo-American Media Connection*, Oxford: OUP.

Turner, G. (2002) *British Cultural Studies*, 3rd edition, London: Routledge.

Turow, J. (1997) *Breaking Up America*, Chicago: University of Chicago Press.

——(2006) *Niche Envy*, Cambridge, MA: MIT Press.

——(2010) *Media Today*, New York: Routledge.

——(2011) *The Daily You*, New Haven, CT: Yale University Press.

UNESCO (2005) *Convention on the Protection and Promotion of the Diversity of Cultural Expressions*, Paris: UNESCO.

Van Cuilenberg, J. (2007) 'Media Diversity, Competition and Concentration: Concepts and Theories' in E. de Bens (ed.) *Media Between Culture and Commerce*, Bristol: Intellect.

Van Cuilenburg, J. and McQuail, D. (2000) 'Media Policy Paradigm Shifts: In Search of a New Communications Policy Paradigm', in B. Cammerts and J.-C. Burgelman (eds) *Beyond Competition*, Brussels: VUB University Press.

van der Wurff, R. (2008) 'The Impact of the Internet on Media Content' in L. Küng, R. Picard and R. Towse (eds) *The Internet and the Mass Media*, London: Sage.

van der Wurff, R. and van Cuilenberg, J. (2001) 'The Impact of Moderate and Ruinous Competition on Diversity: The Dutch Television Market', *Journal of Media Economics*, 14(4): 213–29.

van Dijk, J. (2005) *The Deepening Divide*, London: Sage.

Venturelli, S. (1998) *Liberalizing the European Media*, Oxford: Clarendon.

Voices 21 (2002) 'A Global Movement for Peoples Voices in Media and Communication in the 21st Century' in M. Raboy (ed.) *Global Media Policy in the New Millennium*, Luton: University of Luton Press.

Waetjen, J. and Gibson, T. A. (2007) 'Harry Potter and the Commodity Fetish: Activating Corporate Readings in the Journey from Text to Commercial Intertext', *Communication and Critical/Cultural Studies*, 4(1): 3–26.

Waisbord, S. (2000) *Watchdog Journalism in South America*, New York: Columbia University Press.

Wasko, J. (2004) 'The Political Economy of Communications' in J. D. Downing (ed.) *The Sage Handbook of Media Studies*, Thousand Oaks, CA: Sage.

Wasko, J. and Hagen, I. (eds) (2000) *Consuming Audiences! Production and Reception in Media Research*, Cresskill, NJ: Hampton Press.

Wasko, J., Phillips, M. and Meehan, E. (eds) (2001) *Dazzled by Disney*, London: Leicester University Press.

Wasko, J., Murdock, G. and Sousa, H. (eds) (2011) *The Handbook of Political Economy of Communications*, Chichester: Wiley-Blackwell.

Wayne, M. (2003a) 'Post-Fordism, Monopoly Capitalism, and Hollywood's Media Industrial Complex', *International Journal of Cultural Studies*, 6(1): 82–103.

——(2003b) *Marxism and Media Studies*, London: Pluto.

Wernick, A. (1990) *Promotional Culture*, London: Sage.

Wescott, T. (2011) 'US Leads among Global Top 50 Audiovisual Companies'. Available at http://www.isuppli.com/Media-Research/MarketWatch/Pages/US-Leads-among-Global-Top-50-Audiovisual-Companies;-Comcast-is-No1-with-$36-Billion.aspx (accessed 23 November 2013).

Whish, R. (1989) *Competition Law*, 2nd edition, London: Butterworths.

Williams, K. (2012a) *Read All About it: A History of the British Newspaper*, Abingdon: Routledge.

——(2012b) *Get Me a Murder a Day!: A History of Media and Communication in Britain*, 2nd edition, London: Bloomsbury.

Williams, R. (1958) *Culture and Society 1780–1950*, London: Chatto and Windus.

——(1961) *The Long Revolution*, Harmsworth: Penguin.

——(1974) *Television: Technology and Cultural Form*, London: Fontana.

——(1977) *Marxism and Literature*, Oxford: OUP.

——(1980) *Problems in Materialism and Culture*, London: Verso.

——(1981) *Culture*, London: Fontana.

——(1983) *Writing in Society*, London: Verso

Winfield, B. H. and Peng, Z. (2005) 'Market or Party Controls? Chinese Media in Transition', *Gazette*, 67(3): 255–70.

Winseck, D. (2008) 'The State of Media Ownership and Media Markets: Competition or Concentration and Why Should We Care?', *Sociology Compass*, 2(1): 34–47.

——(2012) 'The Political Economies of Media and the Transformation of the Global Media Industries', in D. Winseck and D. Y. Jin (eds) *The Political Economies of Media*, London: Bloomsbury.

Winseck, D. and Jin, D. (eds) (2012) *The Political Economies of Media: The Transformation of the Global Media Industries*, London: Bloomsbury.

Winseck, D. and Pike, R. (2008) 'Communication and Empire: Media Markets, Power and Globalization, 1860–1910', *Global Media and Communication*, 4(1): 7–36

Yúdice, G. (2003) *The Expediency of Culture*, Durham, NC: Duke University Press.

Zenith Optimedia (2013) 'Google takes top position in global media owner rankings'. Available at http://www.zenithoptimedia.com/wp-content/uploads/2013/05/Top-30-Global-Media-Owners-2013-press-release.pdf (accessed 23 November 2013).

Index

59687955R00148

Made in the USA
Lexington, KY
12 January 2017